OPENING A MOUNTAIN

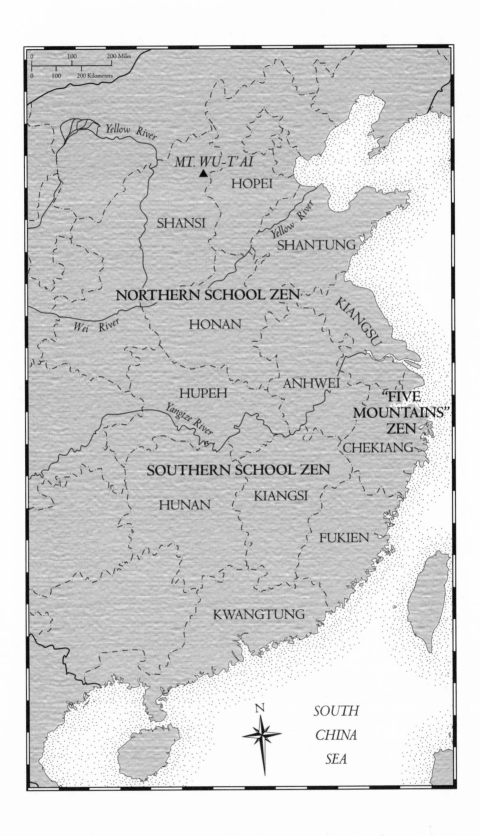

Opening a Mountain

KŌANS OF THE ZEN MASTERS

Steven Heine

OXFORD
UNIVERSITY PRESS
2002

OXFORD
UNIVERSITY PRESS

Oxford New York
Athens Auckland Bangkok Bogotá Buenos Aires Cape Town
Chennai Dar es Salaam Delhi Florence Hong Kong Istanbul
Karachi Kolkata Kuala Lumpur Madrid Melbourne
Mexico City Mumbai Nairobi Paris São Paulo Shanghai
Singapore Taipei Tokyo Toronto Warsaw

and associated companies in
Berlin Ibadan

Published by Oxford University Press, Inc.,
198 Madison Avenue, New York, New York 10016

Oxford is a registered trademark of Oxford University Press

LIBRARY OF CONGRESS CATALOGING-IN-PUBLICATION DATA
Heine, Steven, 1950–
Opening a mountain : kōans of the Zen Masters / Steven Heine.
     p. cm.
     ISBN 0–19–513586–5
     1. Kōan   2. Zen Buddhism.
     I. Title: Kōans of the Zen Masters.   II. Title.
BQ 9289.5 .H438   2001
294.3'927—dc21   2001032151

9 8 7 6 5 4 3 2 1

Printed in the United States of America
on acid-free paper

Chü-chih made a fool of old Tien-lung,

By testing a boy with his sharp knife—

Like a Great Spirit raising its hands,

and without much effort,

Splitting into two the mighty peaks of

Flower Mountain.

—CASE 51,
"CHÜ-CHIH'S ONE FINGER ZEN"

CONTENTS

Contents

SOURCES

CCL *Ching-te ch'uan-teng lu* (Jap. *Keitoku dentōroku*), 1004, Taishō, vol. 50.

DK *Denkōroku*, 13th c., Taishō, vol. 82.

DZZ *Dōgen zenji zenshū*, 7 vols. (Tokyo: Shōnjusha, 1988–1993).

HTC *Hsü tsang ching* (Jap. *Zoku zōkyō*), 150 vols.

EK *Eihei kōroku*, 1236–1253, DZZ, vols. 3–4.

KZK *Kenzeiki*, 13th c., ed. Kawamura Kōdō, *Shohon taikō Eihei kaisan Dōgen zenji gyōjō—Kenzeiki* (Tokyo: Taishūkan, 1975).

KS *Kana Shōbōgenzō*, 1231–1253, DZZ, vols. 1–2.

LL *Lin-chi lu* (Jap. *Rinzai roku*), 12th c., ed. Taishō, vol. 47.

MS *Mana Shōbōgenzō*, 1235, DZZ, vol. 5.

PCY *Pai-chang yü-lu* (Jap. *Hyakujō goroku*), 12th c., *Hsü tsang ching*, vol. 119.

PYL *Pi-yen lu* (Jap. *Hekiganroku*), 1163, Taishō, vol. 48.

SZ *Shōbōgenzō zuimonki*, 1236–1238, DZZ, vol. 6.

Taishō *Taishō shinshu daizōkyō*, 85 vols. (Tokyo: Taishō Issaikyō Kankōkai, 1924–1932).

TJL *Ts'ung-jung lu* (Jap. *Shōyōroku*), 1224, Taishō, vol. 48.

TSL *Tung-shan lu* (Jap. *Tōzan roku*), 13th c., Taishō, vol. 47.

WMK *Wu-men kuan* (Jap. *Mumonkan*), 1228, Taishō, vol. 48.

YY *Yün-men yü-lu* (Jap. *Unmon goroku*), 12th c., Taishō, vol. 47.

PREFACE

This book is a translation with commentary of sixty kōan cases that feature an important supernatural or ritual element selected from a variety of the major and minor Zen Buddhist kōan collections compiled in Sung China and Kamakura Japan. My aim is to demonstrate that the main theme underlying much of kōan (the term is *kung-an* in Chinese, but is better known in its Japanese pronunciation) literature deals with how Zen (Ch'an in Chinese) masters opened or transformed mountains. The mountains harbored spirits, demons, and bodhisattvas, as well as hermits, recluses, ascetics, and other irregular practitioners, and were opened through the use of symbols and rituals of spiritual purification. In contrast to conventional interpretations that view kōans as psychological exercises with a purely iconoclastic intention, the approach here highlights the rich component of mythological and marvelous elements that pervade this genre of literature in a way that complements, rather than contradicts, the demythological or iconoclastic perspective.

This approach to interpretating Zen literature is distinctive and innovative in several respects. It includes the selection of kōan cases emphasizing supernatural symbols—such as mountains, animals, and other natural imagery—based on a strict scholarly standard of translation and the citation of appropriate source materials. It also employs a methodological perspective that is sensitive to the issue of how kōans and kōan collections stand in complex relations with other literary genres. The other Zen genres include transmission of the lamp histories (which contain biographies of multibranched lineages of transmission) recorded sayings texts (which include sermons, verses, and other anecdotes about the life and teachings of individual patriarchs interacting with a variety of disciples), and other kinds of Buddhist and non-Buddhist folklore and hagiographical materials.

The kōans are divided into five sections: 1) magical mountain landscapes of the Northern, Ox Head, and Southern schools, in addition to the mountains inhabited by Tung-shan and the pilgrimage site of Mount Wu-t'ai; 2) diverse sorts of irregular rivals who encountered and challenged the prestige of Zen masters; 3) supernatural experiences involving dreams, visions, and encounters with gods, demons, and magical animals; 4) the use of symbols of authority and transmission, including sticks, staffs, fly-whisks, robes, bells, and a variety of visual and verbal symbols; and 5) confessional experiences through repentance and self-mutilation, as well as death and afterlife encounters with ghosts and relics. The list of sources will be explained at the end of the introduction.

I am grateful for several sources of funding that made possible research on this project, including a National Endowment for Humanities Research Fellowship, the Association for Asian Studies, the American Academy of Religion, and the Division of Sponsored Research and the Institute for Asian Studies at Florida International University. My undying thanks go to Yoshizu Yoshihide and Ishii Shūdō for their insightful understanding of the history of Zen Buddhism. I greatly appreciate Cynthia Read's encouragement and support in shaping the scope of the book. In addition, I am grateful to Carmen Cusack and Patricia Gonzalez for editing the manuscript and for their valuable ideas and suggestions on revisions.

OPENING A MOUNTAIN

INTRODUCTION

What Are Kōans?

STICKS AND STONES, BUT IT'S NO-NAMES THAT HURT

The kōan—a brief, enigmatic anecdote or dialogue between two contesting parties— defines the heart of Zen Buddhism and is the single most distinctive feature in the thought and practice of the Zen sect. Many of the kōan dialogues date back to the "golden age" of Zen in the T'ang era (618–917) of China, and they capture the dramatic and inscrutable encounters between masters and disciples or rivals. These encounters are characterized by quixotic, paradoxical, and often absurd utterances, reprimands, and gestures designed to twist and torment the ordinary rational mind and trigger a spiritual breakthrough to a realm beyond reason.

Kōans are generally known as psychological tools that convey a philosophical message about the meaning of enlightenment. Some of the most prominent examples are questions such as "Does a dog have Buddha-nature?" and "What is the sound of one hand clapping?" However, kōans are much more than that. They are part of a comprehensive body of Zen literature that incorporates mythical and magical elements influenced by popular religious beliefs, symbols, and rites. According to traditional sources, Zen masters were known for encountering and overcoming irregular or heretical religious figures, such as hermits, shamans, and "dangerous women."[1] The irregular recluses and wizards occupied mountain landscapes and practiced some form of meditation or austerity that led to the attainment of supranormal powers, such as mind-reading or the ability to interpret visions. These practitioners resembled the Zen masters, who were also celebrated for taming natural and supernatural forces, including magical animals, local gods, and demons who controlled access to the inner recesses of the mountains and could prevent the opening of the sacrality of the mountain to the Buddhist Dharma.

Zen masters used many methods to prevail over indigenous powers. These included the deployment of powerful symbols, such as staffs, robes, and ceremonial fly-whisks; methods of divination and geomancy; the manipulation of dreams, visions, and apparitions; and exorcism of demons and supernatural stones. The masters also attained spiritual power through acts of repentance, self-mutilation, and dying, as well as travels to the afterlife realm of ghosts and relics.

Dreams and visions, spirits and demons, fantastic symbols and icons, ascetic hermits and witches, sticks, staffs, and stones, and ghosts and apparitions, in addition to sacred or exotic mountain peaks, recesses, valleys, and caves, appear in numerous kōan cases. For instance, there is the sixth patriarch Hui-neng's robe that cannot be moved by any force and convinces his rival chasing him into the mountains of his moral authority (see case 46 in this book); a mysterious, magical fox that undergoes endless reincarnations and appears in the form of a monk before master Pai-chang, who utters a phrase that releases him from karmic bondage (case 38); and a nun toying with the issue of shapeshifting in her dealings with a disciple (case 25). In other examples, master Huang-po observes one of his rivals walking on water (case 28); master Kuei-shan is led by a geomancer to the mountain where he will establish his monastery (case 6); and the wizard P'u-chi eliminates a troublesome god of the hearth (case 31). There is also a fearsome snake that appears in the relic box of the Buddha (case 37); the powers that master Chih-men derives from a magical staff (case 41); and master Lin-chi's shaman-like rival, who departs the earthly realm without leaving a trace of his body (case 57).

The supernatural beliefs and rites in these kōans were borrowed from or influenced by a complex network of factors. One source was the indigenous East Asian religions. These included pre-Buddhist shamanistic techniques of purification and exorcism, Taoist folklore about mountain and other local deities, and generic popular texts on the efficacy of exorcism or turning the power of ghosts and spirits from malevolence to moral purposes. This influence is seen in case 32, in which the master who is supposed to be invisible to local spirits is spotted in his travels by the earth-deity.

Another native contribution was the rhetoric of the "art of war," or martial strategies used to muster spiritual strength against an enemy in battle. In Zen, the opponent might be another monk, an irregular practitioner, or a spirit. For example, a commentary speaks of Te-shan "setting his strategy in motion even while remaining in his tent" during his encounter in the temple of an important abbot (case 7). Another case comments, "The old woman [who challenges master Chao-chou] only sits there in her tent, planning her next campaign, but does not realize that she was being shadowed by a spy" (case 23).

Supernatural beliefs in Zen also reflect some of the fundamental elements of Buddhist meditation techniques imported from India. In the genre of Indian devotional literature known as *avadana*, Buddhist priests who championed the Dharma were shown defeating anomalous rivals in contests of supranormal powers. According to classical sources, the six supranormal powers or *abhijna* (Chinese *shen-t'ung*, Japanese *jinzū*) of a Buddhist monk are omniscient hearing or clairaudience; reading the minds of others or clairvoyance; exceptional physical prowess such as levitation or passing through walls; seeing past karma or knowing one's past lives; understanding the karmic conditioning that affects others and foreseeing their path to enlightenment; and freedom from the outflows of karma and defilement.

The *avadana* tales demonstrate the superiority of Buddhist powers, attained through meditation and based on understanding the emptiness and relativity of all phenomena over powers drawn from otherworldly sources.[2] These Buddhist powers were not to be used unchecked. According to the early Buddhist rules, or Vinaya, one of the four major offenses (*parajika*) against the propagation of the Dharma was the misuse or exaggeration of any of the six supranormal powers, along with the transgressions of murder, stealing, and sexual misconduct.

Another traditional Buddhist source of the supernatural in Zen literature was the model of extreme asceticism practiced by forest monks or itinerant wanderers, as opposed to monks residing permanently in a monastery. These practitioners followed the austerities of *dhutanga* techniques that required extreme self-denial and tormenting the physical body (case 18).[3] Kōan literature also absorbed influences from Chinese Mahayana esoteric religiosity, which used passages from sutras and other sacred writings as *dharani* or chants to cast and ward off spells (case 49).

The voluminous biographical writings on eminent monks in Chinese Buddhism, ranging from meditators, translators, exegetes, and disciplinarians to miracle workers, theurgists, and self-immolators, was another extremely important influence on the kōan tradition. The techniques of meditators and other practitioners who might be expected to use a more rational approach to religious fulfillment often exhibited a mixture of contemplation and magic. The experts in meditation were close in style to miracle workers. Both used a dynamic spiritual communion between the mind and the universal manifestations of the Buddha-nature. The meditation specialists attained this state through thought, and the miracle workers reached it through action.

One of the most important collections of monk biographies was the *Sung kao-seng chuan* or *Sung Biographies of Eminent Monks*. It was compiled in 988, just a couple of decades before the origins of one of the early genres of Zen texts, known as the "transmission of the lamp" records of monks' lives. The first and foremost example of this genre, which would become the primary source of dialogues and anecdotes included in kōan collections, was the *Ching-te ch'uan-teng lu* or the *Record of the Transmission of the Lamp in the Ching-te Era* (1004). The *Sung kao-seng chuan* chronicles monks representative of all the Buddhist schools and styles; the *Ching-te ch'uan-teng lu*, like subsequent transmission of the lamp records, tells exclusively of Zen monks. However, the *Ching-te ch'uan-teng lu* does embrace masters of diverse Zen houses rather than focusing on a particular school. Many of the accounts in this text were excerpted from the *Sung kao-seng chuan*. Both texts are essentially mythological in method and evangelical in outlook. The kōan case records usually consist of snippets of dialogues extracted and adapted from monks' lives in the lamp records, and they reflect and evoke the mythical context from which they emerged.

On the Conventional Understanding of Kōans

The mythological dimension of Zen literature has been neglected by translators and critics of kōans in both East Asia and the West.[4] Supernatural elements, mythical narratives, and ritual structures might seem antithetical to the irreverent and iconoclastic character of the Zen practice of studying kōans as a psychological discipline. The customary understanding of kōans is epitomized in Lin-chi's command, "If you see the Buddha, Kill the Buddha!" and in reprimands such as "Thirty blows of the stick whether you speak or remain silent, or whether you answer yes or no!" It is also found in stories in which masters burn sutras or icons, or in the minimalist design of Japanese rock gardens. Kōans are usually understood as enigmas that during meditation can trigger a spontaneous awakening experience or realization of sudden enlightenment (*satori*). They are considered anti-supernatural, opposed to ritual and magic.

The conventional view of kōans focuses on instances of Zen masters shouting at, slapping, striking, or otherwise rebuking their disciples in order to bring about a spiritual breakthrough. Water pitchers are kicked over, fingers and arms are cut off, cats are sliced in half and shoes are placed on the head, buffaloes are shoved through windows, and people leap off high poles. These widely different episodes are invariably given a single line of interpretation that emphasizes the severing of all attachments and ignorance. Supernatural and ritual elements that appear in kōan records and commentaries are stripped away, and mythical imagery is considered only an outer symbol for internal awareness.

According to this standpoint, the words and phrases used in kōans are devoid of significance and meaning. They function not as names for ideas, people, or things, but as "no-names" in a sense recalling Lao Tzu's famous saying, "The Tao that is spoken is not the true Tao." Words are a kind of "poison to counteract poison," or a way to fight the fire of inherently mis-leading discourse through the mechanism of discourse itself. This is a para-doxical, self-deconstructing approach to discourse. Words are used in a penetrating and often devastating fashion as a means to overcome any trace of reliance on language.

The conventional view seems appropriate for numerous kōan cases that create a double bind, forcing one into an intellectual impasse in which both sides are considered equally wrong and yet some response is required. For instance, in case 15 master Pi-mo asks everyone he sees, "What kind of demons made you become a Buddhist priest? What kind of devil forced you to take up this pilgrimage? You will die from my pitchfork even if you explain it. You will die from my pitchfork even if you do not explain it. Now speak up quickly! Speak up quickly!" In case 60, Ch'ien-yüan taps on a coffin and asks the master, "Alive or dead?" Tao-wu replies, "I won't say it's alive, and I won't say it's dead." Ch'ien-yüan then says, "Why won't you say?," and Tao-wu responds, "I just won't say, I just won't say." Another classic example of a double-bind kōan from the *Wu-men kuan* collection has a master holding up a stick and daring his disciples, "If you call this a stick you will be clinging, and if you do not call this a stick you are ignoring the obvious. So, now, tell me, what do you call it?" In three consecutive cases of the *Pi-yen lu* collection, Pai-chang taunts his disciples, "Keeping your tongues still and lips closed, how will you speak?" In these kōans, all possibilities for thought and speech are eliminated at their root as fundamentally misleading, inadequate, or delusory.[5]

These mystifying, contradictory modalities fall into several patterns. In one pattern, the questions asked by disciples differ but the master's answer is always the same and remains indecipherable—holding up one finger, shaking his staff, or voicing a single word or syllable. In another pattern, two disciples respond with identical answers to the question posed by a master, often with an ambiguous gesture like raising a fist, but one disciple receives approval and the other is denied it. The same answer is given by both parties, but for some reason one is considered right and the other is wrong. In a variation of this pattern two different or even opposite answers are offered, and both are considered correct. In still other variations, a master reverses the implication of his question, or the disciple reverses his answer, or the master's reaction to the disciple's answer is so inscrutable that it is impossible to tell whether he is indicating approval or denial.[6]

Judged on these examples, kōans are rhetorical devices that use paradox, wordplay, and ambiguity to communicate a message about the maddening quality and inherent limitations of language. The absurdities, contradictions, negations, and double negations, as well as the gestures, demands, and demonstrative behavior that characterize this discourse, point to a direct, unimpeded realization of the true nature of reality liberated from all illusion, pretension, and attachment.

Marvelous and Ritual Elements in Kōans

But does this understanding exhaust the full significance of koans? Or is it a partial view that misses key elements of supernaturalism, ritualism, and other mythological and magical features that belong to the overall context of kōan discourse? In other words, does the tradition that utilizes koans understand their function appropriately, or does it contribute to a forgetting of the origins of the tradition? The bias toward a uniformly demythological approach appears to have begun in the early history of the kōan tradition in Sung China. Leading Zen thinkers were in competition with the rational focus of Confucian philosophers and needed to distance themselves from supernaturalism to forestall the critique of rationalist rivals. Chu-hsi, the most prominent neo-Confucian thinker, was very critical of Zen, although he and others did absorb Zen influences.

In the early modern period of Japanese history, especially the eighteenth and nineteenth centuries, Zen was again competing with neo-Confucianism recently imported from China, and therefore emphasized a more rational approach to kōans. For example, the great Tokugawa era Rinzai Zen master Hakuin organized a systematic method of kōan exercises based on levels of difficulty. In the modern period, the iconoclastic slant has been reinforced by the desire of Zen Buddhist thinkers to place their philosophy of religion on a par with mainstream trends in Western philosophy and psychology, including the anti-supernaturalism of secularism and scientific reasoning.[7]

However, apart from iconoclasm, there are several other dimensions of kōan discourse that reflect the context of medieval Chinese religion and society. These need to be understood in order to appreciate the remarkable range and diversity of the narrative structures embedded in kōan records. The legal system of China exerted an important influence on Zen. The Chinese term *kung-an* (kōan is Japanese) refers to the "public records" or precedents that were routinely consulted by local magistrates judging a legal case. This procedure was a model for the ideal of the Zen master acting like a judge in the "court" of the Dharma, testing and evaluating the case record of his disciple's spiritual attainment.

As the postscript to the *Wu-men kuan* collection suggests, "The sayings and doings of Buddhas and Patriarchs have all been correctly judged, as if they were crimes confessed by criminals. From the beginning there are no extra words, I have taken the lid off my skull and bulged out my eyeballs. I ask you to grasp 'it' directly and not to seek for it outwardly." Moreover, the frequent sayings attributed to Te-shan and other masters about dealing "thirty blows"—usually whether the disciple answers correctly or not—are taken straight from the punishments that local magistrates meted out.[8] Furthermore, there is a medieval genre of detective story literature based on tales of intricate, suspenseful legal investigations that is also known by the term "kung-an." Most people in modern China recognize the term as referring to this literary genre, and the significance of *kung-an*/kōan for Zen is less well known.

Another dimension of kōan discourse is political. Following the great suppression of Buddhism in 842–845, in which tens of thousands of temples were shuttered or burned and hundreds of thousands of monks and nuns were returned to lay life, Zen emerged as the dominant religious institution in China. Beginning in the eleventh century, it prevailed for several hundred years and spread to Japan and Korea. The brief but devastating period of persecution is referred to explicitly in case 34 on the role of protector spirits, and indirectly in case 14 on the worship of the bodhisattva of wisdom, Manjusri. The allusive, poetic, mysterious style of kōans, which was so different from traditional Buddhist sutras, rites, and ceremonies, proved to be useful for communicating doctrine in an atmosphere of suppression by the government. The success of Zen in the period of conflict between Buddhism and the state was due to the ability of kōan literature to convey an independent, creative message free of controversial connections to other schools and styles of religious practice.

Kōan discourse also relies on the modalities of esoteric Buddhist training that is characterized by intense subjectivity. This dimension includes the profound intimacy of the master–disciple relation based on intuitive insight and hermetism, as well as an aura of secrecy and inscrutability projected toward outsiders. The esoteric dimension is featured in a case on the mind-reading ability of a monk whose authenticity is challenged by the National Teacher (case 17), and in the way dreams psychically link two masters prior to their actual meeting (case 30).

The legal, political, and esoteric dimensions of kōans reflect the fact that they contain or are part of narratives dealing with complex factors of Chinese religion and culture. This understanding helps us tell the story behind the story that kōans tell. The aim of this volume is to recapture yet another crucial dimension of kōan literature: the mythical and ritual narrative structure underlying the many cases that tell of encounters with strange practitioners, anomalous spirits, magical animals, and dangerous women, as well as confessional experiences of self-mutilation and death. These kōans record the way charismatic Zen patriarchs were challenged by a rich variety of spiritual rivals, followers, forces, and icons located in remote mountains. These encounters tested the Zen claims to legitimacy and authority.

Therefore, the kōan cases cited in this volume express an engagement with the images and symbols of popular religions. The supernaturalism depicted in Zen kōans is comparable to what Jacques LeGoff characterizes as the "marvelous" in his study of medieval Christian religious literature.[9] This category encompasses the supranormal (or a realm transcending ordinary physical reality), and the magical (a manifestation of divine energy in the ordinary world). It is distinguished by its eminently moral, edifying purpose from the superstitious, which manipulates spiritual forces for personal gain.

Kōan discourse emerged in a context in which the efficacy of supernatural practices, such as being haunted by or exorcising ghosts and demons, was taken for granted. Zen kōans were in many ways one of the most important intellectual rebellions against accepting supernaturalism as a key to the religious quest. But the irreverence of Zen almost always conveys a sense of irony and ambiguity—rather than rejection or denial—of super-naturalism. Seen in this light, the motif of opening a mountain influenced by Taoist practices represents a spiritual adventure into the realm of the supernatural that mirrors a physical journey. Sometimes the phrase refers to a symbolic endeavor or pilgrimage, rather than to literal traveling, and the image of reaching the mountain peak functions as a metaphor for an experience of awakening.

The approach to kōan literature expressed here may appear to stand in contrast to the conventional standpoint based on the value of iconoclasm and the priority of silence. But this approach actually complements and enhances the conventional view. It shows that there is fundamentally a two-fold structure operating in Zen discourse, or a mixture of mythical and iconoclastic dimensions. The symbolism of sticks and stones is an example of the two-fold structure. The most famous Zen stones are those in rock gardens that represent stark simplicity, such as Ryōanji temple in Kyoto, and the best-known sticks are those used in the meditation hall to awaken slumbering monks. Yet there are also stones depicted in kōans as powerful icons (see discussion of case 49) and staffs that turn into dragons (case 42).

While the sticks and stones wielded by Zen masters can either conjure visions or inflict pain, in the end it is the no-names based on irreverence and iconoclasm that pack the punch and deliver the real damage. No-names subvert, invert, or convert the literal meaning of the images and icons, transmuting their significance into a message about enlightenment. The communicative power of kōans derives from the creative tension between two levels, with one level embracing supernaturalism, myth, and ritual and the other level detaching from these elements. Clarifying the supernatural component provides a balanced, neutral methodological standpoint. It is sensitive to the socio-historical context from which the tradition of kōan literature emerged, and enhances our understanding of the rhetoric of irony pervasive in kōan collections.

The Case of Chü-chih Cutting Off a Finger

An intriguing example of the two-fold structure is the case "Chü-chih's One Finger Zen (case 51 in this volume)," which is included in different versions in the prominent *Wu-men kuan*, *Pi-yen lu*, and *Tsung-jung lu* kōan collections. The kōan seems to epitomize the irreverent outlook in which an act of violence is purely metaphorical.[10] A master cutting off the finger of a disciple who imitates his gesture symbolizes the eradication of attachments and the attainment of enlightenment.

However, there are supernatural and ritual elements in the narrative background that are crucial for understanding the full meaning of the kōan case. First, the basic act of violence must be seen in light of the continuing popularity of the practice of self-mutilation. This practice was taken as a sign of the perfection of ascetic training and a sacrifice in the physical realm for the sake of the propagation of the Dharma. As John Kieschnick notes in his study of monk biography literature, "Just as enduring [as copying sutras in blood] among Chinese monks is the practice of cutting or burning off one or more fingers, a practice that has continued into the twentieth century. . . ."[11] Therefore, the severing of the finger is not merely an external symbol for some internal realization or psychological state of mind. Rather, it is an important ritual practice, although it is clear that the kōan does not necessarily endorse the technique but refers to it in an ironic way.

Furthermore, the narrative in the transmission of the lamp records from which the kōan case was extracted highlights the crucial role played by other mythical elements, including a hermitage, a mysterious nun, a spirit, a dream, a bodhisattva, the casting of spells, and a powerful staff. The kōan record that appears in the *Pi-yen lu* and the *Ts'ung-jung lu* collections is a highly abbreviated version that does not refer to the act of mutilation, but the prose commentaries allude to the transmission of the lamp narrative. The version in the *Pi-yen lu* also contains several additional sections, including a "pointer" or introductory segment that uses a concrete metaphor of cutting and dyeing a single thread to make a philosophical argument about the identity of particularity and universality. The *Pi-yen lu* pointer and case are cited below, along with selected passages from the prose commentary (note that the story of the mutilation that is central in the *Wu-men kuan* version of the main case is included in the prose commentary in the *Pi-yen lu*).

Pointer

> With the arising of a single speck of dust, the great earth is manifested. When a single flower blooms, the whole world comes into existence. But at the time before the speck of dust appears or the flower opens, what do you see? Thus it is said, "It's like cutting a skein of thread: when one strand is cut, all are cut. It's like dyeing a skein of thread: when one strand is dyed, all are dyed." At this very moment you must cut off all entanglements and

awaken to the treasure hidden within you. You will be able to respond to the presence of each and every phenomenon above and below, without discrimination of past and future. If you still don't get it, look into the following case.

Main Case

Whenever any question was asked, Master Chü-chih would simply hold up one finger.

Prose Commentary

Master Chü-chih was from Chin-hua in Wu-chou in Chekiang province. While he was dwelling in a hermitage, there was a nun named Shih-chi who came to his hut. She walked straight in, and without taking off her broad rain hat she circled around his meditation seat three times holding her staff. "If you can speak," she said, "I'll take off my rain hat." She questioned him like this three times, but Chü-chih still had no reply. Then as she was leaving Chü-chih said, "The hour is rather late. Would you stay the night?" The nun said, "If you can speak, I'll stay over." Again Chü-chih had no reply. The nun then walked out. Chü-chih sighed sorrowfully and said, "Although I inhabit the body of a man, still I lack a man's spirit." After this he aroused his zeal to clarify this matter.

Chü-chih wanted to abandon his hermitage and travel to various Zen temples to call on the teachers there to ask for instruction, so he wrapped up his things to travel by foot. But that night the spirit of the mountain told him, "You do not have to leave this place. Tomorrow a flesh and blood bodhisattva will come here and expound the truth for you. Please stay right here and wait."

The following day master T'ien-lung came to the hermitage. Chü-chih welcomed him ceremoniously and gave a full account of the events that had recently taken place. T'ien-lung simply held up one finger to instruct him. Suddenly Chü-chih experienced a great enlightenment. Since Chü-chih was a very determined and single-minded seeker, the bottom of his bucket fell out easily. Later, whenever he was asked any question, Chü-chih simply held up one finger.

In the narrative cited in the prose commentary, there is a movement back and forth between supernatural and iconoclastic elements based on the hermit's contest of spiritual powers with the nun. The name given for this threatening woman, Shih-chi, literally means "Reality." The very presence of the nun wearing a hat and wielding her staff seems imbued with a charismatic spiritual power that challenges the hermit's manhood and renders him speechless, which is a false sense of silence. But how could a monk be defeated by a nun, since women were considered inferior if not necessarily disqualified from attaining an enlightenment equal to that of men? The nun is one of the so-called dangerous women of traditional China, where "sacred women, whatever the school, inherit a constellation of traits: magic travel, horrific self-sacrifice, divine language. . . ."[12] The narrative also carries a sexual implication regarding the request for the nun to stay the night in Chü-chih's hermitage. It is fascinating to note that Zen texts considered it possible for a female practitioner to prevail over a man, a possibility that was denied in most other forms of Buddhism.

The hermit is led to his realization through the guidance of a mountain spirit, which appears to him in a dream, and the incarnation of a bodhisattva, who offers silent instruction at his mountain retreat. The *Pi-yen lu*'s prose commentary also stresses the relation between the supernatural elements of casting spells or shaking powerful staffs and the meaning of teaching by raising one finger. All are examples of "single method" teaching techniques that established the precedent for the Zen use of kōans. The first passage has Chü-chih's casting a three-line spell, as reported by another hermit known as the One-Eyed Dragon of Ming-chao:

> The One-Eyed Dragon of Ming-chao asked his "uncle," Shen of Kuo-t'ai, "A patriarch said that Chü-chih just recited a three-line spell and thereby became more famous than anyone else. Can you quote the three-line spell for me?" Shen also just held up one finger. Ming-chao said, "If I had not experienced this teaching method today, how would I have gotten to know this borderlands traveler? Now, tell me, what does the teaching mean?"

In the next passage, a staff is used by another irregular practitioner, Pi-mo, who lived on Mount Wu-t'ai in northern China, which was considered the earthly abode of the bodhisattva Manjusri. Manjusri was said to bestow spectacular visionary experiences to believers that could be observed only on selected mountain peaks or in caves in Mount Wu-t'ai. These visions were apparently so vivid and enticing that they frequently attracted Zen pilgrims, even though Lin-chi, Yün-men, and other patriarchs declared the site off limits for their disciples.[13] This passage shows that staffs were considered an especially important symbol of a master's authority. Staffs were cut from wood that was found in the forest during a mountain retreat or pilgrimage. They became the main possession of wanderers and were said to contain wondrous powers in vanquishing demons and defeating rivals. According to the *Pi-yen lu*:

> Pi-mo simply used a forked-branch all his life. The Earth-Beating Teacher would just hit the ground with it one time whenever he was asked any question. Once someone hid his staff and then asked, "What is Buddha?" The teacher just opened his mouth wide. This was another kind of single teaching method used for a whole lifetime without its efficacy ever being exhausted.

The significance of single-method teaching is also emphasized in a philosophical passage from the *Pi-yen lu* prose commentary, which reinforces the conclusion in the pointer: "Penetrate one place, and at once you penetrate hundreds of thousands of places. Clearly understand one device, and at once you clearly understand hundreds of thousand of devices." Yet in another section of the prose commentary, *Pi-yen lu* editor Yüan-wu ironically criticizes Chü-chih for being "rather crude" in only learning one single pedagogical device and using it on every occasion without variation or exception. Thus, it is clear that this contempt for unimaginative routine is the real source of the devastating impact of the case, and not just the story of mutilation.

THE MYTHOLOGICAL BACKGROUND OF KŌAN LITERATURE

The two-fold nature of kōan discourse is reflected in its literary structure. Brief, iconoclastic "encounter dialogues" were the core literary unit of the vast majority of kōan cases. As previously discussed, kōan literature draws from the influence of diverse genres, including pre-Buddhist shamanism manuals and Taoist scriptures, Mahayana Buddhist sutras and sectarian commentaries, and non-Buddhist folklore collections and writings such as the art of war or detective story materials. The kōan cases themselves usually revolve around an encounter dialogue that captures an intensely dramatic, almost combative face-to-face contest between enlightened master and unenlightened disciple or rival. The dialogue usually culminates in a show of irreverence or iconoclasm, such as a slap, shout, or the severing of a finger. But the dialogues were originally contained in mythological narratives included in the transmission of the lamp records.

According to Yanagida Seizan, for many years the preeminent Japanese scholar in studies of the formative period of Zen Buddhism in China, the encounter dialogue is a spontaneous, intuitive repartee between accomplished master and aspiring disciple that formed the basis of the distinctive literary style of the records of Zen patriarchs.[14] This style began with the recorded sayings of Ma-tsu and his Hung-chou lineage, the most important subdivision of the Southern school. In the pedagogy of Ma-tsu and his followers, gestures and demonstrations like shouting and striking were used to get a point across in a compelling way. The aim of Zen literature was not the formal articulation of doctrinal principles, but the informal, oral expression of a dynamic, experiential pedagogical encounter. The term for encounter dialogue (Ch. *chi-yüan wen-ta*, Jap. *kien-mondō*) literally refers to a "decisive, spontaneous opportunity for question and answer." The encounter dialogue, or "oral instructions uttered in different specific situations" by which its participants "could grasp truth," took place during a dramatic meeting that was uniquely conducive to a spiritual breakthrough.[15]

The opportunity for the encounter was sudden and unpredictable, yet the exchange was neither accidental nor predetermined by karma. It was a consequence of a multiplicity of factors that led to a highly charged, interactive situation. The encounters occurred when two parties were ready for the exchange to ignite the spark of inspiration: the enlightened master was given a chance to get his message across to a receptive follower, and the unenlightened disciple or rival was enabled to cross a spiritual threshold by means of the meeting. From the Zen perspective, truth is suited to particular individuals in specific situations, but it cannot transpire in isolation. The process of transmitting the Buddhist Dharma is utterly dependent on the context of an "I and Thou" relationship. One party emerges from the contest as victorious or dominant. The Zen master seeks to overcome the techniques of the hermits or spirits he challenges by showing that he can succeed in their realm. Yet he transforms the main symbols of these beings into an expression or manifestation of the Dharma.

Some scholars have argued that the prototypical encounter dialogue associated with the Southern school's emphasis on sudden enlightenment may have had antecedents in the literature of the Northern school that was dominant prior to sixth patriarch Hui-neng. Northern school literature contained rhetorical questions and pithy admonitions referred to as "questions about things" or "pointing at things and asking the meanings" (*chih-shih wen-i*).[16] However, despite a relatively minor disagreement about the origins of the dialogues, most scholars concur that the efficacy of the encounter derives from the charismatic quality of the Zen master who combines inno-vative pedagogical techniques with an irreverent, tables-turning outlook.

The earliest version of the Zen monastic rules was attributed to Ma-tsu's main disciple, Pai-chang. The rules require that Zen training revolve around the leadership of the monastery abbot. The master is referred to as the living "honored one" (Ch. *ts'un*, Jap. *son*), a term that is usually reserved for an image of Sakyamuni or another Buddha. As opposed to almost every other form of Buddhism, Zen rules dispensed with the Buddha Hall, nor-mally used to display an impressive icon often constructed of gold or some other precious material. Instead, the activity was focused on the Dharma Hall as a place for the delivery of the abbot's regular round of sermons before the full assembly of monks. Zen distinguished its approach because the master was by no means an isolated entity but was "defined almost entirely by the kind of interaction he had with his students."[17]

The encounter dialogue, a genuinely concrete and personal rather than an abstract or theoretical form of expression, is designed to liberate "someone paralyzed and religiously impotent by his dependence on some pre-determined religious position."[18] In the encounter, "an enlightened master displays an uncanny knack for exposing and overcoming the con-ceptual impasse of a disciple by using a rhetorical device, such as homo-phone, punning, paradox, absurdity, or non sequitur, or some nonverbal gesture, such as the iconoclastic, anti-authoritarian 'sticks and shouts' of Te-shan and Lin-chi."[19] The impact of these actions is to force a degree of humiliation, ridicule, or hazing that paradoxically enables the disciple to overcome the final psychological obstacle of ego—a false image of selfhood that has been preventing the attainment of liberation.

The dialogues first appeared in the transmission of the lamp records of Zen masters, including the *Ching-te ch'uan-teng lu* as the first main example of the genre.[20] They were embedded in a complex narrative context, often with supernatural or magical elements, concerning the life and teachings of Zen masters participating in the process of lineal transmission. As Andy Fer-guson remarks, "the lamp records provide a more extensive context for some well-known Zen stories than what appears in the [classic kōan collections]."[21]

The transmission records were, in turn, influenced by two other genres that developed outside but were highly influential on Zen. One main genre was non-denominational monk biography texts. The *Sung kao-seng chuan* of 988 was the third main representative of the monk biography genre, following the *Kao-seng chuan* (from the sixth century, around 520) and its supplement, the *Hsü kao-seng chuan* (667). Each of the three monk hagiographies dealt with ten categories of Buddhist practitioners. The category that primarily included Zen patriarchs was the meditator. The other influential genre was non-Buddhist folklore collections, including the *T'ai-p'ing kuang-chi* (978), one of the main compendiums that covered over five hundred years of folk tales. Folklore collections contained stories of the magical exploits and exorcisms performed by Buddhist priests that were sometimes integrated into Zen records.

The formation of Zen transmission of the lamp records was greatly affected by several key changes of emphasis in the development of the monk biography texts over the centuries. From the time of the *Kao-seng chuan* to the *Sung kao-seng chuan*, a dramatic shift took place from an emphasis on scholasticism to practice. Translators and exegetes were highlighted in the early text, but with Buddhism now firmly established in China meditators and miracle workers were emphasized in the later text.[22] The categories that encompassed scholars and scholastic experts that had been as high as 65 percent of the total number featured in the monk biography of 520 were reduced to 20 percent by the time of the 988 text. The percentage of translators was lower by half, and the figure for exegetes was reduced to a quarter of the original number. At the same time, the percentage of meditation specialists increased threefold to become the single largest representative group at 20 percent. Miracle workers similarly tripled to 17 percent and became the second highest category (although the percentage for this had been as high as 19 percent in 667). In addition, disciplinarians increased two and a half times, to 10 percent, and the categories of evangelizers who performed good works and proselytizers who gave sermons increased four times.

Influenced by the *Sung kao-seng chuan*, the marvelous elements in the *Ching-te ch'uan-teng lu* and related transmission records were characterized by the creative distortions and disruptions typical of a mythological approach. These included idealization, exaggeration, fantasy, the conflation or deliberate fusion of reality and illusion, and melodramatic themes. The transmission records were commissioned by imperial authorities for an audience consisting of the more elite classes of Chinese society. They clearly were not intended as factual history. In these texts, "Myth, magic and facts are tightly fused. . . ."[23] Nor were these records primarily philosophical or theoretical. Rather, they crafted legend with an underlying iconoclastic flavor to propagate a vision of Zen as a spiritually powerful, freethinking and yet highly structured and well disciplined institution.

The transmission records refer to ritual techniques for locating and defining sacred space, such as divination and geomancy, and miraculous events such as monks walking on water and surviving poison or overflowing streams. There are masters who remain so unmoved by the threat of floods that their calm is the reason the water recedes, and practitioners who cause water to flow from a stone. The records also refer to the surmounting of death, including disappearing corpses, corpses rising from the coffin, and corpses that remain unchanged and can avoid decay or retain the appearance of living. Other accounts depict supernatural intercessions, such as a stupa door opening by itself without any apparent cause; the appearance of auspicious clouds, heavenly music, sudden storms or rainbows when a master passes away; and the emergence of valuable relics (*sarira*) at the time of the cremation of a master's body. Moreover, masters transform hostile deities into manifestations of the Dharma, subdue demons, tame tigers, and handle deadly snakes. In addition, mountain and other local gods appear as a large python or some other magical animal and weep at death or express repentance for their behavior.

According to Jacques LeGoff's account of medieval European religiosity, saints and hermits who adventure in the uncharted territory of the wilderness/desert/forest/mountain are able to realize the marvelous quality in natural objects and images. Animals and magical beasts, mysterious sites and mythical domains function as symbols of spiritual trial and self-reflection. The pilgrimage of the Zen master as a mountain opener functions as the agent for manifesting the marvelous, a realm that "stands at the crossroads where religion, literature and art, philosophy, and sensibility meet."[24] That is, the internal, psychological, aspect of kōans is complemented by the social, external aspect, or the encounter between Zen with forms of religiosity that are different, alien, challenging, or threatening to the principles of Zen. As Gail Ashton writes of Christian hagiographies, "Without doubt hagiography is a textual representation that is ultimately also a cultural and historical construct. An interrogation of this genre is likely to reveal something about late medieval culture, its power relations, its discourse, its ideology. As with any text, what at first sight might appear to be a stable, fixed entity might also be a place where meanings are contested or resisted."[25]

The psychological function involving the irreverent, iconoclastic aspect of master–disciple relations is an important but by no means exclusive aspect of kōan discourse. An emphasis on this feature alone does not do justice to the sources of the literature. In Zen texts, a demythological approach is inseparable from the context of a pervasive mythology. In the terms of poststructuralist philosopher Michel Foucault, who highlights the inseparability of claims for truth and bids for power, kōans have a multi-level quality. Conventional readings stress the "truth" of kōan discourse, whereas the interpretation in this volume focuses on the role of "power" underlying the truth claims.[26]

The transmission of the lamp records also influenced another important genre of Zen works created during the Sung era—the "recorded sayings" of individual masters (Ch. y_x-lu, Jap. goroku), which present the records of the verse and prose teachings of particular teachers. The recorded sayings texts cite dialogues to reveal the pedagogical style of the leading patriarchs. The kōan collection commentaries culled dialogues from both transmission records and recorded sayings texts in order to highlight their philosophical significance with a variety of styles of prose and verse commentaries.

The following table illustrates the influence on the formation of the classic kōan collections of various Zen, Buddhist, and non-Buddhist literary genres:

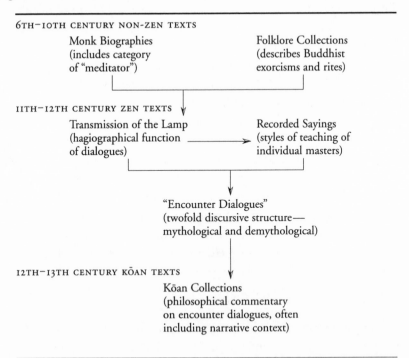

6TH–10TH CENTURY NON-ZEN TEXTS

Monk Biographies
(includes category
of "meditator")

Folklore Collections
(describes Buddhist
exorcisms and rites)

11TH–12TH CENTURY ZEN TEXTS

Transmission of the Lamp
(hagiographical function
of dialogues)

Recorded Sayings
(styles of teaching of
individual masters)

"Encounter Dialogues"
(twofold discursive structure—
mythological and demythological)

12TH–13TH CENTURY KŌAN TEXTS

Kōan Collections
(philosophical commentary
on encounter dialogues, often
including narrative context)

TABLE 1. This diagram shows the evolution of the role of encounter dialogues vis-à-vis the interconnectedness of the three main genres of Zen texts as well as the influence of pre–Zen Buddhist writings.

Mythological motifs come to the surface in many kōans dealing with the testing and/or contesting between two masters, one a regular high priest or realized master and the other an irregular hermit or solitary *pratyeka buddha*, or a meditator who has not trained under or been sanctioned by a legitimate lineage. According to case 18, for example, a monk who has not taken the tonsure builds a hermitage at the foot of Mount Hsüeh-feng and lives there for many years practicing meditation on his own outside the monastic system. He is living as a "wild fox" in the Zen sense of an unusual, eccentric, or perhaps deceitful practitioner. In China, "Recluses were the personifications of the mountains themselves: lonely, untamed, unkempt—storehouses of the secrets of nature. Caves, huts, and mountain temples were their lairs. From ancient times, the mysterious recluses had mysterious powers. They were often referred to as immortals; they could confer on the fortunate supplicant everything from military secrets . . . to medications for healing and for transcendence. . . ."[27] But what are the real intentions of the recluse? Is he an authentic practitioner, or not? Only a regular master can tell for sure by testing, evaluating, and judging the level of his understanding.

Encounter dialogues reveal Zen masters engaging elements of diversity, division, disparity, or dissension, including the anomalous, strange, and perplexing. Zen masters demonstrate the superiority of their supranormal powers derived from meditative discipline over those gained through other modalities. Yet Zen literature also expresses a fundamental ambiguity in striving for a balance between accepting and rejecting supernatural perspectives. Zen seeks to establish its priority over local cults that rely on magic and folklore, but at the same time it tries not to eliminate but to transform these perspectives. In acknowledging a degree of validity in the alternative approaches, Zen utilizes and refashions their images and idioms to articulate its own outlook.

The standpoints of otherness that Zen contends with range from alternative Buddhist meditative disciplines, such as forest asceticism and esotericism, to diverse forms of popular religiosity, including influences from Taoism, shamanism, and other types of trance and exorcism. The symbols, images, icons, and rites that play a key role in numerous kōan cases reflect an interaction with various sects, cults, and movements in China. Some of the symbols are associated with Zen monastic rituals and authority. These include the master's ceremonial staff or fly-whisk that transmutes into or chases down dragons, the fan that circulates in celestial realms, and the monk's robe that is immovable as a rock. Other examples are sermon techniques allowing masters to bridge heaven and earth, and funeral rites that preserve a relation to the otherworldly realm or ward off ghosts. There are also symbols that derive from esoteric Buddhist traditions, such as bodhisattvas, sutras, or dharani chants, each of which has the power to offer salvation. Other symbols stem from non-Buddhist traditions, especially Taoism and folk religions, such as shapeshifting animals that need to be tamed or exorcised, sacred mountains or caves wherein spirits or demons lurk, or stones that have magical attributes. An additional category includes symbols that represent a convergence of traditions, such as oneiric and visionary experiences suggesting an entrance into a liminal realm conducive to spiritual transformation.[28]

Zen Masters and Their Mountains

Mountains, which have a numinous, utopian quality resonating throughout the history of Chinese religions, were the primary symbol evoked by Zen masters that defined their identity and enhanced the vibrancy of their authority in a competitive religious context. Zen masters, known as "mountain openers," had a complex relation with mountains. Many of the masters began their spiritual search as itinerant wanderers, pilgrims, or hermits, who gravitated to the sacred landscape of mountains to avoid the secularization and corruption of urban life in pursuit of special resources of spiritual power. In so doing, they were influenced by (as well as in a rivalry with) local shamans and wizards whose practices were associated with Taoism or folk religions. Many of these alternative religious figures were able to manipulate demonic forces or reflected a "negative charisma," in the terminology of I. M. Lewis.[29] From the Buddhist standpoint, the negative energy of these forces needed to be transmuted into expressions of the Dharma, as shown in several cases featuring the encounters of Northern school masters with spirits haunting remote mountain domains (cases 1, 2, 3, and 31). These troublesome spirits are converted, sometimes through their own repentance, to the Buddhist Way.

The multidimensional significance of mountains that influenced Zen is described in William Powell's account of master Tung-shan, one of the founders of the Ts'ao-tung (Jap. Sōtō) school, and the mountain landscapes where he wandered:

> Mountains in China have been seen as a particularly powerful aspect of sacred geography. They are sometimes the dwelling places of the dead or of local divinities. . . . Mountains are filled with dangers, such as ferocious

beasts, but they also hold a magnetic attraction to which the wealth of Chinese landscape painting and poetry bears testimony. In entering the mountains the pilgrim is often entering another reality. . . . In addition to being regarded as an external, physical sacred space, mountains have also been seen as images of internal, subjective sacred geography. [30]

Powell notes that the distinction between descriptions of natural scenery and the rhetoric of nature (identified as an inner spiritual journey) "seems to be left intentionally ambiguous, or the emphasis shifts really from external to internal and back again."

Mountains in China have long been a locale for seeking religious experience by pilgrimage. This was especially true for Taoism, which had already explored and defined many of the mountains that Buddhists rediscovered and re-encoded. A prime example was Mount Wu-t'ai in northern Shanxi province, with its multiple peaks and grottoes that are depicted as the dwelling place of bodhisattva Manjusri (cases 13, 14, and 15). The spiritual significance of mountains in China encompasses popular and elite—as well as the ritual and personal—levels of meaning.

Mountains that have mighty summits piercing the clouds where deities dwell represent a divine manifestation, or the experience of something mysterious and awe-inspiring. They are believed to contain both the tablets of fate and elixirs of life, according to popular Taoism. Mountain landscapes provide the key to immortality and other secrets kept by mountain deities. These landscapes feature the intrinsic numinosity of nature found in peaks, cliffs, vistas, caves, grottoes, springs, rocks, or trees, which inspire the building of stupas, tombs, inscriptions, ritual arenas, shrines, and pavilions, as well as the creation of sculpture and paintings. Mountains in Buddhism are uniformly decorated with a "mountain gate" that demarcates the transition from mundane reality to an entry into a spiritual domain.

Mountain landscapes are originally uncultivated, untamed, and primordial, beyond the limits of society or the fringes of civilization. For some travelers, mountains function as the site of an idyllic retreat for recreation or aesthetic appreciation, enjoyment, and communion with nature. In the end, this experience may amount to little more than a creative escape and a way to kill time for the jaded elite. In China, pilgrims travel to mountains in order to "see a vision of the deity, perform a penance, ask for heirs or cures, or pray for good health and long life for themselves and their family members."[31] Pilgrims seek to obtain blessings and avert calamities. They also try to appease dead ancestors viewed as powerful spirits requiring ritual attention through regular visits, as well as the construction of mound-shaped temples built to resemble mountains.

Huts, hermitages, and retreats—some primitive and others more elaborate—provide a transient dwelling for tourists and lay pilgrims in addition to those on a more serious quest. For determined seekers, such as Taoist and Buddhist poets, the pristine natural setting of mountains offers relief from the turmoil of urban life. For example, the famous verse essay by T'ao-ch'ien Yüan-ming (365–427), "Peach Blossom Spring" ("T'ao-ch'ien ching"), describes a fisherman who serendipitously wanders to a utopian village where people dwell in harmony, longevity, and prosperity, and without conflict or suffering. This is one of the earliest examples in the history of world literature of depicting a utopia based on nature.

Furthermore, transcending the romantic, idealized social conception of mountains as the basis of a new vision of society, mountain landscapes became the object of artistic contemplation for philosophical Taoists and meditative Buddhists. Mount Lu, located near the heart of the Southern Zen school temples, was a famous gathering place for Buddho–Taoist contemplatives. Many hermits dwelling in deep reclusion remain withdrawn from any traces of social involvement. In their solitude, recluses gaze upon and contemplate the purity, simplicity, silence, and cyclicality of nature. The ideal of solitary contemplation is expressed by a poet of the T'ang era, Wang-wei (699–759), who makes an ironic use of supernatural imagery in the final line of the verse:

> I didn't know where the temple was,
> Pushing mile upon mile among cloudy peaks;
> Old trees, unpopulated paths,
> Deep mountains, somewhere a bell.
> Brook voices choke over craggy boulders,
> Sunrays turn cold in the green pines.
> At dusk by the bend of a deserted pond,
> A monk in meditation, taming poisonous dragons.[32]

Wang-wei's verse is echoed by Shih-t'ou, an important patriarch during the formative period of the Southern school who evokes the ideal of living in a "ten-foot square hut" that was first described in the *Vimalakirti Sutra*:

> I've built a grass hut where there's nothing of value. . . .
> The person in the hut lives here calmly,

not stuck to inside, outside, or in between. . . .

Though the hut is small, it includes the entire world

In ten square feet, an old man illumines forms and their nature.[33]

In Chinese history recluses often moved back and forth, staying within and yet moving frequently outside of mainstream society. When "leaders of early Chinese culture needed to get in touch with natural forces, and go outside the city wall and inside the human heart, they turned to hermits. Hermits could talk to heaven. They knew its signs, they spoke its language. Hermits were shamans and diviners, herbalists and doctors, adepts of the occult and the manifest."[34]

The importance of mountain reclusion for Zen is indicated in an exchange in which a monk asked fifth patriarch Hung-jen, "Why can't the study of the Buddha Dharma take place in cities where there are many people, rather than only deep in the mountains?" Hung-jen answered, "You must seek refuge for your spirit in remote mountain valleys, escaping far from the troubles of the dusty world."[35] Countless other prominent Zen masters have exhorted their disciples to practice in deep mountain recesses, far removed from the world of distractions. From an early period, Zen masters realized that to open a mountain as the appropriate location for the fulfillment of the ideal of reclusion, they had to overcome obstacles and hindrances imposed by the gods, spirits, and rival figures lurking in these remote locale. This is illustrated in a case about the transmission from fourth patriarch Tao-hsin to Niu-t'ou Fa-jung, founder of the early Ox Head school (case 4). Fa-jung had studied the Confucian classics as well as the *Nirvana Sutra*, and was ordained as a Buddhist priest. He became a hermit on a secluded mountain, where every day hundreds of birds with flowers came to pay homage to him. Tao-hsin, led to the site of Fa-jung's hermitage by a celestial sign, explained the Zen approach to the Dharma and Fa-jung was converted. After that, the birds disappeared along with other portents.

Another early Zen movement, the Northern school, was largely an urban phenomenon in the capital cities of Chang-an and Luo-yang, but it was also very popular in mountain temples. In cases 1 and 2, Northern school masters demonstrate their prowess by outsmarting a local god who claims to have power over life and death or besting a mischievous spirit that had been deceiving people for years with magical sights and sounds. As the Zen sect began to flourish through the lineage initiated by Ma-tsu, which became the dominant Southern school movement, most of the temples were located on remote mountain sites known for their numinosity and beauty. These temples, in addition to the masters, took their names from the mountain location. For example, T'ang–era masters Pai-chang, Huang-po, Kuei-shan, Yün-men, and Tung-shan, among many others, had names based on the mountain where they established a temple.

Therefore, when a mountain name is used in Zen literature it might refer to any one or a combination of three factors: the mountain itself, the temple or the site of its location, or the master who founded the temple. There is an identity between monastic institution, mountain, and master, although in some cases a master would move to a new mountain and take with him the name of his former temple site. In Zen rhetoric, the terms "entering a mountain" or passing through a "mountain gate" refer to embarking on a spiritual journey, usually in a mountainous domain where monasteries or hermitages are located. As time went by, all Zen temples were considered mountains regardless of whether they were actually located in the countryside or on hills; temples in valleys or even in urban areas were still referred to as "mountains."

The Southern school began to build monasteries according to the "seven-hall" style. This approach tended to reduce the number of buildings in a temple compound, and emphasized the role of several primary structures. These included the Monks Hall, where the assembly gathered for meditation, and the Dharma Hall, where the abbot presented his daily round of formal sermons. Another key building was the Abbot's Quarters, also known as the ten-foot-square hut, where the master often gave special, private instruction to selected disciples. One of the most important mountains in the formative period of Ma-tsu's Hung-chou lineage was Ta-hsiung Peak, the largest summit in the area of Mount Pai-chang (which literally means "a hundred fathoms"). This was the location of the temple founded by Pai-chang, who was known for creating the first Zen monastic rules text as well as frequently retreating from the temple compound to a mountain hermitage in the isolated splendor of Ta-hsiung Peak.

Pai-chang, the direct heir of Ma-tsu, whose lineage also gave rise to Lin-chi, founder of the Lin-chi (Jap. Rinzai) sect, was memorialized by an inscribed rock still standing on the mountain that says, "Rules prevail throughout the world." When Pai-chang first met Huang-po, who became his foremost disciple and Lin-chi's teacher, he was practicing in a Ta-hsiung hermitage. The dialogue in case 5 plays on the deliberate ambiguity about the identity of mountains and master. According to the kōan, Pai-chang was asked by a monk, "What is the most extraordinary thing?" He replied, "Sitting alone on Ta-hsiung Peak," which can also be translated, "I sit alone on Ta-hsiung Peak." Because of the ambiguity of the main subject in Pai-chang's terse reply, the answer could be read as "I, Ta-hsiung, sit alone."

The symbolism of this mountain functions on a more pervasive level of ritual and supernatural significance. First, Pai-chang was not the only hermit to climb Ta-hsiung Peak for a period of isolation. According to traditional accounts, there were numerous hermitages scattered about the mountainside, some for austere ascetics and others for idyllic retreats. A prose commentary in the *Pi-yen lu* indicates that there was a sub-lineage of four hermits who trained there under Lin-chi. The hermits were renowned for practicing an extreme asceticism that led to the accrual of magical powers. In a dialogue recorded in Pai-chang's sayings, supernatural symbolism suggests that Huang-po was able to defeat magical tigers on the mountain, a practice that may have been *de riguer* in early Zen history. According to this passage, Pai-chang, also known for his dedication to the principle of "a day without work is a day without food," took up his axe and made a gesture of chopping. Huang-po, who had returned from wandering on Ta-hsiung Peak, grabbed the tool and immediately slapped the master. That evening, Pai-chang said approvingly of his disciple, "Listen, there is a tiger on the mountain. Watch out for his comings and goings. This morning I myself got bit by him!"

These dialogues illustrate the interweaving of the double folds of Zen discourse. An understanding of the paradoxicality and iconoclasm of kōan rhetoric is enhanced by an awareness of the mythical elements in the narrative background. Neither aspect of the discursive structure excludes the other, or is sufficient in itself to encompass the totality of the significance of kōan cases. Rather, both levels of meaning, which play off of one another, must be clarified in tandem. The twofold structure highlights the ironic dismissal yet acceptance of the supernatural context from which kōan literature at once emerged and rebelled.

KŌAN THEMES AND SOURCES

Kōan cases are literary records expressing the vitality and dynamism of the Zen tradition in its formative period. Charismatic leaders not only displayed wisdom and wit in expressing a realization of emptiness but an ability to manipulate various popular religious symbols. This ability appealed to potential disciples in the competitive religious environment of medieval China and Japan. The examples cited here showcase the atmosphere of testing and contesting with rival spiritual elements and leaders.

This volume introduces sixty kōans that highlight a central underlying theme: how Zen masters "open a mountain," or establish a new monastery or teaching lineage. This is achieved through encountering and ultimately domesticating powerful yet wild and erratic spiritual forces in remote mountain landscapes. Once the transformation has been completed, the previously untamed forces became protectors and providers of the Buddhist Dharma. The transforming of spiritual forces that had been closing off the mountains into manifestations of sacred space in Zen was referred to in Chinese as *kuai-shan* (Jap. *kaizan* or *yama o hiraku*).

Therefore, this volume represents one of the first attempts to provide a systematic selection, ordering, and analysis of kōan cases according to supernatural and ritual themes. Kōans were presented in the classic collections in a random fashion without apparent order or sequential design.[36] The cases translated and interpreted here have been selected from a variety of sources published during the classical period of Zen writings in Sung China (960–1279) and Kamakura Japan (1185–1333), especially the eleventh through thirteenth centuries. The cases represent over a dozen sources, including kōan collections, transmission of the lamp records, recorded sayings texts, and monk biographies. These texts dealt primarily with the masters of lineages that thrived in an earlier, more formative and dynamic period in the development of the Zen sect in the sixth through ninth centuries that encompassed the T'ang "golden age" period (618–917).[37]

Themes

Some of these cases presented here are well known and have been included in different versions in numerous texts of the various genres as well as in modern translations. Other cases are more obscure and appear in only one or two examples of the early sources of kōans. The translated cases cover five main themes:

1. SURVEYING MOUNTAIN LANDSCAPES. This section contains cases that focus on the role of mountains and the spirits encountered by Zen masters. It treats four topics, including the early Northern and Ox Head schools for which supernatural images are the most vivid; the Southern school, especially the role of Ta-hsiung Peak, which was known for its hermits and hermitages; the mountains explored by Tung-shan, one of the founders of the Ts'ao-tung (Jap. Sōtō) school; and Mount Wu-t'ai, a

place for visionary experiences in northern China generally considered off limits to iconoclastic Zen practitioners.

2. CONTESTING WITH IRREGULAR RIVALS. These cases include encounters with rivals within the Zen lineage as well as practitioners outside the monastic order, such as hermits, shamans, wizards, mind-readers, and miracle workers, and dangerous women including nuns and Zen grannies.

3. ENCOUNTERING SUPERNATURAL FORCES. This section concerns the experiences of the supranormal realm of dreams, visions, and apparitions, in addition to meetings with spirits, gods, demons, and bodhisattvas. It also treats strange, anomalous, or magical entities like the snake and fox, which have the power to shift shape into human form in order to deceive or to bless.

4. WIELDING SYMBOLS OF AUTHORITY. These cases illustrate how Zen masters wield or wear symbols of charisma and authority, including sticks, staffs, and fly-whisks, to which are often ascribed miraculous powers. Furthermore, it treats the ritual significance of important symbols used in monastic ceremonies and rites, such as robes, fans, bells, screens, icons, and portraits.

5. GIVING LIFE AND CONTROLLING DEATH AS CONFESSIONAL EXPERIENCES. This section includes cases that depict a spiritual transformation through the experiences of confession or repentance, including the extreme example of self-mutilation, as well as the realm beyond death populated by ghosts and relics.

These categories are by no means mutually exclusive, but should be seen as overlapping; many cases could well fit into two or more categories. The placement of kōans in a particular category is based on an evaluation of the main or overriding theme, or the primary message expressed by the case.[38] For each group of kōans, the cases in which supernatural imagery is more overtly expressed are placed at the beginning of the section, and the cases in which the imagery is more indirect or is evoked ambiguously or ironically are placed toward the end. Also, it is interesting to note how case narratives interweave with one another to paint a picture of a particular master such as Tung-shan, or a specific sacred site such as Ta-hsuing Peak or Mount Wu-t'ai. In other instances, a master or a site is known only by a single story, such as Iron Grindstone Liu (case 13), Mo-shan (case 25), Chü-chih (case 51), or Lotus Flower Peak (case 44).

Sources

The following is a list of the main sources cited in this translation. All of these texts, which form the Zen "canon," are from the critical period of the eleventh through fourteenth centuries in Sung China and Kamakura Japan. Note that the texts generally were published several centuries after the lives of the masters they depict. Also, many of the kōans appear in two, three, or more of the texts on this list as well as additional Zen texts of the various genres.[39]

CCL *Ching-te ch'uan-teng lu* (Jap. *Keitoku dentōroku*), 1004, Taishō, vol. 50. The earliest and most influential of the transmission of the lamp histories that was commissioned by the imperial government and helped propel Zen into the status of a kind of state religion in Sung China.[40] Cases cited: 1, 2, 3, 4, 31, and 50.[41]

DK *Denkōroku*, 13th c., Taishō, vol. 82. A Japanese Sōtō sect version of a transmission of the lamp record composed by fourth patriarch Keizan that tends to highlight the importance of his sect's lineage. Case cited: 54 (also in EK).

EK *Eihei kōroku*, 1236–53, DZZ, vols. 3–4. The recorded sayings of Dōgen covering his abbacy at Kōshōji temple in Kyoto and the last ten years of his life when he was founding abbot of Eiheiji temple. The ninth of ten volumes is a collection of ninety kōans with verse (*juko*) commentaries composed in 1235 while Dōgen was at Kōshōji. Cases cited: 8, 17, 18, 32, 45, 48, and 54.

KZK *Kenzeiki*, 13th c., ed. Kawamura Kōdō, *Shohon taikō Eihei kaisan Dōgen zenji gyōjō—Kenzeiki* (Tokyo: Taishūkan, 1975). The most important of the many traditional Sōtō biographies of Dōgen composed by master Kenzei. It includes some of the famous anecdotes and dialogues that are later cited as kōan cases in the Sōtō tradition. Case cited: 55.

KS *Kana Shōbōgenzō*, 1231–53, DZZ, vols. 1–2. *Kana Shōbōgenzō* (or *Shōbōgenzō* composed in Japanese), the master work of Dōgen, is a hybrid genre that includes commentaries on dozens of cases as part of Dōgen's sermons on thematic topics. Cases cited: 25 and 26.

LL *Lin-chi lu* (Jap. *Rinzai roku*), 12th c., ed. Taishō, vol. 47. The recorded sayings text of master Lin-chi (Jap. Rinzai), founder of the Lin-chi/Rinzai school, that includes important dialogues that are cited in subsequent works as kōan cases. Cases cited: 16 and 57.

MS   *Mana Shōbōgenzō*, 1235, DZZ, vol. 5. *Mana Shōbōgenzō* (or *Shōbōgenzō* composed in Chinese) is Dōgen's collection of three hundred kōans, which is a list of cases without commentary that he composed in 1235. It became the basis for many of his prose commentaries included in the KS. Cases cited: 9, 10, 15, 26, 30, 41, 42, and 52.

PCY   *Pai-chang yü-lu* (Jap. *Hyakujō goroku*), 12th c., HTC, vol. 119. The recorded sayings text of Pai-chang, a disciple of Ma-tsu and teacher of Huang-po, who was known for devising the first set of monastic rules in Zen. Case cited: 38 (also in WMK).

PYL   *Pi-yen lu* (Jap. *Hekiganroku*), 1163, Taishō, vol. 48. The most prominent collection of one hundred kōans first compiled by Hsüeh-tou with verse and prose comments, and then expanded a century later by Lin-chi school master Yüan-wu, with pointer, capping verses, and notes. It has a complex, intricate, multilayered style of commentary. Cases cited: 5, 7, 13, 14, 20, 24, 28, 33, 36, 39, 40, 42, 44, and 60.

SZ   *Shōbōgenzō zuimonki*, 1236–1238, DZZ, vol. 6. The sayings of Dōgen at Kōshōji temple that were recorded by his main disciple, Ejō. Case cited: 37.

TJL   *Ts'ung-jung lu* (Jap. *Shōyōroku*), 1224, Taishō, vol. 48. Resembling the complex structure of the *Pi-yen lu* (but without the section of notes), this collection of one hundred cases was first compiled by Ts'ao-tung master Hung-chih and then further commented on by Wan-sung. Cases cited: 22, 34, 47, and 49.

TSL   *Tung-shan lu* (Jap. *Tōzan roku*), 13th c., Taishō, vol. 47. The recorded sayings of the founder of the Ts'ao-tung school. Cases cited: 11, 12, 35, 58, and 59.

WMK   *Wu-men kuan* (Jap. *Mumonkan*), 1228, Taishō, vol. 48. Perhaps the best known of the major kōan collections, it contains forty-eight cases with four-line verse comments and brief prose commentary. Cases cited: 6, 19, 21, 23, 27, 29, 38, 43, 46, 51, 53, and 56.

YY   *Yün-men yü-lu* (Jap. *Unmon goroku*), 12th c., Taishō, vol. 47. The recorded sayings of master Yün-men. Case cited: 42 (also in PYL).

The larger compilations from which many of the above texts are cited include:

DZZ *Dōgen zenji zenshū*, 7 vols. (Tokyo: Shunjūsha, 1988–1993). The collected works of Dōgen.

HTC *Hsü tsang ching* (Jap. *Zoku zōkyō*), 150 vols. (Taipei: Shin Wen Feng, n.d.). The supplement to the Taishō that contains many important Zen works.

Taishō *Taishō shinshū daizōkyō*, 85 vols. (Tokyo: Taishō Issaikyō Kankōkai, 1924–1932). The authoritative collection of Buddhist works in Chinese and Japanese, with several volumes containing seminal Zen texts.

ON READING KŌANS

The translations vary in the extent of commentary included for each of the kōans.[42] This reflects the variation in the commentarial styles of the traditional sources. Most of the kōan collections, like the *Wu-men kuan*, include prose and verse commentaries. But several important collections only have verse commentary, and some collections like Dōgen's *Mana Shōbōgenzō* are just a listing of cases without any commentary.

The *Wu-men kuan*, which contains a four-line verse and a brief prose paragraph, has a fairly simple and straightforward structure when compared with two other major collections, the *Pi-yen lu* and the *Ts'ung-jung lu*. Both collections contain multiple levels of commentary provided by two editors: an original compiler of the cases composed commentaries in prose and verse, and then a later editor further commented, sometimes line by line, on the original commentaries. These collections also include an introductory comment or "pointer," in addition to verse and prose commentary sections that are lengthier than the *Wu-men kuan* comments. The *Pi-yen lu* and *Ts'ung-jung lu* also contain another distinctive style of commentary: "capping phrases," which usually make ironic allusions to other Zen or non-Buddhist texts in commenting on the main case or on the verse or prose commentary. The *Pi-yen lu* contains an additional style of commentary, "notes," which are usually ironic remarks on key phrases or passages of the main case.

This translation does not attempt to provide the complete set of commentaries available for all of the kōans. Rather, it highlights the main cases and selects representative commentary sections to illustrate various interpretive styles and themes. The section of commentary included in the translation is based on the translator's selection process and thus varies from case to case. The "discussion" section that follows the translation of every case explains the source text from which the kōan is cited. The main components of kōan records are:[43]

> POINTER. This section of commentary, included in the *Pi-yen lu* and *Ts'ung-jung lu* collections, provides introductory philosophical commentary on the main case.
>
> MAIN CASE. The main case consists of an encounter dialogue usually excerpted from one of the transmission of the lamp records or recorded sayings texts. It is fair to assume that the Zen monks studying kōan collections in Sung China and Kamakura Japan would have been very familiar with the source texts. Collections with longer sections of prose commentaries like the *Pi-yen lu* and *Ts'ung-jung lu* usually recapture the fuller narrative background from the source.
>
> PROSE COMMENTARY. Prose commentary or *nien-ku* (Jap. *nenko*) can be as short as a brief paragraph or considerably longer (several pages in English translation). The shorter commentaries generally focus on philosophical themes, while the longer commentaries usually reproduce the narrative background of the encounter dialogue.
>
> VERSE COMMENTARY. Known as *sung-ku* (Jap. *juko*), the original style of commentary included in the earliest kōan collections was a four-line verse (this still appears in the *Wu-men kuan* and Dōgen's *Eihei kōroku*). Other major collections often contained longer verses of eight or ten lines with capping phrases. There were also special collections, not translated here, that compiled all of the available verses on a given kōan.
>
> CAPPING PHRASES. This is one of the most innovative styles of commentary that epitomizes the Zen approach to hermeneutics. Used throughout the *Pi-yen lu* and *Ts'ung-jung lu* collections and further perfected by Japanese Rinzai master Daitō, "a Zen capping phrase is something of a cross between a kōan and a footnote. . . . [It] is supposed to be able to make a comment, resolve a specific conundrum, convey a Zen insight, transform another's awareness, resonate like a line of poetry, or perform several of these functions simultaneously."[44] The capping phrase is generally one to twenty-five words, with quotations from sutras, recorded sayings, other kōans, Chinese poetry, Confucian and other religious texts, or popular proverbs.
>
> NOTES. Another innovation in the *Pi-yen lu*, the notes on key phrases of the main case usually offer an ironic allusion or comment.

The translation of each kōan also includes:

DISCUSSION. This is the translator's analysis of the main case and commentaries that examines the source texts as well as the role of supernatural and ritual imagery in understanding the kōan and its narrative background.

Notes

1. See Victoria Cass, *Dangerous Women: Warriors, Grannies, and Geishas of the Ming* (Lanham, MD: Rowman and Littlefield, 1999).

2. See the discussion in Kenneth L. Woodward, *The Book of Miracles: The Meaning of the Miracle Stories in Christianity, Judaism, Buddhism, Hinduism, Islam* (New York: Simon & Schuster, 2000), p. 361. The Buddhist strategy was to show the illusory character of all forms as demonstrated by their dependent origination and perpetual transformation into other forms. Therefore, "What looks like magic is in fact a demonstration of the emptiness of all things."

3. The twelve austerities of *dhutanga* practice include: wearing a robe made of rags, wearing a three-layered robe, begging, no excessive eating, eating one meal a day, restrained eating, living in isolation, living by the graveyard, sitting under a tree, sitting outdoors, sitting on the grass, and sitting up and never lying down. See Reginald Rey, *Buddhist Saints in India: A Study in Buddhist Values and Orientations* (New York: Oxford University Press, 1994).

4. Some examples of scholarship dealing with issues presented here include Bernard Faure, *The Rhetoric of Immediacy: A Cultural Critique of Chan/Zen Buddhism* (Princeton: Princeton University Press, 1991); William Bodiford, *Sōtō Zen in Medieval Japan* (Honolulu: University of Hawaii Press, 1993); and Steven Heine, *Shifting Shape, Shaping Text: Philosophy and Folklore in the Fox Kōan* (Honolulu: University of Hawaii Press, 1999). Some of the discussions of kōans in this volume draw on material from the latter book.

5. As Sueki Fumihiko notes, these cases "have to do with a deconstruction of the language of daily life, not with the elimination of language altogether. Quite the contrary, Chinese Ch'an puts great stress on language, though always in such a way as to avoid confusion with our ordinary, everyday way of using words." In "A Reexamination of Critical Buddhism," in *Pruning the Bodhi Tree: The Storm Over Critical Buddhism*, ed. Jamie Hubbard and Paul L. Swanson (Honolulu: University of Hawaii Press, 1997), p. 332.

6. For example, Ma-tsu was known for the teaching "This very mind itself is Buddha," but later reversed himself by declaring "No mind, no Buddha." See WMK cases 30 and 33.

7. See the analysis by Bernard Faure, *Chan Insights and Oversights: An Epistemological Critique of Chan* (Princeton: Princeton University Press, 1993), especially pp. 52–125.

8. See T. Griffith Foulk, "The Form and Function of Koan Literature: A Historical Overview," in *The Kōan: Texts and Contexts in Zen Buddhism*, ed. Steven Heine and Dale S. Wright (New York, Oxford University Press, 2000), pp. 15–45.

9. Jacques LeGoff, *The Medieval Imagination*, trans. Arthur Goldhammer (Chicago: University of Chicago Press, 1988).

10. See the discussion in Katsuki Sekida, *Two Zen Classics* (New York: Weatherhill, 1977), p. 35.

11. John Kieschnick, *The Eminent Monk: Buddhist Ideals in Medieval Chinese Hagiography* (Honolulu: University of Hawaii Press, 1997), p. 41.

12. Cass, *Dangerous Women*, pp. 65–66.

13. See Robert M. Gimello, "Chang Shang-ying on Wu-t'ai Shan," in *Pilgrims and Sacred Sites in China:*, ed. Susan Naquin and Chün-fang Yü (Berkeley: University of California Press, 1992), pp. 89–149; and Steven Heine, "Visions, Divisions, Revisions: The Encounter Between Iconoclasm and Supernaturalism in Kōan Cases about Mount Wu-t'ai," in *The Kōan*, pp. 137–167.

14. Yanagida Seizan, "The 'Recorded Sayings' Texts of Chinese Ch'an Buddhism," trans. John R. McRae, in *Early Ch'an in China and Tibet*, ed. Whalen Lai and Lewis R. Lancaster (Berkeley: Berkeley Buddhist Studies Series, 1983), pp. 185–205.

15. Yanagida, "The 'Recorded Sayings' Texts of Chinese Ch'an Buddhism," p. 189.

16. John R. McRae, *The Northern School and the Formation of Early Ch'an Buddhism* (Honolulu: University of Hawaii, 1986), pp. 93–97. The main difference is that these were not conversations but monologues or one-sided pronouncements of masters only, without any interaction with disciples. See also McRae, "The Antecedents of Encounter Dialogues in Chinese Ch'an Buddhism," in *The Kōan*, pp. 46–74.

17. McRae, *The Northern School and the Formation of Early Ch'an Buddhism*, p. 95.

18. Yanagida, "The 'Recorded Sayings' Texts of Chinese Ch'an Buddhism," p. 190.

19. Steven Heine, *Dōgen and the Kōan Tradition: A Tale of Two Shōbōgenzō Texts* (Albany: SUNY Press, 1994), p. 27.

20. Another important text was the precursor to the transmission of the lamp records, the *Tsu-t'ang chi* (Jap. *Sodōshū*) of 952. This text was preserved in Korean and reconstructed in Chinese in modern times.

21. Andy Ferguson, *Zen's Chinese Heritage: The Masters and Their Teachings* (Boston: Wisdom, 2000), p. 11.

22. Albert Welter, *The Meaning of Myriad Good Deeds: A Study of Yung-ming Yen-shou and the Wan-shan t'ung-kuei chi* (New York: Peter Lang, 1993), pp. 9, 11–12.

23. Ferguson, *Zen's Chinese Heritage*, p. 3.

24. LeGoff, *The Medieval Imagination*, p. 11.

25. Gail Ashton, *The Generation of Identity in Late Medieval Hagiography: Speaking the Saint* (London: Routledge, 2000), p. 2.

26. See Michel Foucault, *A Foucault Reader*, ed. Paul Rabinow (New York: Pantheon, 1970).

27. Cass, *Dangerous Women*, p. 17. In addition, in his study of hermits in modern mainland China, especially in the region of the Chung-nan mountains, Bill Porter comments, "I concluded that if Buddhism were to survive in China, as anywhere else, it would depend not so much on monks and nuns living in temples as it would on them living in huts and caves." In *Road to Heaven: Encounters with Chinese Hermits* (San Francisco: Mercury House, 1993), p. 9.

28. Bernard Faure emphasizes the role of "dreams, thaumaturgy, death, relics, ritual, and gods . . . usually silenced or explained away—both by the tradition itself and by its scholarly replication—by means of notions such as the Two Truths," in *The Rhetoric of Immediacy*, p. 305.

29. I. M. Lewis, *Religion in Context: Cults and Charisma* (Cambridge: Cambridge University Press, 1996).

30. William F. Powell, trans., *The Record of Tung-Shan* (Honolulu: University of Hawaii Press/Kuroda Institute, 1986), p. 17.

31. Susan Naquin and Chün-fang Yü, "Introduction: Pilgrimage in China," in *Pilgrims and Sacred Sites in China*, p. 12.

32. In Burton Watson, trans., *Chinese Lyricism: Shih Poetry from the Second to the Twelfth Century* (New York: Columbia University Press, 1971), p. 175. The dragons are usually interpreted as representing passions, but the scene could certainly be a supernatural encounter. The description of nature makes an interesting contrast with the following verse by utopian essayist T'ao-ch'ien, who also affirms the role of transcendence amid urban life in "Hermit Among the Flowers."

> I built my cottage among the habitations of men,
> And yet there is no clamor of carriages and horses.
> You ask: "Sir, how can this be done?"
> "A heart that is distant creates its own solitude."
> I pluck chrysanthemums under the eastern hedge,
> Then gaze afar toward the southern hills.
> The mountain air is fresh at the dusk of day;

The flying birds in flocks return.
In these there lies a deep meaning;
I want to tell you, but have forgotten the words.

33. Taigen Daniel Leighton, trans. *Cultivating the Empty Field: The Silent Illumination of Zen Master Hongzhi* (San Francisco: North Point Press, 1991), p. 57. The need for a separation from society accompanied by an appreciation of solitude is expressed by writers of many cultures, and the Chinese approach greatly influenced Thoreau's writing in *Walden*.

34. Porter, *Road to Heaven*, p. 25.

35. Taishō 85:1283.

36. Some of the leading thinkers in the Zen tradition subsequent to the classic period have created a curriculum for the study of kōans by devising a set of categories for grouping cases selected from among various collections. Perhaps the best known example is the system created by Rinzai master Hakuin that has five categories encompassing several hundred cases: realizing the Dharmakaya (the absolute or ultimate level of the Buddha-nature); conveying dynamism; emphasizing verbal expression; requiring difficulty to pass through; and attaining nonattachment. See Akizuki Ryūmin, *Mumonkan o yomu* (Tokyo: Tosho insatsu, 1990), pp. 211–221. Many additional types of curriculum using a particular sequence of cases as the basis of a study program have been developed but remain unpublished or in the private possession of a particular teacher or teaching lineage. These programs are generally designed to foster a special, secretive tutelage relationship between teacher and disciple.

37. The golden age of Zen is generally considered to be the T'ang era (618-907) when many of the most creative and noteworthy masters lived, whereas the Sung era (960-1279) is considered a less dynamic, more scholastic and regimented period. However, the Sung was the time of the great production of Zen texts, so in that sense it also enjoys a golden age status.

38. For example, cases 13, 27, and 56 are appropriate in the category of dangerous women, cases 34 and 59 deal with Tung-shan, case 11 deals with a symbol of authority, and cases 31 and 50 are representative of the Northern school.

39. The following is a list of translations that have been consulted: CCL—partial translation by Sohaku Ogata, trans., *The Transmission of the Lamp: Early Masters* (Wolfeboro, NH: Longwood, 1990), and selections in Chang Chung-yuan, trans., *Original Teachings of Ch'an Buddhism* (New York: Vintage, 1969). DK—Thomas Cleary, trans., *Transmission of Light: Zen in the Art of Enlightenment* (San Francisco: North Point Press, 1990). EK—Yūhō Yokoi, trans., *The Eihei-kōroku* (Tokyo: Sankibō Buddhist Bookstore, 1987). KZK—none available. KS—Gudo Wafu Nishijima and Chodo Cross, trans., *Shobogenzo*, 4 vols. (Tokyo: Windbell Publications, 1994–1999). LL—Ruth Fuller Sasaki, trans. *The Recorded Sayings of Ch'an Master Lin-chi Hui-chao of Chen Prefecture* (Kyoto: The Institute of Zen Studies, 1975), and Burton Watson, trans., *The Zen Teachings of Master Lin-chi* (Boston: Shambala, 1993). MS—Gudo Wafu Nishijima, trans., *Master Dōgen's Shinji Shōbōgenzō*, vol. 1 (Tokyo: Windbell Publications, 1990), plus an unpublished typescript of vols. 2 and 3. PCY—Thomas Cleary, trans., *Sayings and Doings of Pai-chang* (Los Angeles: Center Publications, 1978). PYL—Thomas Cleary and Christopher Cleary, trans., *The Blue Cliff Record*, 3 vols. (Boulder, CO: Shambala, 1977), and Katsuki Sekida, trans., *Two Zen Classics* (New York: Weatherhill, 1977). SZ—Reihō Matsunaga, trans., *A Primer of Sōtō Zen: A translation of Dōgen's Shōbōgenzō Zuimonki* (Honolulu: The University Press of Hawaii, 1975). TJL—Thomas Cleary, *Book of Serenity* (Hudson, NY: Lindisfarne Press, 1990). TSL—William F. Powell, trans., *The Record of Tung-Shan* (Honolulu: University of Hawaii Press/Kuroda Institute, 1986). WMK—Robert Aitken, trans., *The Gateless Barrier: Wu-men kuan (Mumonkan)* (San Francisco: North Point Press, 1991); Thomas Cleary, trans. *No Barrier: Unlocking the Zen Koan* (New York: Bantam, 1993); Katsuki Sekida, trans., *Two Zen Classics* (New York: Weatherhill, 1977); Zenkei Shibayama, *Zen Comments on the Mumonkan*, trans. (New York: Mentor, 1974); and Kōun Yamada, trans. Sumiko Kudo, *The Gateless Gate* (Tucson: University of Arizona Press, 1990). YY—Urs App, *Master Yunmen: From the Record of Chan*

Teacher "Gate of the Clouds" (New York: Kodansha, 1994). In addition, selections of Zen records appear in John C. H. Wu, *Golden Age of Zen* (Taiwan: United, 1975), and several cases discussed in this volume have been dealt with in Heine, *Shifting Shape, Shaping Text.*

40. See Heinrich Dumoulin, *Zen Buddhism: A History, Volume 1, India and China*, trans. James W. Heisig and Paul Knitter (New York: Macmillan, 1988), pp. 8–9.

41. Additional texts consulted include several transmission of the lamp records, especially the *Tsung-men t'ung-yao chi* of 1093, *Tsung-men lien-teng hui-yao* of 1163, and *Wu-teng hui-yüan* of 1253, as well as monastic rules texts including the *Ch'an-men kuei-chih* of 1003 and the *Ch'an-yüan ch'ing-kuei* of 1103.

42. In many instances there are a number of different versions of the narrative in the multiple texts of the various genres, so that the same dialogue is often included—usually with some variation—in transmission of the lamp records, recorded sayings texts, and kōan collections.

43. Translations of pointers are included in cases 7, 13, 14, 20, 22, 28, 34, 36, 40, 42, 47, 58, and 60; prose commentary is included in cases 6, 19, 21, 23, 27, 29, 36, 38, 39, 43, 46, 51, 53, and 56; cases with verse commentary include 5, 6, 8, 13, 17, 18, 19, 20, 21, 23, 29, 32, 33, 34, 36, 38, 40, 42, 43, 45, 46, 48, 49, 51, 53, 54, and 56; capping phrases are translated in cases 7, 14, and 44 (as commentary on the main case), and in cases 40 and 49 (as a second, interlinear level of commentary on the verse commentaries); and notes are translated in case 39.

44. Kenneth Kraft, *Eloquent Zen: Daitō and Early Japanese Zen* (Honolulu: University of Hawaii Press, 1902), p. 2.

[ONE]

Surveying
Mountain
Landscapes

The cases in this chapter deal with encounters that Zen masters had with images and symbols of nature animated by supernatural properties that are reflected in popular religious beliefs. These kōans demonstrate that while Zen masters admired mountains as a realm of purity and transcendence where they could practice meditation in seclusion or establish a new monastery, they also had to contest with, overcome, or assimilate magical forces—including spirits, gods, and bodhisattvas as well as demons—that controlled the entranceway to those domains. This was done through the power of Zen rituals, contemplation, and rhetoric that was able to challenge and successfully overcome diverse and dispersed supernatural elements in the mountain landscape and ultimately transform them into representations of the Buddhist Dharma.

The term "mountain" in Zen can refer to real places where monks journey in search of an ideal location for a hermitage retreat. Or, the term implies a sacralized sense of space populated by supernatural forces and engaged by pilgrims and other travelers. Mountains, with their towering, misty peaks and valleys below, with their rushing streams and lush vegetation, represent interiority and the progressions and digressions of the spiritual path. According to traditional Buddhist cosmology, mythical Mount Sumeru was the central structure of the universe, and a kōan in the *Pi-yen lu* (case 23) cites a passage from the *Avatamsaka Sutra* concerning the "Wondrous Mystic Peak," a symbol for ultimate reality, that is identified in the case with here-and-now reality. In general, kōan records and commentaries vacillate between asserting/affirming the supernatural context explicitly or implicitly and the iconoclastic tendency to negate and transcend supernaturalism as the only conceptual sphere, or to reorient this imagery from a demythological perspective.

Supernatural imagery stemming from the influence of the hagiographical context of monk biography texts is most clearly evident in the first group of kōans in this chapter attributed to masters of the Northern and Ox Head schools. The Northern school was dominant in the early eighth century until it was surpassed by the followers of sixth patriarch Hui-neng. The first two cases in this section deal with the threatening presence and conversion of local gods and demons. However, the third case shows a transition from an emphasis on an engagement with supernatural elements to the importance of an encounter dialogue between monks that transmutes supernaturalism into a symbol for interior realization. The case representing the Ox Head or Niu-t'ou school, another early Zen movement located on the mountain of the same name and led by master Niu-t'ou Fa-jung, also reveals a shift from a reliance on supernaturalism to iconoclasticism.

By the time of the hegemony of the Southern school in the late eighth and ninth centuries, supernatural implications were placed in the background of kōan discourse while the rhetoric of irony and demythology appreared at the forefront. The emphasis shifted to the role of ritual and rhetoric as a way for a master to establish and declare his leadership of a mountain domain. The dialogues involving Tung-shan Liang-chieh, who established his own important lineage that later flourished in Sung China and Kamakura Japan, reveal the subtle games of wordplay and purposeful ambiguity concerning the meaning of mountain landscapes that Zen masters play. Beginning in the late tenth century, the center of the Southern school became the "Five Mountains" monastic system in Chekiang province.

The final section highlights the encounter between the visionary, supernatural realm of Mount Wu-t'ai in northern Shansi province, which represented an entirely different style of Buddhism based on esoteric or tantric beliefs, and the iconoclastic trends of Zen contemplation that resisted but could not help but be attracted to the Mount Wu-t'ai brand of religiosity. Although many prominent Zen masters tried to prohibit their disciples from making the long trek, the potential for receiving visions of the bodhisattva Manjusri had a powerful appeal that appealed to a steady stream of seekers.

Northern and Ox Head Schools

1. Yüan-kuei Subdues the Mountain God

Main Case

Master Yüan-kuei of Mount Sung used divination to choose a cottage in a valley deep in the mountains as a site to practice a life of reclusion. One day, a strange man appeared in the deep mountains wearing formal attire and accompanied by a large retinue of attendants. He demanded to see the master. Yüan-kuei, noticing that his visitor had a strange and unusual manner, greeted him, "Welcome, friend, why have you come here?"

The man answered, "Master, don't you recognize me?" The master replied, "I view Buddha and sentient beings equally. Why should I distinguish you from the rest of them?" The man declared, "I am the god of the mountain, and can make people live or die. How can you regard me as just one more being?"

The master said, "I am originally unborn. You claim to be able to make me die, but I see you beyond any discrimination as empty of selfhood and you see me beyond any discrimination as empty of selfhood. Even if you can destroy emptiness and yourself, I will remain unborn and undying, so why should I accept your claim to control my living and dying?"

The god bowed down to the floor in reverence and said, "I am the most confident and upright of the gods. But I didn't realize that you possessed such eloquence and wisdom. Please grant the true precepts that will enable me to transcend the world." The master replied, "When you ask about the precepts you are already observing the precepts, because there are no precepts apart from seeking out the precepts."

Discussion

This dialogue is cited from CCL vol. 4 (Taishō 51:233b), a section in the earliest transmission of the lamp history that includes a listing of the hagiographical records of many of the Northern school patriarchs, usually without any form of additional commentary. Although the Northern school was centered in the twin capital cities of Chang-an and Luo-yang, it also flourished at nearby Mount Sung. This case incorporates elements of ritual and supernaturalism along with an emphasis on Zen iconoclastic rhetoric expressing a nondual philosophy. In the end, it is the rhetoric of nonduality that wins the day by overcoming the manifestations of supernaturalism based on the contemplation of emptiness and absence of selfhood.

The case begins with Yüan-kuei guided to his site of reclusion in the mountains by a magical process of divination. He finds himself in the "deep mountains," a term used repeatedly in Zen literature to refer to the inner recesses of a mountain range where traces of civilization vanish and one faces only the forces of untamed nature as well as the lurking presence of the supernatural. In the deep mountains of Mount Sung, deities appear as snakes or some other shapeshifting apparition and weep at death or express repentance for their misdeeds as an avenue for their conversion to the Buddhist Dharma.

Here the deity takes on a human appearance that gives away its true identity by manifesting a "strange and unusual manner" and asserts its power over life and death. Yüan-kuei responds by evoking the ultimate equality of living and dying from the standpoint of the "unborn," a notion of the empty ground of existence that becomes important for later Zen thinkers, especially the Japanese master Bankei. When Yüan-kuei's assertion of the meaning of emptiness proves effective in transforming the deity, who then asks to receive the precepts, the master makes a very interesting comment about the essential uselessness of the precepts in relation to Zen contemplation. This approach is actually quite similar to the Southern school philosophy.

In traditional Buddhist practice, taking the precepts, or ascribing to the list of 250 ethical vows, is the centerpiece of the ordination process that is renewed during a fortnightly repentance ceremony that functions as a kind of Buddhist Sabbath. Another important time for renewal of the precepts is the end of the three-month rainy season retreat. While the Zen monastic institution has always adhered to the formal practice of taking the Buddhist precepts, it also gained prominence by advocating a new philosophical position that the precepts—as specific codes of conduct or commandments—were essentially unnecessary and even counterproductive if considered a means to the end of attaining enlightenment. Zen philosophy argues that the genuine meaning of the precepts is nothing other than ongoing contemplation of the unborn.

On that issue, despite the sectarian rivalry that led to its demise, the Northern school's outlook expressed in this dialogue is consistent with the philosophy of Hui-neng's *Platform Sutra*. This text makes a basic distinction between "repentance about things," which is considered an inferior approach, and "repentance about the principle (of emptiness)," based on nonduality. However, the CCL narrative later indicates that in the end, Yüan-kuei allows the deity to repay his indebtedness by magically transplanting cedar trees on the mountain. Yüan-kuei even warns his disciples against talking about this incident for fear of being accused of supporting the supernatural by competitors from other religious schools.

2. Tao-shu and the Trickster

Main Case

Master Tao-shu, in seeking the Dharma, decided to go on a pilgrimage to visit places he had never seen. After studying at various sites he returned to Northern school patriarch Shen-hsiu, who enlightened him with a single word. Tao-shu understood the subtle meaning of Shen-hsiu's teaching, and in later years he became a good vessel for the Dharma. Using divination to find a dwelling place, he built a humble hermitage at the Three Peaks of the Shou State to continue his practice in solitude. He attracted a following of young disciples.

There lived on the mountain a strange, mischievous spirit, who frequently appeared as a beggar talking and laughing, and at other times manifested in the figure of a bodhisattva or a hermit. Sometimes, the spirit produced radiant lights or spoke in strange voices and echoes. Although the young monks saw and heard them, none of them were able to fathom what these phenomena really were. After ten years of tricks, the spirit vanished once and for all, and no more shadows, figures, or voices ever appeared.

Master Tao-shu told the assembly, "That trickster deceived many people with his pranks. There was only one weapon against his antics—the 'way of non-seeing and non-hearing.' The talent of playing tricks is limited and eventually exhausted. But the capability of non-seeing and non-hearing is limitless and inexhaustible."

Discussion

Also cited from CCL vol. 4 (Taishō 51:232b), this kōan highlights the rhetoric of emptiness in an encounter between a master and the spirit of the mountain that has a menacing, persistent presence. Tao-shu begins his path as a pilgrim who is enlightened by a "single word" from the main patriarch of the Northern school, Shen-hsiu. Like Yüan-kuei in case 1, he continues his journey by using divination to discover an ideal site for reclusion in the deep mountains. Yet Tao-shu's solitary practice in a "humble hermitage" attracts a following of young monks who are disturbed by the tricks of the spirit and turn to their teacher for solace, so that this encounter becomes a test of his own powers.

In contrast to case 1, in which the spirit is lured to appear in human form by the presence of an accomplished meditator and quickly repents and converts, this entity manifests as a trickster for many years. It appears by either shapeshifting into the form of a beggar, hermit, or bodhisattva—which is also a power that Buddhist deities utilize for compassionate pedagogical purposes—or taking on a quasi-physical appearance as a radiance or a sound. In any case, the spirit is illusory and deceptive. But, in a way that is very similar to the previous case, Tao-shu performs an exorcism that eliminates the mischievous appearance of the spirit through the power of his contemplation and rhetoric of nonduality. The master overcomes the spirit by preaching a message of "non-seeing and non-hearing." Like the notion of the unborn, this refers to a fundamental identity of form and formlessness, illusion and reality, or what is perceptible to the senses and what is beyond the realm of sense perception.

Evoking the way of non-seeing and non-hearing proves effective in vanquishing the spirit. This could imply Tao-shu's ignoring of the spirit by acting as if it were only an illusion that did not deserve or require any more attention. Or it could support a holding fast of his mental energy to offset the force of negativity represented by the spirit's presence. The other monks, who were aware of the trickster's manifestations but never had an understanding of their origins or meaning, are relieved and impressed by the master's capabilities. The master eliminates the troublesome obstacles to the genuine opening of the mountain, so that the landscape is now able to receive the presence of the Dharma.

3. Master Chiang-mo, Subjugator of Demons

Main Case

Master Chiang-mo Ts'ang of Yen-chou hailed from Chao county. His surname was Wang, and his father was a government official. He was ordained as a novice at the age of seven. At that time, there were numerous strange, abnormal, or supernatural beings lurking in the fields, but he fearlessly handled them, so he was given the name Subjugator of Demons (Chiang-mo). He later received the transmission from master Ming-tsan of Kuang-fu Temple. Some time after this, Chiang-mo decided to be ordained and to study the Dharma seriously with the Northern school, which was flourishing in the country at that time. Chiang-mo resolved to gird up his robe and enter their Dharma Hall.

Master Chiang-mo was challenged by master Shen-hsiu, "You are called the Subjugator of Demons. Here there are no spirits lurking in the mountain or ghosts haunting the trees. What kind of demons will you subjugate?" Chiang-mo replied, "If there are Buddhas, then there are also demons." Shen-hsiu said, "Perhaps you are one of the demons. Then you would surely dwell in a mysterious, unthinkable realm." Chiang-mo said, "The realm of the Buddhas is empty. What other kind of realm can there be?"

Shen-hsiu commented, "I'm sure you will leave relics at your burial mound!"

Discussion

This dialogue is cited from the same section of CCL vol. 4 (Taishō 51:232b–c) as are the previous two kōans, but this case reveals a significant shift in focus from the process of claiming a mountain through an encounter with the local god or demon to an exchange with Shen-hsiu, who as leader of the monastic institution challenges an irregular monk's supranormal powers. Shen-hsiu, the main patriarch of the Northern school, is depicted as the true liberator and arbiter of the mountain domain, although the teaching of emptiness and the equality of opposites—in this instance, the unity of Buddhas and demons—remains consistent with the basic message of the previous dialogues. However, the case concludes with a spotlight on the popular religious practice of venerating relics.

Chiang-mo takes his name from his reputation for subjugating or exorcising demons—that is, the strange, mysterious supernatural beings lurking in the fields, but he has not yet become an ordained Zen priest. Apparently, he wishes to relinquish his independent, solitary status and become part of the institutional mainstream. In order to gain this status and enter into the lineage of the Northern school by earning the right to wear his robes, Chiang-mo must face an encounter with Shen-hsiu inside the gates of the Dharma Hall. Shen-hsiu proclaims that the sense of space is radically different—iconoclastic and free of supernaturalism—in the

Dharma Hall. There are no mountain spirits or tree ghosts lurking, and therefore nothing to be subjugated.

At first Chiang-mo responds to Shen-hsiu's challenge by asserting the validity of the supernatural realm—"If there are Buddhas, then there must be demons"—thereby seeming to fall into the patriarch's trap. But he escapes this predicament by evoking the rhetoric of emptiness and iconoclasm, even denying the existence of Buddhas. Shen-hsiu proclaims his approval by declaring that Chiang-mo's corpse will reveal relics (*sarira*), which are rare, jewel-like deposits left in the cremated remains of Buddhist saints and stored in special monuments or stupas. Buddhist relics are considered to possess magical properties for healing, divination, and fortune-telling.

Following this encounter, according to the account in the CCL, Chiang-mo eventually entered Mount T'ai, and while he taught there for several years "students gathered around him like clouds." One day the master told his students, "I have gotten old and in the way. Let me return to a place where all things reach their limit." Just as he finished speaking he passed away while sitting in the lotus position, at the age of ninety-one, an early Zen master who could control the manner and timing of his dying.

4. Does Niu-t'ou Need the Flowers?

Main Case

How was it that before Niu-t'ou encountered the fourth patriarch Tao-hsin, the birds used to flock to him with flowers in their beaks, whereas after their meeting the auspicious phenomenon ceased?

Discussion

This kōan is based on a passage in CCL vol. 4 (Taishō 51:226c–227b) that deals with Niu-t'ou Fa-jung, the founder of the Ox Head or Niu-t'ou school. Along with the Northern school, the Ox Head school was a successful early Zen movement in the seventh century, before the Southern school became dominant through the efforts of Hui-neng and his evangelical disciple Shen-hui. The Ox Head school was known for advocating a standpoint based on "formless precepts" that was influenced by the Madhyamika philosophy of emptiness, and also became a factor influencing Tendai Buddhism brought to Japan by Saichō. The influence of Zen on the

Japanese Tendai sect was short-lived, however, and it was not until the thirteenth century that Zen began to flourish in Japan based on the Sōtō teachings of Dōgen and the Rinzai teachings of Eisai.

As with the Northern school, the Ox Head literature was close in style to the hagiographical materials in the monk biography texts. This case emerged from a fascinating narrative about the encounter between Niu-t'ou, who was then a hermit, and fourth patriarch Tao-hsin, who came to visit his mountain hut near the northern cliff of the temple. Every day, hundreds of birds flocked to Niu-t'ou with flowers in their beaks, as a sign of nature paying homage to the meditation master. Also, a huge snake once came into his hut and stayed for a hundred days without harming the monk.

Although he was residing some distance away, Tao-hsin became aware of these auspicious phenomena and traveled to check out the master who was receiving so much adulation. When Tao-hsin arrived in the area, he asked a monk if there was a "man of Tao" in the vicinity, and was told that on the mountain one would be hard-pressed to find someone who was not a man of Tao. But when asked to identify such a person in a more specific or concrete way, the monk was at first speechless. He then suggested that Tao-hsin venture another ten miles to find "Lazy Jung," so called because he did not bother to rise from his sitting position to greet visitors.

Tao-hsin indeed discovered Niu-t'ou in his monastic cell sitting in the lotus posture, oblivious to everything and everyone. When Niu-t'ou realized the importance of his guest, he took Tao-hsin to see his hermitage where there were tigers and wolves prowling around that protected the meditator from any harm. Tao-hsin made a gesture of fright in order to liberate Niu-t'ou from his excessive isolation. When that tactic failed, he inscribed the word "Buddha" on the stone seat Niu-t'ou used for meditation. This had a kind of exorcistic effect that focused the attention of Niu-t'ou, who gazed in reverential awe at the insignia, on the significance of Tao-hsin's message.

Tao-hsin then delivered a sermon that is crucial to understanding the transition in early Zen from a reliance on supranormal powers to the rhetoric of anti-supernaturalism. The patriarch explained patiently that supranormal powers are based on the mind of contemplation that is free of karmic hindrances, making judgments, or indulging in illusory distinctions between right and wrong. On hearing these words Niu-t'ou attained enlightenment, and the supernatural appearance of birds carrying flowers as well as other magical animals ceased and dissolved altogether. Now that he understood the meaning of emptiness as the root and basis for the manifestation of supranormal powers, Niu-t'ou apparently became invisible to the spirits, one of the abilities attributed to attributed to advanced Zen masters (also seen in case 32).

SOUTHERN SCHOOL

5. Pai-chang Meditates on Ta-hsiung Peak

Main Case

A monk asked Pai-chang, "What is the most extraordinary thing?" Pai-chang said, "Sitting alone on Ta-hsiung Peak."
The monk bowed, and Pai-chang hit him.

Verse Commentary (by Hsüeh-tou)

> In the realm of the patriarchs, the heavenly colt goes galloping by,
> Among his styles of teaching, enfolding and unraveling are two
>   different modes,
> He flashes the ability to shift with circumstance like a bolt of
>   lightning or a spark struck from a stone,
> It's laughable how an ordinary monk thinks he can just grab the
>   tiger by its whiskers!

Discussion

This case is cited from PYL 26 (Taishō 48:166c–167b), along with four-line verse commentary by Hsüeh-tou. As the Southern school gained hegemony, numerous monasteries were opened and established, especially in the mountainous regions south of the Yangtze River. The monasteries often were large compounds, in some cases with dozens of buildings expanding from the seven-hall base structure that housed hundreds of monks. But outside the grounds of the temple, the mountains remained untamed and populated by irregular practitioners, magical animals, and other supernatural forces. The dialogues of Southern school masters rarely mention supernaturalism directly, but it forms the background or narrative context for the iconoclastic rhetoric of numerous kōans.

In this brief case, the key element is Ta-hsiung (literally, "Great Sublime") Peak, a high, rocky promontory that was located behind or just to the northwest of Mount Pai-chang ("Hundred Fathoms High"). The area running between the monastery of master Pai-chang, who was the founder of the system of Zen monastic rules emphasizing the role of the abbot as the "living Buddha," and Ta-hsiung Peak was apparently filled with huts and hermitages. These huts were mostly for irregular practitioners, although some were used by monks from the temple. A number of prominent hermits are referred to in the prose commentary on a *Pi-yen lu* kōan (case 85 in that collection), in addition to magical tigers that lurked near the summit. According to a famous dialogue involving Pai-chang and his main disciple Huang-po, the masters talked about whether Huang-po had to subjugate any tigers during a trip to the peak. Then, following the disciple's irreverent response, Pai-chang referred to Huang-po as a tiger.

The leading question in this case inquires of Pai-chang, "What is 'extraordinary' (Ch. *ch'i*, Jap. *ki*)?," using a term found throughout Chinese folklore that refers to the mysterious and anomalous realm of existence including spirits, sprites, and otherworldly beings. The meaning of this term is very similar to Jacques LeGoff's sense of the marvelous in medieval European hagiographical literature. The implication of the monk's question is that it is expected that supernatural, marvelous elements transpire on Ta-hsiung. But Pai-chang interprets this as a query about the role of spiritual training. He dramatically slaps the disciple, apparently for being overly deferential rather than independent in his outlook.

Pai-chang's response to the question is somewhat surprising in that he cites an activity that takes place outside the gates of the temple system he wholeheartedly endorsed. His emphasis on solitary meditation reveals the interplay between the realms of regularity and irregularity, or the mainstream institution and the domain of raw, untamed nature. The opening line of the verse commentary refers to Pai-chang, the disciple of Ma-tsu whose name literally means "horse," as a galloping heavenly colt. The last line identifies Pai-chang as a tiger whose whiskers cannot be grasped.

This case gained prominence because it served as a topic for important commentaries by Dōgen and his Chinese mentor Ju-ching. Ju-ching reconsidered the leading query and rewrote the response as, "It is only to eat rice in a bowl at Ching-tsu-ssu temple on Mount T'ien-t'ung." He thereby shifted the focus from solitary zazen to everyday activities, as well as from Mount Pai-chang to his own mountain temple.

Dōgen reflected on this case at least five times in his works. In the earlier writings, he cited Ju-ching's comments approvingly. But during a later sermon, Dōgen spontaneously rewrote the case by raising his staff, then throwing it down, and stepping off the dais. Several years later, he again rewrote the case with the remark that the most extraordinary thing is "delivering sermons at Eiheiji temple." This is intriguing in that Dōgen is primarily known for his emphasis on zazen meditation through the doctrine of "just sitting" (*shikan taza*) rather than for delivering sermons, whereas Pai-chang is known for stressing sermons in his monastic rules text that makes little mention of the need for sitting meditation.

6. Kuei-shan Kicks Over the Water Pitcher

Main Case

When Kuei-shan was studying under master Pai-chang, he worked as chief cook of the monastery. Pai-chang wanted to appoint him abbot of a new monastery to be built on Mt. Ta-kuei. He instructed Kuei-shan and the head monk of the assembly to each offer a few words showing their understanding of Zen. The most capable one would be sent to open the new monastery.

Pai-chang picked up a water pitcher and set it on a rock, asking: "Without calling it a water pitcher, let's see what you will call it?" The head monk said, "It cannot be called a wooden sandal." Pai-chang then asked Kuei-shan. Kuei-shan strode forward, kicked over the pitcher, and then walked away from the scene.

Pai-chang said, "The head monk has lost to Kuei-shan." And so he sent Kuei-shan from the monastery to open the new mountain.

Prose Commentary

Kuei-shan was courageous but he could not escape Pai-chang's trap. On careful investigation, he selected what is heavy rather than what is light. How? Think about it! He removed his headband, and put on an iron yoke.

Verse Commentary

> Tossing aside bamboo baskets and wooden ladles,
> He makes a direct strike and cuts off entanglements.
> Pai-chang's double barrier cannot stop him,
> The tip of his toe creates innumerable buddhas.

Discussion

This kōan, cited from WMK case 40 (Taishō 48:296a), appears to epito-mize the iconoclastic approach with the kicking of the pitcher of water by Kuei-shan, an act that is admired and praised by master Pai-chang. Pai-chang approves of Kuei-shan's dramatic, rebellious gesture, just as he also accepts Huang-po's slap in the epilogue to case 38. He declares the head dis-ciple "the loser" of the contest, and Kuei-shan succeeds in establishing the new monastery. However, the kōan really revolves around a figure who is hidden from the dialogue in the main case and only appears in the narra-tive background that was originally included in several of the transmission of the lamp records beginning with CCL vol. 9 (Taishō 51:264b–266b).

The primary figure in this episode is neither Pai-chang nor Kuei-shan but Ssu-ma, an irregular monk also involved in notable dialogues with Kuei-shan about the "fox kōan," who was known as an expert in *dhutanga* or ascetic practices and who was also skilled in indigenous occult arts such as geomancy, divination, and physiognomy. Therefore, this case is a prime example of how important it is to recover a deleted or suppressed narrative structure encompassing supernatural elements in order to understand a kōan's overall meaning and significance.

The key to the two-fold discursive structure is in the *Wu-men kuan* prose commentary, which says that "after careful consideration, Pai-chang selected what is 'heavy' rather than what is 'light.'" Prior to the testing and evaluation of the two disciples, Ssu-ma, based on his occult powers, had already selected Kuei-shan for stewardship of Mount Ta-kuei. Pai-chang had asked the geomancer to determine the fate of the Ta-kuei mountain temple. Ssu-ma felt that Mount Ta-kuei was ideally suited to the formation of a formi-dable monastery with a large assembly of over a thousand monks, but he rejected Pai-chang, a gaunt man with ascetic habits, who he considered too retiring for the post. He had also tested the head disciple, Hua-lin, by asking him to cough deeply and walk three paces, and found him wanting. But he approved of Kuei-shan, "a mountain of flesh" with a vigorous personality, on first sight, even without putting him through an ordeal. Thus, the encounter dialogue between Pai-chang and Kuei-shan was a staged affair, with its result predetermined in large part by the supernatural powers of Ssu-ma rather than philosophical analysis or spiritual insight.

This situation is hinted in the *Wu-men kuan* prose and verse commen-taries. The prose commentary suggests that Kuei-shan "could not escape Pai-chang's trap," but was selected anyway. . . . How? "Think about it (*chien*)!" The last term in this passage, also used in the prose commentary of case 21, suggests the practice of providing a protection from ghosts (*chien* is a character that is posted near graves and other sites to ward off prowling spirits). In addition, the verse commentary refers to "the tip of [Kuei-shan's] foot kicking out myriad buddhas."

What transpires in the *Ching-te ch'uan-teng lu* narrative subsequent to the dialogue preserved in the kōan record is equally interesting and important for its use of supernatural imagery that is usually interpreted in a strictly iconoclastic vein. Kuei-shan lived for several years like a hermit on the peak of Mount Ta-kuei, which had previously been an inaccessible and forbidding region far from any sign of human habitation, and he subsisted on wild nuts and berries with only animals, including monkeys and birds, as his companions and friends. Nevertheless, his reputation for genuine spirituality spread and eventually the villagers in the valley below gained support from government officials in their efforts to construct for him a monastery on the mountain. Once established, Kuei-shan received numerous visitors seeking instruction in the Dharma, including the prime minister as well as Zen monks, such as Yang-shan, who became his main disciple. In one lecture that emphasized a literal view of karmic causality, Kuei-shan cautioned his followers to reject the teaching of an originally pure Buddha-nature that could never be contaminated by karmic defilements and to strive constantly to remove evil thoughts and deeds. This sermon was against the grain of Hui-neng's famous verse in the *Platform Sutra* on the primal purity of human nature unaffected by karma.

In addition, a version of the hagiography not included in the CCL highlights the role of the supernatural. Prior to his successes in the monastery, Kuei-shan got discouraged after eight years of solitude and decided to leave the mountain. On the pathway down, he met a friendly tiger, which appeared to beckon him to return to the peak. Kuei-shan followed this omen and shortly thereafter his fortunes improved. Meanwhile his rival, Hua-lin, the former head disciple, also became involved with sacred tigers. He lived as a hermit on another mountain when a visitor asked if he were not disheartened by the absence of disciples. The monk replied that he was not alone but had two attendants and he calls out for Tai-k'ung (J. Daikū) and Hsiao-k'ung (J. Shōkū), which literally mean "Great Emptiness" and "Small Emptiness." In response to the call, two fierce tigers came from the back of the hermitage, roaring ferociously. The visitor became terribly frightened but the tigers, instructed by the monk to be kind and courteous to his guest, crouched at his feet like two gentle kittens.

7. Te-shan Carrying His Bundle

Pointer

Standing out under the blue sky and in the open sunlight, it is not necessary to point to the east or to point to the west. But based on temporal conditions, we still must respond to a disease with the appropriate cure. Now, tell me, is it better to go with the flow or to hold fast? As a test, consider the following. Look!

Main Case (with capping phrases by Yüan-wu)

Te-shan came to see Kuei-shan.

> *Look at him carrying a board on his shoulder. That wild fox spirit!*

He carried his bundle into the Dharma Hall.

> *This can't help but cause people to doubt him. He has already suffered his first defeat.*

Then he crossed from the east side to the west side, and again from the west side to the east side.

> *He possesses the power of Zen, but what good does it do him?*

He looked around and said, "No one is here. There's nothing here," and then he left.

> *Give him thirty blows of the staff! His spirit reaches up to the heavens, but only a real lion cub can roar like a lion.*

[Hsüeh-tou comments: "He checked things out!"]

> *What a mistake, after all.*

But when Te-shan got to the gates of the temple he thought to himself, "I really should not be so crude."

> *Letting it all go, or taking it all in? At first too high, and then too low. When you realize the error of your ways, you should try to correct them. But how many people are capable of doing this?*

So he entered the Dharma Hall once again, with full ceremony, to greet the master.

> *He acts the same way as before. This must be his second defeat. Watch out!*

Kuei-shan just sat there.

> *He's watching that fellow with steely eyes. It takes someone like this to grab a tiger by the whiskers.*

Te-shan held up his teaching mat and said, "Teacher."

> *Switching heads and changing faces, he stirs up the waves even though there is no wind.*

Kuei-shan reached for his fly-whisk.

> *See what kind of person he is, setting his strategy in motion even while remaining in his tent. Nothing can stop him from cutting off the tongues of everyone in the world.*

Te-shan cried out, shook out his sleeves, and abruptly left.

> *This is the understanding of a wild fox spirit. In one shout, he expressed the provisional and the real, the illuminative and the functional. Among all those who can grab onto the clouds and grasp at the mist, he alone is uniquely skilled.*

[Hsüeh-tou comments: "He checked things out!"]

> *What a mistake, after all.*

Te-shan turned from the Dharma Hall, put on his straw sandals, and departed.

> *The landscape is charming, but the case is far from over. Te-shan kept the hat covering his head, but lost the shoes covering his feet. He's lost any chance he may have once had.*

That evening Kuei-shan asked the monk in charge of the Monks' Hall, "Where is the newcomer who was with me earlier."

> *He lost his footing in the east and gave up following the trail in the west. His eyes are gazing to the southeast but his heart is in the northwest.*

The head monk said, "At that time he turned away from the Dharma Hall, put on his straw sandals, and departed."

> *The spirit turtle is dragging his tail, and deserves thirty blows. How many blows to the back of the head does it take for him to get it?*

Kuei-shan said, "After this he will dwell on the summit of a peak all by himself, and build a hut where he scolds the Buddhas and reviles the Patriarchs.

> *Kuei-shan draws his bow after the thief has already gone. No patchrobed monk in all the world will be able to follow after Te-shan.*

[Hsüeh-tou added the comment, "He adds frost to snow."]

> *What a mistake, after all.*

Prose Commentary (selection by Yüan-wu)

When immersed in this kind of Zen, even if the myriad appearances and forms, heavens and hells, and all the plants, animals, and people all were to shout at once, he still wouldn't be bothered. Even if someone overthrew his meditation seat and scattered his congregation with shouts, he wouldn't give it any notice. It is as high as heaven, and as broad as the earth. If Kuei-shan did not have the ability to cut off the tongues of everyone on earth, at that time it would have been very difficult for him to test Te-shan. If he weren't the enlightened teacher of fifteen hundred people, at this point he wouldn't have been able to explain anything. But Kuei-shan was setting strategy in motion from within his tent that would settle victory over a thousand miles.

Discussion

This kōan, cited from PYL case 4 (Taishō 48:143b–144c), along with capping phrase commentary on each line of the main case, is a classic example of an encounter between two masters, one who claims the mountain temple as his own and the other who comes to challenge and test him with an irreverent, tables-turning manner. A key to understanding the case is the ritual context of the monastic institution, for which rules of etiquette regarding proper dress and behavior were prescribed in utmost detail. Although the basic set of Zen monastic rules was set forth in a very short, concise text attributed to Pai-chang in the first half of the ninth century, the lengthy and more detailed rules of the *Ch'an-yüan ch'ing-kuei* was not published until 1103. But it is safe to assume that codes of conduct regulating the attire of monks visiting a temple, including their entrance into the Dharma Hall, the central structure of the monastic compound, and their greeting of the resident master, were at least unofficially in effect at the time of Kuei-shan, one of Pai-chang's main disciples, and his contemporary Te-shan.

Te-shan was originally a member of the Vinaya order (this was a different sect based on monastic discipline, whereas Zen was based on meditation), and he was particularly known as a specialist in the *Diamond Sutra*. Carrying voluminous commentaries on the sutra in his backpack as he traveled from mountain to mountain, Te-shan was proud of his nickname, "King of the Diamond Sutra." Te-shan became part of the Shih-t'ou lineage, which had a Northern school orientation and later gave rise to the Ts'ao-tung (Jap. Sōtō) school. This eventually became the main rival to the Lin-chi (Jap. Rinzai) school that epitomized the Southern school approach. Therefore, Te-shan represented what was at the time the primary rival to the lineage represented by Kuei-shan.

The main difference between approaches was that the Northern school put an emphasis on the interpretation of scriptures or sutras and a more gradual method of attainment through meditation, whereas the Southern school emphasized sudden enlightenment perfected through everyday activities, such as communal labor, as well as a valorization of silence. Several kōans record how Te-shan was traveling south to investigate the Southern school approach with the intention of "going to raid their dens and caves and exterminate the whole crew, in or order to do justice to the compassion of the Buddha." While case 24 shows an elderly laywoman giving Te-shan his comeuppance, the current case indicates that Kuei-shan acknowledges Te-shan as a worthy rival who will soon be able to open and establish his own independent mountain. Therefore, this kōan endorses a multibranched approach to Zen lineal transmission.

By carrying his bundle right into the Dharma Hall, Te-shan shows that he is full of self-confidence, considering himself invincible and willing to disregard the regulations and intrude upon sacred territory by passing to and fro as if he enjoyed perfect freedom to do as he pleased. Then he thinks better, and returns to the Dharma Hall in a courteous and ceremonial manner. Kuei-shan responds by reaching for his fly-whisk, the main symbol of a master's authority and charisma, but it proves an ineffective technique, and Te-shan abruptly leaves, the apparent winner in this contest. Kuei-shan acknowledges the merit of Te-shan's irreverence, although the comment by Hsüeh-tou, the original compiler of the one hundred cases in the *Pi-yen lu*, indicates that his words of praise come too little, too late.

The aim of the capping phrases is to comment ironically on the encounter, first by questioning Te-shan who is repeatedly demeaned as a "wild fox spirit," a deceiver who carries a "board on his shoulder," or cannot move beyond a narrow, one-sided perspective. The capping phrase commentary also refers to Te-shan as a "spirit turtle," which means that he leaves a trail behind after his travels. When a turtle lays eggs in the sand it covers them to hide them but as it leaves its tail makes a track, revealing the hatchling's nest, which is similar to a Zen saying that you can hide a body but the shadow is still revealed. In the prose commentary, Kuei-shan is praised as a kind of general who sets his strategy in motion while remaining in the tent. Yet, at the end of the main case, the capping phrase commentary reverses itself and critiques Kuei-shan as someone who "draws his bow after the thief has already gone."

Meanwhile, the prose commentary (in a section not translated here) is characteristically ambivalent about the winners and losers of the case. The commentary remarks, "People say that Kuei-shan was afraid of Te-shan, but he was not flustered at all. It is said, 'One whose wisdom surpasses a bird's can catch a bird, and one whose wisdom surpasses an animal's can catch an animal, and one whose wisdom surpasses a man's can catch a man.'" Then, this section of commentary suggests, "Te-shan turned his back on the Dharma Hall, put on his straw sandals, and departed. Now, tell me, what was his meaning? Tell me, did Te-shan win or lose? In acting as he did, did Kuei-shan win or lose? In saying 'He checked things out' two times, Hsüeh-tou was like a bystander judging the two men." Finally, the prose commentary casts doubt on Kuei-shan's approval of Te-shan: "Te-shan could scold the Buddhas and revile the Patriarchs, but he would still never escape that cave. The marsh is so wide it can hide a mountain, and the cat is swift enough that it can subdue a leopard."

8. Nan-ch'üan Sweeping on a Mountain

Main Case

One day Nan-ch'üan was doing his chores and sweeping on the mountain. A monk approached him and asked, "Tell me the way to get to Mount Nan-ch'üan." Nan-ch'üan raised his sickle and said, "I bought this for thirty cents." The monk retorted, "I did not ask about the price of the sickle. What I asked about was the path to Mount Nan-ch'üan."

Nan-ch'üan said, "Now, let me get back to chopping down weeds."

Verse Commentary

> The novice came and went on Mount Nan-ch'üan,
> But, in trying to reach the peak, he had a wonderful experience,
> He heard Nan-ch'üan's remark about the sickle and it affected
> him deeply,
> We should keep listening to this dialogue for years to come.

Discussion

This case appears in Dōgen's kōan collection with verse commentary, EK vol. 9 case 81 (DZZ 4:238) and in MS case 154 (DZZ 5:206), and it is also cited in EK vol. 8 and KS "Sansuikyō." It focuses on the importance of communal labor in the self-definition of the Southern school during its formative period in T'ang China. As the large monastic compounds were being established in the isolation and splendor of remote, lofty mountains, demonstrating the strength of the still developing sect, Zen also came under attack from its ideological rivals, particularly the socially minded Confucians who stressed the priority of family oriented values. Buddhism in general, and Zen in particular, was cast as an essentially life-negating, escapist approach that sought the accumulation of property and wealth in mountain hideaways at the expense of the welfare of society as a whole.

In order to combat this image and fend off its critics, Zen cultivated a self-definition as a monastic system in which communal labor was a primary requirement. Nan-ch'üan was a contemporary of Pai-chang, who created the monastic rules text in which the requirement was first enunciated. Both were first-generation disciples of Ma-tsu, founder of the very influential Hung-chou branch of the Southern school that also emphasized encounter dialogues. The seven main principles of Pai-chang's rules, the *Ch'an-men kuei-shih*, are: Zen is a separate lineage, independent of other Buddhist sects; its training revolves around the charismatic abbot, who lives in "ten-foot-square" quarters and delivers two formal sermons a day in addition to providing informal individual instruction; the Dharma Hall as the place for the assembly to meet, for the abbot's sermons takes priority over the role of the Buddha Hall; the Monks Hall serves as the communal lodgings of the assembly; compulsory communal labor is required of all members of the assembly regardless of rank or seniority; monastery officials are assigned specific tasks, including the rector who supervises the Monks Hall; and punishment by excommunication is prescribed for those who violate any of the rules, especially the communal labor requirement, in fact or in spirit.

Although the requirement for communal labor is mentioned only briefly in the *Ch'an-men kuei-shih*, the notion is reinforced by two other kinds of expression: Pai-chang's famous utterance that "a day without work is a day without eating," which is reinforced by the anecdote that when his disciples hid his tools one day to test his commitment to the "no work, no food" rule, Pai-chang refused to eat. Furthermore, Zen monasteries prohibited monks from begging, a practice that had long been central to all other forms of Buddhist monasticism, which forbade monks from sustaining themselves through farming since tilling the soil could result in taking the life of small organisms. The aim of all of these principles was to show its Confucian critics that Zen was a self-supporting, self-sustaining institution that could manage for itself as a mostly autonomous society from economic and legal perspectives, without draining resources (other than human resources) from mainstream society.

In the current case, a wandering monk—referred to in the verse commentary as a "novice" (literally "water and clouds")—sees Nan-ch'üan and, apparently without recognizing him, asks the way to the master's mountain. His asking for the mountain means the same as if he were asking for the person. The monk does not expect that an abbot will be engaged in manual labor, and so he does not realize that he has just met the master he is looking for. When the monk does not get the point of Nan-ch'üan's initial response that emphasizes the importance of working hard with simple tools, the master dismisses the wanderer and gets back to his chore of chopping down weeds. Note that the master's indirect reproach is not the kind of harsh verbal or physical reprimand one might expect, and the verse commentary suggests that the monk probably did have an experience of sudden awakening from this encounter.

9. Hsüan-sha's "One Luminous Pearl"

Main Case

A priest asked master Hsüan-sha Tsung-i of Fu-chou district, "I have heard that you often say, 'The whole universe in ten directions is one luminous pearl.' How are we to understand the meaning of this?" Hsüan-sha replied, "The whole universe in ten directions is one luminous pearl. What is the point in trying to understand the meaning?"

The next day Hsüan-sha asked the priest, "The whole universe in ten directions is one luminous pearl. How do you understand the meaning of this?" The priest said, "The whole universe in ten directions is one luminous pearl. What is the point in trying to understand the meaning of this?"

Hsüan-sha taunted him, "I see you have been struggling like a demon in the cave of a black mountain."

Discussion

This kōan is cited from Dōgen's collection of 300 cases, MS case 15 (DZZ 5:132), and it is also included in EK vol. 9 case 41 (DZZ 4:208–210) and with extensive commentary in the "Ikkya myōjū" ("One Luminous Pearl") fascicle of his main philosophical text, the KS (DZZ 1:76-81). The key supernatural element of the dialogue occurs in the last line when Hsüan-sha reprimands the monk for struggling like a demon in the black mountain cave. When taken out of the context of the narrative background of the case, the final line in this case may seem to represent a rhetorical flourish that is intended to deliver an anti-supernatural message or an inversion of meaning so that supernatural imagery itself comes to represent iconoclasm. However, the narrative context suggests that supernaturalism, in connection with the ritual element of extreme asceticism, plays a very important role in reinforcing the impact of Hsüan-sha's statement.

According to the account in Dōgen's commentary that is based on passages in transmission of the lamp records, Hsüan-sha had been a fisherman who came to understand the precarious, conditional nature of the fleeting world at the age of thirty, when he converted and "entered the mountains." After a period of wandering he began training under master Hsüeh-feng, but was always looked on as a *dhuta*, or a practitioner of the extreme forest ascetic discipline of *dhutanga*. The twelve practices of the *dhutanga* method of training (see Chapter 1, note 3) often were conducted in caves and grottoes, and were considered an effective method of exorcising demons and summoning the presence of beneficial spirits.

Hsüan-sha throughout his career wore a patched robe made of coarse fiber that he mended but never replaced. With a minimum of formal training he eventually became the successor of Hsüeh-feng and was known for his single-method teaching based on the phrase "one luminous pearl," which means that there is a jewel amid the dusty world of samsara or that the samsaric world itself has a bright, jewel-like quality. Dōgen's KS prose commentary stresses a nondual outlook by asserting, "Forward steps and backward steps in a demon's black mountain cave are nothing other than 'one luminous pearl.'" But the reference to the cave of demons, whether implying supernaturalism or anti-supernaturalism, or praise or criticism of the monk's attitude, is better understood through an awareness that caves were the likely lair of Hsüan-sha, the forest ascetic.

Tung-shan's Mountain

10. Tung-shan's "Two Clay Oxen Enter the Sea"

Main Case

Master Tung-shan and Master Mi were traveling in the mountains looking for a place to stay the night and came across the master of Lung-shan. The old monk asked, "This mountain has no path, so how did you two monks get up here?" Tung-shan said, "That's true, reverend priest, so what did you use to get to this mountain?" The old monk said, "I did not follow the clouds and water."

"How long have you been staying on this mountain, reverend priest?" Tung-shan asked. "I don't pay attention to the passing of spring and autumn," replied the master. "Were you, reverend priest, residing here first? Or was it the mountain that was abiding here before you?" Tung-shan asked. "I don't know," replied the old monk. Tung-shan asked, "Why is it that you don't know?"

"I didn't come here to follow the gods or people," replied the old monk. "Then for what reason have you come to take up staying on this mountain?" asked Tung-shan. The monk said, "I saw two clay oxen fighting each other until they both fell into the sea. From that point on, there has been nothing new that has happened."

Discussion

This kōan is cited from Dōgen's MS case 222 (DZZ 5:242). It appears in a slightly different version in the TSL (Taishō 47:508c) as well as the CCL vol. 8 (Taishō 51:263a) and the *Hung-chih lu* vol. 4 (Taishō 48:35b), along with the collected works of Ta-hui and other transmission of the lamp records. Tung-shan is traveling in search of a metaphorical, as well as an actual, mountain where enlightenment can be attained. According to some versions, Tung-shan and his companion see a sign while they are wandering in the mountains—a vegetable leaf floating in valley stream—and think that someone who practices Buddhism must be in their presence, so they go looking for a hermit in a hut. However, while several versions indicate that they are deliberately seeking out a practitioner who might be able to guide them, the version cited here and elsewhere suggests that they were lost and stumbled upon the hermit.

In any case, the hermit is an irregular monk who declares that he has never gone through the novice training in a Zen lineage ("I did not follow the clouds and water," which travel from the top of the mountain down), and therefore he is not officially a Buddhist monk. His dialogue with Tung-shan reflects an important encounter and contest over who can claim rights to the mountain, which "has no path." The mountain remains unopened and not yet established from the standpoint of incorporating the official Buddhist Dharma. The reference to the term "mountain" could be interpreted in an entirely symbolic or metaphorical way as representative of the process of attaining enlightenment, or it might reflect the need for the appearance of a mountain-opener to overcome rivals or usurpers of the Dharma.

Each of Tung-shan's queries seems to elicit a reply demonstrating that the hermit has the upper hand. The hermit, in his state of transcendence, does not need to pay attention to the passing of spring and autumn or to the dictates of the gods or people, and his statement "I don't know" evokes Bodhidharma's irreverent response to the emperor who asks him his name, as recorded in PYL case 1. The hermit's final reference to "clay oxen" alludes to traditional ritual objects that are used to mark the beginning of spring or the new year, and can be interpreted here as symbolic of monks encountering and challenging each other. According to the hermit's retort to Tung-shan, he has transcended the need to engage in disputation and testing among quarreling monks. This reveals that Zen literary records are willing to preserve and venerate an account of an irregular monk prevailing, for the time being, over a regular monk who would eventually become an acknowledged master and one of the major patriarchs of the tradition.

11. Yün-yen's "Non-Sentient Beings Can Hear It"

Main Case

Tung-shan left Kuei-shan, with whom he had been studying for some time, and then went to meet master Yün-yen. Referring to a previous encounter with Kuei-shan, he asked, "When non-sentient beings preach the Dharma, what sort of people are able to hear it?" Yün-yen said, "Non-sentient beings are able to hear it."

Tung-shan asked, "Can't you hear it?" Yün-yen replied, "If I could hear the preaching of the Dharma by non-sentient beings, then you would not be able to hear the Dharma that I preach." "Why couldn't I hear the Dharma that you preach?" Tung-shan asked.

Yün-yen raised his fly-whisk and said, "Well, do you hear this?" Tung-shan said, "No, I don't hear anything." Yün-yen said, "You can't even hear it when I preach the Dharma. How do you expect to hear it when a non-sentient being preaches?" Tung-shan asked, "In which sutra is it taught that non-sentient beings preach the Dharma?" Yün-yen replied, "You mean you haven't read this? In the *Amitabha Sutra* it says, 'Water, birds, trees, and forests, all without exception, recite the Buddha's name and preach the Dharma.'"

Reflecting on this, Tung-shan composed the following verse.

> How extraordinary! How extraordinary!
> The preaching of the Dharma by non-sentient beings is a
>   mystery,
> If we listen for it only with the ear, there is no chance of
>   hearing it,
> But when sound is heard with the eye, then it can be
>   understood.

Discussion

This case, cited from the TSL (Taishō 47:507c), is a classic example of an encounter between master and disciple that becomes an instance of a "satori" dialogue, in that it marks the sudden and final breakthrough experience to enlightenment for someone who has been wrestling with and obstructed by a particular conundrum for a long period of studies with several masters. For Tung-shan, the key question is whether non-sentient beings preach the Dharma, as the devotional or Pure Land-oriented *Amitabha Sutra* asserts, in a way that can be heard and acknowledged by sentient beings. The conventional distinction is that sentient beings are living or animate and non-sentient beings are non-living or inanimate. But this view is challenged by the shamanistic quality of the Mahayana Buddhist notion of the universality of the Buddha-nature, which argues that not only can animals and plants preach the Dharma but non-sentient beings such as rocks, lands, seas, and mountains are vibrant and dynamic and, therefore, in a sense alive. Thus, the Mahayana doctrine, which in many ways is a throwback to preliterate animistic beliefs in an all-pervasive vital energy or life force, maintains that there is no distinction between the sentient and non-sentient.

Furthermore, from the standpoint of attaining enlightenment, non-sentient beings take priority in that they have no emotional attachments—the term for non-sentience can also be glossed as "non-attachment"—a state that Buddhist seekers, as sentient beings, aspire to attain. On the other hand, even though the sentient and non-sentient are fundamentally the same and of equal capacity in preaching the Dharma, for the unenlightened the sound of the non-sentient cannot be heard. According to Buddhist lore, only enlightened sentient beings that have attained supranormal powers, such as bodhisattvas, saints, and Zen masters, are able to hear the preaching of non-sentient beings because they have the synesthetic or crossover ability to hear with their eyes and see with their ears.

Tung-shan had apparently worked on this issue under master Kuei-shan, who was unable to help him resolve it and recommended that he go to study with Yün-yen who became his master. Yün-yen's response to Tung-shan's query, which asserts that only non-sentient beings can hear the preaching of the non-sentient, seems to reinforce a duality that is denied by the Mahayana doctrine of Buddha-nature yet affirmed by Buddhist folklore about the capacity of supranormal powers that enlightened masters have attained. When Tung-shan remains confused, Yün-yen raises his fly-whisk (which is the maneuver to which Kuei-shan had resorted when challenged by Te-shan in case 7), and asks rhetorically if Tung-shan can hear the preaching of this instrument. The point is that preaching is not a matter of words or even sounds, and thus "hearing" does not refer to a particular sense perception but to the phenomenon of gaining intuitive insight into the true nature of reality. This insight reflects an ability that is based on the supranormal, synesthetic power of hearing with the eye rather than the ear and of seeing with the ear rather than the eye.

12. Yün-chü Wandering the Mountains

Main Case

Master Tung-shan asked Yün-chü, "Where are you coming from?" Yün-chü replied, "I've been wandering about in the mountains." "Which mountain did you stay on?" the master asked. "I didn't stay on any particular mountain," Yün-chü answered.

The master said, "Is that so? Have you wandered about on every single mountain in the whole country?" Yün-chü said, "No, not really."

The master said, "In that case, you must have found a special pathway by which to enter the mountains." Yün-chü replied, "No, I didn't find any such pathway." The master asked, "If you didn't find such a pathway, then how have you come here to see this old monk?" "If I had found such a pathway, then there would be a mountain standing between us," Yün-chü replied.

The master said, "From now on, a thousand people, or even ten thousand people, will not tie Yün-chü down to one spot."

Discussion

This kōan, cited from the TSL (Taishō 47:513a), is one of several cases in which Tung-shan, now that he is enlightened and has opened his own mountain, challenges seekers who wander into his domain. Yün-chü meets with the master's approval and becomes the foremost disciple in his lineage. As with case 10, the reference to mountains can be interpreted in a purely symbolic way as representative of the path to enlightenment, so that not staying "on a particular mountain" means that Yün-chü has not yet trained formally under a legitimate teacher and the "special pathway" for entering the mountains refers to a specific method or technique for training. When Yün-chü says in the penultimate line of the dialogue that "there would be a mountain standing between us," he indicates that he has no links to other masters that stand in the way of his openness to receiving the teaching and transmission directly from Tung-shan. Therefore, the repartee about finding or not finding mountain pathways is a kind of verbal mating dance between parties destined to become partners in the process of transmitting the Dharma lineage.

In a similar kōan known as "Tung-shan's 'Did You Reach the Peak?'," which appears in MS case 49 (DZZ 5:150) as well as the TSL, the master asked a wandering monk, "Did you reach the peak of any of the mountains?" "Yes, I reached the peak," the monk replied. "Was there no one else at the peak?" the master asked. "No, there was not," the monk said. "In that case, you must not have reached the peak," the master said. "If I had not reached the top of the mountain, how else would I know that no one was there?" the monk asked. The master replied, "Reverend priest, why don't you stay for a while in this temple?" The monk said, "I'd be happy to stay in this temple, but it would not be in accord with the wishes of the sage of India."

The penultimate line of this case is a reference to the "Entering the Dharma-Realm" chapter of the *Hua-yen Sutra*. It appears by the end of the encounter dialogue that the anonymous, itinerant monk has won this round of repartee about mountain peaks, gained Tung-shan's approval, and yet snubbed the master by indicating that he does not intend to stay on his mountain because it would not accord with the teachings of first patriarch

Bodhidharma. One of the commentaries issues a put-down to the monk: "I've been having my doubts about him all along." As with case 7, the question of who has really won or lost the contest is deliberately left vague and ambiguous by most of the other commentaries.

MOUNT WU-T'AI

13. "Iron Grindstone" Liu Goes to Mount Wu-t'ai

Pointer

Stand on the peak of the highest mountain, and no demon or non-believer can lay a hand on you. Walk on the bottom of the deepest sea, and even the eyes of the Buddha will not be able to spot you. Even if your eyes are like shooting stars and your effort is exerted like a flash of lightning, you are still like the spirit turtle that cannot avoid dragging its tail. At such a juncture, what do you do? Examine the following case.

Main Case

Iron Grindstone Liu reached Kuei-shan. Kuei-shan said, "Old buffalo, so you've come here?" Iron Grindstone Liu said, "Tomorrow, there'll be a great communal feast on Mount Wu-t'ai. Master, will you be going?"

Kuei-shan lay down on the ground and stretched out. Then Iron Grindstone Liu departed right away.

Verse Commentary

> Riding an iron horse, the general entered into the castle,
> The imperial edict proclaims that the six kingdoms are at peace,
> Still gripping a golden whip, he prods the returning troops,
> In the dark of night, no one else dares go with him through the
>   streets of the king.

Discussion

This kōan, with pointer and verse commentary from PYL case 24 (Taishō 48:165a–c) also appears in TJL case 60 (Taishō 48:64c–265a) as well as several transmission of the lamp records, and features two main elements of hagiographical literature that infiltrate and influence the two-fold discursive structure of Zen kōans. One element is the role of women, in this case a nun living as a hermit, who outsmart their male counterparts, and the other is the importance of Mount Wu-t'ai as a pilgrimage site for visionaries in northern China.

The nun Liu was known as "Iron Grindstone" because of her ability to defeat opponents in Dharma-combat as if they were crushed or ground into fine powder. According to the prose commentary on PYL case 17, Liu gained a reputation for being ornery or arrogant but was eventually beaten in a contest by Tzu-hu, who struck her while her words of response to one of his questions "were still hanging in midair." After this, she built a hut near Kuei-shan's mountain and one day paid him a visit. Given her reputation for being "severe and dangerous," according to the PYL prose commentary, Kuei-shan must have sensed immediately that she was ready for a contest, and he seems prepared to disarm her with his words.

Kuei-shan's response to her arrival accomplishes two things. First, it makes a playful insult. Kuei-shan often told a story that he expected to be reincarnated as a buffalo branded with his name, so that people would wonder if this was a really a buffalo or a Zen master. By calling Liu a buffalo, he is indicating ironically an intimate connection with her in a way that also puts her on the defensive. In saying "so you've come here?," Kuei-shan shows that he was expecting and anticipating that this dangerous rival would show up one day and declares his readiness. Note the combative tone in the art-of-war style of rhetoric of the verse commentary.

Liu questions the master about whether he would be attending a festival on Mount Wu-t'ai. The PYL prose commentary suggests that this is a rather surprising query since Mount Wu-t'ai is so distant from Mount Kuei-shan. Mount Kuei-shan is in the southern district in Hunan Province below the Yangtze River, while Mount Wu-t'ai is to the north, in Shansi Province near Mongolia (north of modern Beijing). However, the gap between these places is not so much a matter of geographical as of theological or ideological distance. Kuei-shan, at that time (two generations after Ma-tsu), was the leading monastery of the Zen Southern school where Te-shan and others came to challenge the master. Mount Wu-t'ai (literally "five peaks" because it is a collection of mountains and terraces rather than a single main promontory) was the bastion of Northern style Buddhism.

"Northern style" in this sense does not refer to the Northern school of Zen, which advocated a gradual approach through the study of scriptures in contrast to the Southern school's emphasis on suddenness and silence. Rather, Northern style Buddhism was a very different approach to

Mahayana theory and practice that incorporated the influences of esoteric, tantric, lamaist religiosity, in which visionary experiences and exotic rituals played a primary role in the spiritual path. In that sense both schools of Zen, Northern and Southern, appear to be radically different than Northern style Buddhism, which is the antithesis of Zen iconoclasm. Numerous leading Zen masters, especially Lin-chi, Chao-chou, and Yün-men, emphasize in their recorded sayings a refutation of Mount Wu-t'ai religiosity and prohibitions against their disciples being allowed to visit the location in search of a different approach to spiritual fulfillment.

On one level, Liu's question about attendance the following day at the festival in an era of premodern technology is simply absurd and can easily be dismissed. However, the real significance of the question is whether or not Kuei-shan, as the leading current patriarch of Southern school Zen, would be willing to entertain Northern Buddhist style practice. Coming from a female hermit, the query highlights the dangerous, subversive elements that are at once threatening and a part of Zen discourse. The verse commentary suggests that Kuei-shan is victorious; since his "six kingdoms are at peace" (symbolic of the six senses or six activities of consciousness, including seeing, hearing, feeling, tasting, smelling, and knowing), he is able to offset the attacking general who is not accompanied by sufficient supporting troops. Orthodoxy is upheld.

14. Manjusri's "Three by Three"

Pointer

Distinguish between dragons and snakes, discriminate jewels from stones, and separate the complex and simple decisively and without delay. But if you do not have an eye on your forehead or an amulet under your arm, you will keep on missing the point right in front of you over and over again. If right here and now your seeing and hearing are not obscured so that sound and form are perceived without impediment, I will still ask you: "Is this black or white?", or "Is this crooked or straight?" Show me how you are able to discriminate.

Main Case (with capping phrases by Yüan-wu)

Manjusri asked Wu-cho, "Where are you from?"
> *Under the circumstances, the question must be asked.*

Wu-cho said, "The South."

> *Wu-cho's head pokes up from his nest in the weeds, but why must he raise his eyebrows? There is nothing beyond the one vast realm, and yet there exists a place called "the South."*

Manjusri asked, "How is the Buddha Dharma being upheld there?"

> *It would have been a terrible mistake to ask anyone but him. The question still lingers on his lips.*

Wu-cho replied, "In the Age of Decline, monks have little regard for ethics (Sila) or the monastic rules of discipline (Vinaya)."

> *It is hard to find such a truthful person.*

Manjusri asked, "Are the congregations large or small?"

> *Right then and there he should have given Manjusri a shout. He would have hit the mark right off.*

Wu-cho replied, "Some have three hundred, some have five hundred."

> *It's obvious from the way he said it that they are all nothing but wild fox spirits.*

Then Wu-cho asked Manjusri, "How is the Dharma being upheld in these parts?"

> *What a blow! He pushes the spear in and turns it round and round.*

Manjusri responded, "Unenlightened people and sages dwell together; dragons and snakes intermingle."

> *The tide is turned. He's tripping over his own feet and his hands are flailing.*

Wu-cho asked, "Are the congregations large or small?"

> *The phrase comes back to haunt me, Manjusri is thinking. But Wu-cho couldn't hold it in any longer.*

Manjusri said, "In front three by three, in back three by three."

> *An extraordinary statement! But, are the congregations large or small? Even a thousand arms of great compassion could not count all the people.*

Verse Commentary (with capping phrases by Yüan-wu)

> A thousand peaks swaying with the color of indigo.
> *Can you see Manjusri?*
> Who says that it was Manjusri that was conversing with him?
> *Even if it were Samantabhadra, it wouldn't matter. He's already slipped by.*
> It is laughable to ask, "Are the congregations on Mt. Ch'ing-liang large or small?"

Let me ask, what's all this laughter about? It exists prior to any discourse.

In front three by three, and in back three by three.

Take a look and see it below your feet, but beware of the thorns in the muddy ground. A teacup falls on the ground and splinters into seven pieces.

Prose Commentary (selection by Yüan-wu)

The One-Eyed Dragon of Ming-ch'ao also wrote a verse commentary that enveloped heaven and earth:

> Extending throughout the whole universe is the marvelous monastery,
> The Manjusri that fills the eyes is the one conversing;
> Not knowing to open the Buddha-eye on hearing his words,
> Wu-cho turned his head and saw only the green mountain crags.

Some time after the dialogue, Wu-cho decided to stay on Mount Wu-t'ai and was serving as cook in a monastery. Every day Manjusri appeared above his cauldron of rice, and each time Wu-cho struck him a blow with the bamboo stick used for churning the porridge. But that is like drawing the bow after the thief has already fled. At the right time, when asked "How is the Buddha Dharma being upheld in the South?" he should have hit Manjusri on the spine—that would have accomplished something!

Discussion

This kōan, cited from PYL case 35 (Taishō 48:165c–166c) with pointer, capping phrase commentary on the main case, verse commentary with capping phrases, and a selection from the prose commentary that includes a verse attributed to the One-Eyed Dragon of Ming-ch'ao, also appears in MS case 127 (DZZ 5:194–196) and was commented on by Lin-chi. The dialogue between bodhisattva Manjusri and an anomalous Zen pilgrim to Mount Wu-t'ai named Wu-cho (which literally means "no attachment") is particularly intriguing because it seems to be directly influenced by a vast body of non-Zen Buddhist hagiographical literature on mountain pilgrims in search of visions and a direct encounter with Manjusri, who was one of the four main bodhisattvas venerated in China and was said to make Mount Wu-t'ai his earthly abode. A common theme in this literature is that pilgrims, who are drawn by stories of miraculous visions and events, as well as the presence of strange, beautiful plants and animals occurring on the mountain landscape, approached the Diamond Grotto or the cave where Manjusri resided with his celestial attendants. Some visionaries who experienced an apparition of the bodhisattva and a supernatural temple where he preached were inspired to build an actual structure based on a deep belief in an invisible, though an apparently compellingly visualizable, reality.

The narrative context for this case included reports of several notable visionary builders recorded in the *Kuang Ch'ing-liang chuan*, a text devoted to Mount Wu-t'ai pilgrimages, who either did enter the Diamond Grotto or were able even without entering to realize their vision through the construction of an actual temple. The PYL has altered the story of Wu-cho from what appears in the hagiographical text, in which he does succeed like the others, apparently by conflating it or perhaps by deliberately blurring the distinction with the account recorded in the monk biography text, the *Sung kao-seng chuan*, of another monk named Wu-cho who arrived at Mount Wu-t'ai a few decades later and failed to enter the grotto after its location was revealed by a servant boy.

According to the account in the PYL prose commentary, after the dialogue with Manjusri, Wu-cho is shown an apparitional temple by a servant and turns his head in a moment of doubt, and when he looks again he finds suddenly that the illusory temple the boy conjured had disappeared completely, and all that remains is an empty valley. Another version of the case in the *Yu-hsuan yü-lu*, a later kōan collection text, follows the *Kuang Ch'ing-liang chuan* record in explaining that Wu-cho originally met Manjusri in the form of a beggar even before the dialogue in the main case, and recognized that this was the bodhisattva only after the apparitional temple mysteriously vanished following the conversation with the servant boy, a common motif in visionary builder literature.

In the encounter dialogue between the monk and the deity, Wu-cho's reference to the "South" can be considered to imply Southern style Buddhism or, more specifically, the Southern school of Zen. The Age of Decline they discuss is the view that was especially strong in the Pure Land devotional branch of Mahayana Buddhism, which claimed that about 1,500 years after the life of Sakyamuni a period of degeneration would occur due to people's fundamental ignorance and deficient karma. The Age of Decline would last for a period of 10,000 years, during which no one could gain enlightenment through his or her own self-effort alone. The term "wild fox spirits" as a comment on Wu-cho's response is borrowed from folklore about magical, shapeshifting foxes, and functions as a conventional epithet used to critique those who claim a false, inauthentic enlightenment. The crucial saying "three by three" in front and in back alludes to a phrase used in the *Hsüan-hsa kuang-lu* (Jap. *Gensha kōroku*), which could be interpreted to mean "six in front or before, and six in back or behind"—six may refer to the six senses, which are gateways for the perception of the world of external stimuli.

The two-fold discursive structure of the kōan is well expressed in the verse by the One-Eyed Dragon. The final line can be read as a criticism of the pilgrim for not paying attention to the vision and words of the bodhisattva who "fills the eyes" and ears, thereby supporting an acceptance of the supernatural. But the prose commentary shows that this line can also be interpreted as a negation of the literal standpoint, or as a simple descriptive expression of natural beauty beyond both literal and metaphorical implications. It thus counteracts the supernatural claims that the mountain crags alone constitute the place for the realization of emptiness. Wu-cho no longer needs to rely on visions or dialogues with otherworldly beings in order to experience the true nature of the world.

Yet the final section of prose commentary is deliberately ambiguous about whether the winner is Manjusri or Wu-cho. The monk is said to strike the now diminutive deity that appears in his rice cauldron, but this action is too little and too late—like "drawing the bow after the thief has already gone." But who, in the end, has the last laugh?

15. Pi-mo's "You Shall Die from My Pitchfork"

Main Case

Master Pi-mo Yen, who lived in reclusion on Mount Wu-t'ai, used to carry a forked stick. Whenever he saw a Buddhist monk coming by, he would hold up the pitchfork and say, "What kind of demons made you become a Buddhist priest? What kind of devil forced you to take up this pilgrimage? You will die from my pitchfork even if you explain it. You will die from my pitchfork even if you do not explain it. Now speak up quickly! Speak up quickly!"

Discussion

This kōan, cited from Dōgen's MS case 73 (DZZ 5:102–04), also appears with a brief commentary in CCL vol. 10 (Taishō 51:280a–280b), and a different version is included in the verse commentary on case 51 (case 19 in the PYL collection). Pi-mo was a ninth-century follower of Manjusri who took up residence on Mount Wu-t'ai after the suppression of Buddhism was lifted in 845. Mount Wu-t'ai was one of the few Buddhist institutions to continue to thrive in the period immediately following the era of suppression, whereas the Zen movement as a whole did not regain its status and become a dominant sect for at least another century. It is not clear whether Pi-mo was a Zen practitioner, but he used a Zen-style single method of teaching while living in a hermitage on Mount Wu-t'ai, which was populated by Zen pilgrims despite the fact that it represented a kind of religiosity that seemed antithetical to Zen. Pi-mo placed any disciples or rivals that came his way in a double bind by threatening to strike and kill them with his pitchfork whether they answered or did not answer him correctly.

The PYL prose commentary on "Chü-chih's One Finger Zen" cites Pi-mo as another example of someone who uses only one method of teaching on every occasion: "Pi-mo just used a forked branch all his life. The Earth-Beating Teacher would hit the ground once whenever he was asked any question. Once someone hid his staff and then asked, 'What is Buddha?' The teacher just opened his mouth wide. This was another kind of method used for a whole lifetime without ever being exhausted."

The case as it appears in the CCL cites commentaries by three masters who offer brief responses to Pi-mo. Master Fa-yen commented, "Instead of becoming a monk I would beg for my life"; Master Fa-teng commented, "Instead of becoming a monk, I would stretch out my neck and offer it"; and master Hsüan-chia commented, "Instead of becoming a monk, I would give up on the idea of leaving home. Now, old man, throw that fork away!" These remarks, especially Hsüan-chia's challenge, indicate that Zen's irreverent discourse was alive and well in the heart of Northern style Buddhism.

In addition, according to another encounter dialogue in CCL vol. 9, an irregular monk announced that he would be leaving the monastery where he had been studying on Mount Wu-t'ai after having a sudden realization one night. When pressed by the temple abbot to offer an explanation of what he realized, the monk said, "A nun is naturally a woman." This reinforces the notion expressed in cases 13 and 23 that Mount Wu-t'ai was threatening and yet also appealing to Zen because it was a hospitable environment for female practitioners.

[TWO]

Contesting with
Irregular Rivals

The kōans in this chapter are records of encounters and contests between masters and irregular practitioners. This category includes hermits, shamans, and wizards who are non-Buddhists or quasi-Buddhists—that is, they give the appearance of practicing Buddhism without having received an authentic transmission—as well as Buddhists who train outside the confines of the mainstream institutional structure as recluses, solitary wanderers, or forest ascetic, who may be of questionable authenticity. The chapter also contains a couple of kōans in which the master himself is the hermit (as in case 20) or with masters engaging other masters, including case 21 on Jui-yen interacting or having an encounter dialogue with himself or a side of his personality. In addition, the chapter covers women, who are often considered dangerous or subversive in Buddhism and Chinese religious culture at large.

Throughout history and long before the arrival of Buddhism, the Chinese mountain landscapes were populated with a variety of religious practitioners who were involved in using techniques such as trance, mediumship, exorcism, divination, and geomancy in order to commune with and manipulate supernatural forces, including ancestor spirits, ghosts, gods, demons, sprites, and magical animals. Many of these techniques resembled meditation or the results or by-products of meditation, especially the six supranormal powers of clairaudience, clairvoyance, using the body to break through barriers at will, knowing past karma, predicting future enlightenment, and liberation from karma. Also, the training methods for attaining these psychic states were similar to the way Buddhists practiced by wandering from ordinary society to secluded, remote, or exotic territories free of the secularization, commercialization, and corruption of urban centers. Many of the hermits and wizards were part of teaching apprenticeships, while others followed eclectic or self-directed styles of practice.

When Buddhism came to China it brought the category of the *pratyeka buddha*, which refers to solitary ascetics who practice and claim enlightenment without undergoing formal instruction or incorporation into the official assembly. These itinerant monks, including those training in the twelve exercises of *dhutanga*, were looked on as suspicious from the standpoint of mainstream monastic institutions. Subsequently, authentic Zen masters constantly sought to prove themselves by taking up the challenge of confronting and contesting with varieties of irregular practitioners, regardless of whether they claimed to be Buddhists. In some cases, the irregular monks might be more proficient at meditation than the legitimate master. Or they might have gained a reputation for accomplishment in some type of trance or exorcism that closely resembled Buddhism and provoked the masters to test them. The ultimate aim of the encounters with irregular practitioners was either the defeat or the assimilation of unaffiliated monks into the institutional lineage. The encounter between masters and followers, who attempt to outwit, one-up, tweak, outrage, disprove, or dishearten each other, is a distinctively dramatic pedagogical style used in Zen's primary ritual of instructing disciples and guiding them to an experience of spontaneous awakening.

Another set of irregular practitioners includes women: either nuns who were officially Buddhists but could not normally be considered equal, let alone superior, to their male counterparts; or what is often referred to by the tradition as Zen "grannies," or elderly laywomen who could demonstrate that they were more knowledgeable and wise than the Zen masters, or at least able to outsmart the masters in a distinctive, creative, tables-turning way. Zen literature generally excluded women from official accounts of monastic life, although nuns did play an important role. This is not surprising given that most Buddhist sects denied women access to enlightenment. At the same time, however, Zen preserved numerous stories highlighting the spiritual attainment of certain unusual or threatening female practitioners. These passages show women giving monks their comeuppance through a mastery of verbal prowess or wordplay that may stem from or reflect a shamanistic power or an eremitic ability to surpass the state of meditation in the mainstream Buddhist institution.

HERMITS, WIZARDS, AND OTHER MASTERS

16. P'u-hua Kicks Over the Dining Table

Main Case

P'u-hua accompanied master Lin-chi to a patron's house to eat dinner. Lin-chi asked, "It is said that a single hair swallows up the huge sea and a single mustard seed encompasses Mount Sumeru. Is this a manifestation of supranormal power, or is it just a reflection of the natural state of things as they are?"

P'u-hau turned over the dinner table. Lin-chi said, "That's too crude!" P'u-hua said, "This is the realm of mystery. Why do you reduce it to a matter of what's crude and what's refined?"

The next day, Lin-chi once again went with P'u-hua, this time to eat a noontime meal that was being provided by a lay believer. He said, "How does today's meal compare with yesterday's?" P'u-hua again turned over the dinner table. Lin-chi said, "That's too crude!" P'u-hua said, "Blind man! Why talk about crude and fine when trying to express the Buddha Dharma?"

Lin-chi stuck out his tongue.

Discussion

This kōan, from LL record 26 (Taishō 47:503b), is also contained in MS case 96 (DZZ 5:174), and it is included in different versions in a number of the transmission of the lamp records, including the CCL. The dialogue appears in the "Testing" section of the LL and is a fascinating example of the interaction of one of the most prominent of the early patriarchs, considered the founder of what became the dominant Zen school in China, Korea, and Japan, with an intriguing but highly controversial irregular monk, featured in several other anecdotes in the Lin-chi records, who probably represents a Taoist style of practice.

The name P'u-hua (Jap. Fuka) literally means "universal transformation," and the second part of the name, *hua* (Jap. *ka*, also pronounced *bakeru*), generally refers to a shapeshifting spirit or a manifestation that can transform itself from one state of existence to another, such as from animal to human or from human to divine (or the reverse). The shapeshifter's ability is usually constrained by several factors, including the incapacity to change back successfully from a state of existence to which a transformation has occurred and a mixture of beneficent and demonic moral intentions underlying the changes. The implication for this dialogue is that P'u-hua is a wizard with magical powers, probably derived from practices outside the Buddhist tradition. He encounters Southern school leadership in its fifth generation, and brings Lin-chi to an impasse without a clear winner emerging from the contest. According to another passage in the LL, observers of P'u-hua said, "He goes around the streets of town every day behaving like an idiot or a madman. Is he a common mortal or a sage?" In several passages, P'u-hua is referred to as someone who assisted Lin-chi in his teachings, rather than as his rival. It is also mentioned in the LL recorded sayings text that he died suddenly and vanished mysteriously, "body and all," as if a Taoist immortal (see case 57).

Lin-chi was one of the most rigorously iconoclastic of the Zen patriarchs. He attained enlightenment only after mustering the bravado to slap his mentor Huang-po, who was known for striking his teacher Pai-chang in the epilogue to case 38, and he regularly practiced a style of verbally accosting and punching unwary disciples, enjoining them to "Kill the Buddha!" Lin-chi also adamantly refuted Mount Wu-t'ai religiosity and insisted that Manjusri not be found in visions but within the inner sanctum of one's true nature, and he interpreted the six supranormal powers as the ability to enter the realms of form, sound, odor, taste, touch, and consciousness without being deluded by realizing their essential condition of emptiness. In addition, Lin-chi regularly evoked the saying attributed to Layman Pang, "What are my supranormal powers and marvelous activities—carrying water and chopping firewood!"

Yet it is clear from the series of dialogues with and about P'u-hua that Lin-chi's own status as an emphatic iconoclast is being challenged at the same time that he seeks to assimilate the wizard into the fold of the regular lineage. In one of the dialogues, Lin-chi called P'u-hua a donkey and he responded by braying; in another, P'u-hua asked, "You tell me, am I a common mortal or a sage?" and then pointed with his finger at Lin-chi and a small group of followers and said, "Ho-yang is a new bride, Mu-t'a is an old Zen granny, Lin-chi is a brat but he's got the eye!" However, while the usual interpretation of the final phrase is that it praises Lin-chi for possessing the "eye" or "[Dharma-] eye" of intuitive insight, it could also be interpreted as the put-down, in effect, "Lin-chi can only see out of one eye."

In the current case, it appears that P'u-hua has the upper hand in turning back Lin-chi's insult that he is "too crude" or coarse, a sarcastic remark often used in Zen dialogues, especially in cases dealing with border-line practitioners. P'u-hua gives Lin-chi a dose of his own medicine by turning over the table (note that in traditional Buddhist monasticism, the last meal of the day was at noon) while Lin-chi relies on words. It is P'u-hua who effectively evokes nonduality, whereas Lin-chi's comments create a polarity of right versus wrong, appropriate versus inappropriate. Yet the version of the dialogue included in the record of Lin-chi has the master get-ting the last laugh by sticking out his tongue, thus preserving the superi-ority of the monastic institution. But several passages later the text reports that P'u-hua travels around ringing a hand bell and saying, "Approach from the bright side and I'll hit you on the bright side. Approach on the dark side and I'll hit you on the dark side." Again, the irregular monk expresses a clearer vision of the unity encompassing a differentiation of bright and dark, and clear and concealed.

17. The Tripitaka Monk Claims to Read Others' Minds

Main Case

The Tripitaka master Ta-erh came to the capital all the way from India and proclaimed, "I have the Dharma-eye that reads others' minds." Emperor Tai-tsung ordered the National Teacher Hui-chung to put him to a test. When the Tripitaka monk saw the National Teacher he at once bowed and stood to his right side.

The National Teacher said, "Do you have the power to read others' minds?" The monk responded, "No, far from it." "Tell me where I am right now." "You are a National Teacher. How can you see the boat race in the West River?"

The National Teacher repeated the question, "Tell me where I am right now." The monk said, "You are a National Teacher. How can you see the people playing with monkeys on the Tien-tsin Bridge?" When the teacher asked the same question for a third time, the Tripitaka monk remained silent for a while, apparently not knowing how to answer.

The National Teacher scolded Ta-erh by saying, "You wild fox spirit! Where is your power to read others' minds?" But the monk still remained silent.

Verse Commentary

> Pai-yan reproaches his great friend Tzu-chi for not coming,
> And Te-yün stays alone on Mount Miao-feng.
> The mind is beyond the reach of ten thousand valleys.
> What a pity that this Buddha was nothing but a wild fox.

Discussion

This kōan, which originally appears in CCL vol. 5 (Taishō 51:244a), is cited from Dōgen's EK vol. 9 case 27 (DZZ 4:198–200) and it is also the main subject of the "Tajinzū" fascicle of Dōgen's KS (DZZ 2:41–252). The dialogue concerns the meeting, at the behest of the emperor, between an early T'ang master, National Teacher Hui-chung, who was a disciple of Hui-neng, and a maverick practitioner from India known as Ta-erh. This is particularly interesting because Hui-chung, prior to attaining his status as an imperial priest, was famous for becoming enlightened on his own through a remarkable manner of ascetic training that lasted for forty years in the seclusion of a mountain valley. Once established as National Teacher, he was asked by the emperor to "test" the abilities of a foreign priest, who claimed to have mastered the supranormal power of reading others' minds. After failing to answer Hui-chung's questions correctly the first two times, Ta-erh remains silent the third time, and he is finally scolded by the National Teacher for being no better than a shapeshifting creature.

This kōan revolves around the traditional Buddhist doctrine that the six supranormal powers (the translation of the term in Chinese literally means "spiritual penetrations"), including reading the minds of others, are a by-product of the enlightenment experience. The Tripitaka monk from India represents the old, remote Hinayana tradition that was never accepted in Chinese Mahayana Buddhism. He seems to be a type of maverick who corresponds to what Mahayana Buddhism has labeled the *pratyeka buddha*, or the practitioner who is self-enlightened through a mixture of Buddhist and non-Buddhist practices and lives as a recluse without the need for either teacher or disciples in the chain of transmission. At its worst, the maverick is a reckless and at times harmful monk with unharnessed or misused powers (or a "wild fox," in the sarcastic words of the National Teacher) that evoke a Zen tradition of referring to the magical animal as a standard criticism of rogue or renegade priests. Although the great Zen masters like Pai-chang in case 5 often spent time in retreats or hermitages to attain or perfect their spiritual realization, as leaders of monastic communities they warned their followers against wayward independence and threatened to expel the unworthy who could infiltrate and disrupt the legitimate community. Yet, the National Teacher and others still needed to remain open to test and, in some cases acknowledge, the merits of irregular practitioners.

This case is discussed extensively in the *Shōbōgenzō* "Tajinzū" ("Reading Others' Minds") fascicle. Dōgen refutes what evolved as the typical interpretation—which seems to reverse the overt meaning of the dialogue—that the Tripitaka monk's first two answers are actually correct and that even the silent response in the third part of the dialogue may be considered acceptable. Dōgen considers several commentaries by leading masters that justify why the Tripitaka master was silent at the end. For example, he discusses Chao-chou's remark that the Tripitaka monk did not see the National Teacher in the third question because the master "was standing right on the monk's nostrils" and was therefore too close to be perceived. He also considers another comment that the National Teacher had gone into a state of *samadhi* or profound absorption and was imperceptible to the monk. According to Dōgen, all of these are convoluted ways of trying to reconcile the monk's inability, and he returns to a literal reading of the case.

Dōgen maintains an iconoclastic view with several components. According to Dōgen, supranormal powers do not lead to and are not really the result of enlightenment, and therefore they are not comparable in merit to everyday activities and simple chores, such as chopping down weeds. Also, reading minds is symbolic of intuitive insight, which is beyond having or not having powers, and knowing about others is actually based on self-knowledge. Therefore, reading the mind of another can only take place on the basis of "reading one's own mind" (*jijinzū*), or realizing one's true nature. The first two lines of Dōgen's verse commentary refer to similar situations of mindreading in other Zen dialogues or Chinese Buddhist anecdotes, and the final lines reiterate the National Teacher's critique of Ta-erh as someone who is fundamentally deceptive.

18. A Hermit's "The Mountain Torrent Runs Deep, So the Ladle Is Long"

Main Case

A monk built a hermitage at the foot of Mount Hsüeh-feng and lived there for many years practicing meditation, but without having his head shaved. Making a wooden ladle, the solitary monk drew and drank water from a mountain torrent.

One day, a monk from the monastery at the top of the mountain visited the hermit and asked, "What is the meaning of Bodhidharma's coming from the West?" The hermit responded, "The mountain torrent runs deep, so the handle of a wooden ladle must be appropriately long." The monk reported this to the master of Hsüeh-feng temple, who declared, "He sounds like a strange character, perhaps an anomaly. I'd better go at once and check him out for myself."

The next day, master Hsüeh-feng went to see the hermit while carrying a razor and was accompanied by his attendant monk. As soon as they met he said, "If you can express the Way, I won't shave your head." On hearing this, the hermit at first was speechless. But then he used the ladle to bring water to have his head washed, and Hsüeh-feng shaved the hermit's head.

Verse Commentary

> If someone asks the meaning of Bodhidharma coming from the
>   West,
> It is that the handle of a wooden ladle is long, and the mountain
>   torrent runs deep;
> If you want to know the boundless meaning of this,
> Wait for the wind blowing in the pines to drown out the sound
>   of koto strings.

Discussion

This kōan is cited from Dōgen's EK vol. 9 case 71 (DZZ 4:230), and it is also included in his MS case 183 (DZZ 5:218). Although it does not appear in the major kōan collections, the case is contained in a wide variety of sources including other transmission of the lamp records, especially the *Tsung-men t'ung-yao chi* vol. 8 and the *Tsung-men lien-teng hui-yao* vol. 3, as well as the *Cheng-fa yen-tseng* (Jap. *Shōbōgenzō*) kōan collection of master Ta-hui. In addition to citing it in the EK and MS collections, Dōgen discusses the case in several KS fascicles, including "Gyōji," "Bodaisatta shishōbō," and especially "Dōtoku."

The dialogue involves a hermit who seems to represent the *pratyeka buddha* model that Zen, as a form of Mahayana Buddhism, sought either to discredit or assimilate. The solitary ascetics were in some cases rivals to the Zen patriarchs. In other cases, they were like wild foxes that resembled authentic masters but could mislead the family-oriented Confucian elite by conveying the wrong impression that Zen was an essentially antisocial ideology. The style of encounter dialogue is particularly suited to expressing the contest between a Zen master and a solitary practitioner.

The monk in this case must have been particularly astute, because his reputation spread and alarmed the leaders of the monastic institution situated on the mountain. The monastery monk asks the hermit the classic question about the meaning of Bodhidharma's "coming from the West" (that is, what brought Zen Buddhism to China from India). He is given a characteristically indirect, even absurd, though eminently practical response: "A mountain torrent runs deep, so the handle of a wooden ladle must be appropriately long." This Zen style of response piques the curiosity of master Hsüeh-feng, who decides to go and test the irregular monk. Hsüeh-feng brings a razor along with him, indicating that he is confident that he will be able to shave the bearded hermit who has not heretofore taken the tonsure. As in case 17, the hermit's inability to respond illustrates that silence is sometimes an ineffective or inappropriate response.

In an extensive discussion in *Shōbōgenzō* "Dōtoku," Dōgen characteristically alters the significance of the hermit's status by remarking that Hsüeh-feng should not and would not have asked or expected the irregular practitioner to "express the way" (*dōtoku*), unless he already knew that the hermit was enlightened. Unlike his interpretation of case 17, in which he asserts the literal meaning of the dialogue that refutes the Tripitaka monk's powers, this time Dōgen reverses the literal standpoint in both the EK verse commentary and the KS prose commentary by arguing that the hermit should not be considered a *pratyeka buddha*. Dōgen accepts the hermit's authenticity but he also agrees that the silent response indicates the superiority of Hsüeh-feng despite the hermit's considerable spiritual attainment. Hsüeh-feng earns the right to be testing and domesticating the hermit. The verse commentary steers from endorsing or disputing the spiritual powers of the irregular practitioner, who has been adopted through the master's administration of the tonsure into the legitimate Zen lineage.

19. Chao-chou Checks Out Two Hermits

Main Case

Chao-chou went to where a hermit was staying and asked, "Are you there? Are you there?" The hermit raised his fist. Chao-chou said, "A ship cannot anchor where the water is shallow," and then he left.

Chao-chou later came upon where another hermit was staying and called out, "Are you there? Are you there?" This hermit also raised his fist. Chao-chou said, "You have the ability to give and to take, to kill and to give life," and then he bowed.

Prose Commentary

Both hermits raised a fist. Why did Chao-chou approve of the one and disapprove of the other? What is the meaning of this contradictory behavior? If you are able to capture it in a turning word, then you will realize that Chao-chou's tongue has no bone and he can freely give the one hermit a boost and give the other a put-down. But do you also realize the flip side, that Chao-chou is being checked out by the hermits? If you suggest that either of the hermits is superior or inferior, then you do not display the eye of Zen. Or, if you suggest that there is no distinction whatsoever between the hermits, then you do not display the eye of Zen.

Verse Commentary

> An eye like a shooting star,
> A spirit like lightning,
> The sword that kills is also
> The sword that gives life.

Discussion

This kōan is cited from WMK case 11 (Taishō 48:294b), and it also appears in MS case 281 (DZZ 5:266). Chao-chou was featured in more dialogues and anecdotes that came to be included in the classic kōan collections, especially the WMK, than any of the other leading patriarchs. He is the key figure in many of the better known kōan cases, including "Does a dog have Buddha-nature? *Wu!* (Jap. *Mu*, or No!)" in WMK case 1; "Go wash your breakfast bowls" in WMK case 7; and "Why did Bodhidharma come from the West? An oak tree in the garden" in WMK case 37. Yet Chao-chou's career was somewhat anomalous because he trained for a very lengthy period in the south and also traveled extensively on pilgrimages, including to Mount Wu-t'ai, but did not become an abbot until he took over as leader of a monastery in the north at the age of eighty, according to traditional sources.

This case is a classic example of a double bind situation in that Chao-chou receives identical responses from two hermits yet he offers contradictory reactions, and the prose commentary insists that the hermits cannot be understood as respresenting either correct or incorrect standpoints. Apparently the master has heard that these hermits have attained a special level of spiritual accomplishment, and he decides to visit them in their huts or caves to test their abilities. When asked the question, "Are you there"—meaning, in effect, "demonstrate your power!"—both hermits give the same non-verbal response by holding up a fist somewhat defiantly. But they receive opposite evaluations from the master: the first hermit is criticized as being like "shallow water," and the second is praised for being able to "give and take life" like a double-edged sword, as mentioned in the verse commentary.

This interaction seems to demonstrate the pattern of the neither/nor logic of nonduality (or the transcendence of conventional logic) that was expressed by Chao-chou's teacher, Nan-ch'üan, in a more analytic fashion in WMK case 19 (Taishō 48:295b): "Tao belongs neither to knowledge nor to no-knowledge. For knowledge is but illusive perception, while no-knowledge is mere confusion. If you really attain true comprehension of the Tao, unaffected by the slightest doubt, your vision will be like infinite space, free of all limits and obstacles." The pattern expressed in the dialogue of two monks giving one answer and receiving opposite evaluations also recalls, but represents the flip side of, another encounter dialogue that Chao-chou had with two disciples: one said that he had visited the temple previously and the other said he had not, but Chao-chou's response to both was to offer a cup of tea.

The key ritual element in this kōan is the master's relation to the hermits. Who are these mysterious figures? In the previous cases in this chapter the irregular practitioners were either a Taoist immortal (P'u-hua), a Buddhist wizard (Ta-erh), or a *pratyeka buddha* (the hermit with the ladle). But the hermits in the current case are very likely enlightened followers of a Zen lineage, though not necessarily Chao-chou's own branch, who have secluded themselves after their main period of training in the Zen monastery in order to fortify their spiritual state to prepare for a return to everyday society. That is, they have not skipped over or avoided the stage of receiving transmission, as have the practitioners in the previous cases. The hermits are already legitimate members of the sect who need to be "checked out" by a master.

In one of the English translations the case is titled "Chao-chou Sees the True Nature of Two Hermits" (Zenkei Shibayama, *Zen Comments on the Mumonkan* [New York: Mentor, 1973], p. 88), which probably conveys the result of the process but does not necessarily express the extent and significance of the contest of wills that underlies the encounter dialogue. After all, it seems that Chao-chou is defeated by the second hermit, or at least he acknowledges the merit of the second hermit's aattainment. But on what basis is the judgment, pro or con, being made about the two hermits, especially the positive conclusion about the second one? The evaluations are a double-edged sword, according to the prose commentary, and may be seen as demonstrating the effectiveness—or perhaps lack of it—of Chao-chou's own supranormal power to gain insight into the past karma and current status of the hermits' spiritual state.

20. Hsüeh-feng's "What Is This?"

Pointer

As soon as you make a judgment about right or wrong, your mind falls into hopeless confusion. But if you do not commit to ranking, then you are groping in the dark. Tell me, which is preferable: letting go, or holding fast? At this very moment, if you follow the path of interpretation, you will remain trapped in the realm of language. If you cling to words, you will end up like a ghost roaming the fields and haunting the thickets. Even if you free yourself from this constraint, you will still be tens of thousands of miles from your homeland. Can you attain such freedom? If not, then it's simply another clear-cut case to be reflected on. Now consider the following.

Main Case

When Hsüeh-feng was living in his hermitage, two monks came to pay their respects. Seeing them approach, Hsüeh-feng pushed open the gate of the hut with his hand and standing before them said, "What is this?" One of the monks replied, "What is this?" Hsüeh-feng lowered his head and went back inside the hut.

Some time later the monks went to visit Yen-t'ou who asked, "Where are you coming from?" The monks responded, "From south of Mount Lingnan." Yen-t'ou said, "Did you ever go to meet Hsüeh-feng?" The monk said, "Yes, we have been to see him." Yen-t'ou asked, "What did he have to say?"

The monks told Yen-t'ou the whole story of their meeting with Hsüeh-feng. Yen-t'ou said, "Well, what did he tell you?" The monks said that in the end Hsüeh-feng lowered his head and returned to the hut. Yen-t'ou said, "Alas! I regret that I did not teach him the 'last word' when he was studying with me. If I had taught him this, then there would not be anyone on earth who could lay a finger on the master of Mount Hsüeh-feng."

At the end of the summer retreat, the monks brought up the preceding case and asked Yen-t'ou for instruction. Yen-t'ou said, "Why didn't you ask me for this instruction when we discussed it before?" The monks said, "We weren't ready to do so at that time." Yen-t'ou said, "Hsüeh-feng was brought up in my lineage, but he won't die in the same lineage. If you want to know the last word—that's it!"

Verse Commentary (by Hsüeh-tou)

> The "last word"—It is already expressed.
> Light and dark come and go at their own time.
> Born of the same lineage, they share the knowledge,
> Dying of different lineages, they are completely separate.
> Completely separate—
> Even Yellow-Head Buddha and Blue-Eyed Bodhidharma are
>   unable to tell.
> South, North, East, West, all returning to their respective
>   homes,
> And in the dead of the night, you can look out from any direction at the snow falling above thousands of peaks.

Discussion

This kōan, with pointer and verse commentary cited from PYL case 51 (Taishō 48:185c–187c), also appears in TJL case 50 (Taishō 48:258c–259a).

The case contains three encounter dialogues: one between Hsüeh-feng and the two monks from his temple, and the others involving the monks and Yen-t'ou, who meet on two different occasions. Hsüeh-feng and Yen-t'ou were both disciples of Te-shan, so that they would ordinarily be considered Dharma brothers. However, according to the prose commentary in the PYL that is based on materials in transmission of the lamp sources, Yen-t'ou was the one who facilitated Hsüeh-feng's enlightenment by teaching him about the last word of Zen. Furthermore, according to part of the account of their interaction that is also included as WMK case 13, Te-shan was actually taught the last word of Zen by Yen-t'ou, so that the master was referred to as a "toothless tiger" who had run into a "thief," his student. Therefore, Yen-t'ou's superiority is clearly established, but at the same time he only had one main disciple (Jui-yen, who is discussed in the following case) and his lineage expired shortly after that. On the other hand, Hsüeh-feng gave birth to a long-lasting, multibranched lineage, so that history records him as being much more significant in the overall development of the Zen sect in China.

In the current case, there is a significant role reversal in that master Hsüeh-feng, who challenged the *pratyeka buddha* in case 18, is functioning as the hermit who is being greeted and tested by two regular monks from the monastery. Apparently, Hsüeh-feng is in retreat during a minor period of the persecution of Buddhism by the state, although this case occurs several decades subsequent to the major suppression of Buddhism in the mid-840s when hundreds of temples were shuttered and tens of thousands of monks and nuns returned to lay life. The monks who come to his hermitage are likely former disciples who are expecting the encounter to become a situation of training rather than a contest. When they respond to the master/hermit's probing query by simply repeating his words, Hsüeh-feng is disappointed in their behavior. He lowers his head and returns to the sanctuary of his hut.

In the second dialogue, the monks visit Yen-t'ou and relate the whole story of their encounter with Hsüeh-feng. Yen-t'ou reacts by scolding the monks and reiterating his famous "last word of Zen" style of teaching, which is mysterious, elusive, and paradoxically demonstrative rather than strictly verbal. Apparently Hsüeh-feng's silent response to the monks did not reflect a complete understanding. Yen-t'ou's emphasis on the last word style is reinforced by the case pointer, which provides a classic account of the double bind of language: one is condemned for talking or not talking, judging or not ranking. The pointer also includes a supernatural element in its reference to ghosts that roam and haunt the landscape, entangled in the thicket of words and speech.

However, the real message of the kōan, as indicated in the final lines of the main case that are amplified by the third and fourth lines of the verse commentary, involves the issue of lineal transmission and the relation between Hsüeh-feng and Yen-t'ou, rather than language or nonduality. Yen-t'ou, as a Dharma brother, is not in a position of authority to sanction Hsüeh-feng's enlightenment, despite his role as a catalyst. The case record acknowledges indirectly and with some degree of ambivalence that Hsüeh-feng, the junior brother, surpasses both his senior and their mentor Te-shan in his impact on the growth of Zen during difficult political circumstances. Yet, the verse also shows that even the practical issue of the relation between lineages can and should be interpreted in terms of nonduality—the different lines of transmission are neither completely the same nor completely different.

21. Jui-yen Calls Out to Himself, "Master"

Main Case

Every day Jui-yen was calling out to himself, "Master!" And he would answer himself, "Yes?" Then he would say, "Stay awake, remain steadfast!" "Yes," he would answer.

"Don't let yourself be deceived by anyone, at any time or any day!" he would say. "Yes, yes!" he would reply.

Prose Commentary

Old Jui-yen does the selling as well as the buying all by himself. He dons the masks of so many goblins and ghosts. What is this? Hark, ye demons! There are masks for the one who calls out and also for the one who answers, and masks for the one who remains alert and also for the one who is not deceived by others. But if you take any of the appearances before you to be real, you are altogether mistaken. And if you try to imitate Jui-yen, that is nothing other than the standpoint of a wild fox.

Verse Commentary

> Seekers of the Way do not find the truth,
> When they are entangled in discriminating consciousness,

This is the root cause of endless rounds of birth and death,
Yet fools mistake this for the original face.

Discussion

This kōan, cited from WMK case 12 (Taishō 48:294b), appears in MS case 247 (DZZ 5:254–256). It is another case that focuses on the issue of lineage and uses other, more theoretical concerns, such as the matter of overcoming a reliance on language, almost as a pretext to highlight the question of the effectiveness of the authority of transmission.

The kōan evokes the fine line of ambiguity separating the authentic from the inauthentic wildness or irreverence of Zen monks. According to the case record, master Jui-yen, the main disciple of Yen-t'ou who was the last representative of his short-lived lineage, has what seems like a disturbing habit. In an example of deliberate ambivalence, the kōan leaves the reader to wonder whether Jui-yen, who was known to have sat for long periods of meditation on a certain special "zazen stone," is a fool who has perhaps lost his composure from too much isolation, or a worthy successor to Pai-chang, admired for sitting alone on Ta-hsiung Peak, as well as numerous other hermits and eccentric practitioners. Like case 39, this kōan uses anti-supernatural rhetoric against the background of magical fox imagery to show that problematic behavior lies not so much in acting in an eccentric or crazy way, which is often to be applauded, but in blindly following those who do so, whose path is nothing other than the state of a drooling wild fox.

The prose commentary makes two references to supernatural imagery that reveal the importance of the two-fold discursive structure of this kōan. The last line uses typical anti-supernaturalism that relies for its impact on an underlying belief in the supernatural to criticize the imitators of Jui-yen, and this is reinforced by the verse commentary. However, the final sentence of the prose commentary could also be interpreted to mean, "If you follow Jui-yen, you would realize that his understanding is that of a wild fox."

Another interesting supernatural feature of the commentary is the use of the term *chien* (Jap. *nii*), rendered as "Hark!", which can also be translated in a non-supernatural way as "Think about it!" The term is used in other Zen dialogues, including the prose commentary in case 6, as an injunctive to remind disciples to look at or listen to a situation carefully, so that another possible rendering is "Listen!" A Zen master will frequently utter this term for emphasis or dramatic effect. But the term as it appears in the kōan commentary harbors an ambiguity in evoking the original folklore meaning of the word, which refers to what a ghost becomes at death. In popular religious practice, the character for *chien* is written on a piece of paper that is then fastened to a doorway or gate as a charm to prevent and exorcise the appearance of ghosts and goblins (i.e., non-humans, Ch. *fei-jen*, Jap. *hinin*) from intruding on a dwelling.

The real point of criticizing the deficiencies in Jui-yen's approach is to highlight the question of lineal transmission. Jui-yen's is the final representative in the lineage of Yen-t'ou, who was the first patriarch, and this stands in contrast to the transmission of Yen-t'ou's Dharma brother Hsüeh-feng, as discussed in case 20. His lineage spread for many generations and gave rise to multiple branches. In that sense, the commentary mocks Jui-yen's dubious accomplishments, even as it chides those who would inauthentically imitate his actions. It suggests that one should not follow Jui-yen, partly because that would be the slavish imitation (or fox drool) of a great master who is a wild fox in the positive sense of the term, and partly because he is not worthy of admiration since he did not create a lineage and thus represents a fox in the negative sense. Another commentary on the case suggests, "Jui-yen alone can put a stop to this habit, no one else can do it for him."

22. Ti-tsang Planting the Fields

Pointer

Scholars plough with their pens, and orators plough with their tongues. We patchrobed monks sit idly watching a white ox roam freely, not taking note of the abundant, limitless grass. How else do we pass the time?

Main Case

Ti-tsang asked Hsiu-shan, "Where do you come from?" Hsiu-shan said, "From the South." Ti-tsang said, "How is the Buddha Dharma in the South these days?" Hsiu-shan replied, "People are always talking things over." Ti-tsang retorted, "How does that compare to what's going on here, where I am busy planting the fields and preparing rice for meals?"

Hsiu-shan said, "How does that affect the Triple World?" Ti-tsang replied, "Why do you think it's called the Triple World?"

Discussion

This kōan, cited from TJL case 12 (Taishō 48:234c–235b), raises the issue of the relation between "north" and "south" on a number of different levels that are employed indirectly by the encounter dialogue. This polarity is the basis for interpreting the case. In terms of the overall situation of Buddhism in China, the Northern style referred to visionary, esoteric, tantric practices associated with Central Asia, such as worship of Manjusri on Mount Wu-t'ai as depicted in cases 13–15; the Southern style referred to a more simple and iconoclastic approach to the practice of meditation that was associated with Zen, as in case 5. In the early history of Zen, the contrast took on an additional significance, with north, or the Northern school, referring to the first powerful movement of the emerging Zen sect around the beginning of the eighth century that was led by Shen-hsiu. His authority was usurped by the Southern school, led by sixth patriarch Hui-neng. By way of contrast, the Northern school was known for its emphasis on gradualism and the study of sutras, whereas the Southern school was known for emphasizing suddenness and silence. However, these distinctions often functioned more on the level of the rhetoric of polemics than as descriptions of the actual historical condition or spiritual process.

Yet while the Southern school, which defined Zen as a "special transmission outside the scriptures/ Without reliance on words and letters," gained a reputation for repudiating and even destroying the sutras, it also developed the unique style of encounter dialogue literature. For the followers of Ma-tsu, the encounter dialogue style, alluded to in this case by the Hsiu-shan's reference to people in the South "talking things over," was the main method of transmitting and evaluating the legitimacy of transmission. Despite the emphasis on silence, there was also a tremendous interest in the efficacy of a distinctive type of language based on the dialogical context of challenges and contests.

Therefore, Ti-tsang is implicitly critical of the Ma-tsu-style Southern approach in his emphasis on the everyday chores of planting crops and preparing meals, although such activities were also advocated by Ma-tsu's foremost disciple, Pai-chang, and his notion of "a day without work is a day without eating" or "no work, no food." The "Triple World" refers to the basic Buddhist doctrine of the existence of the worlds of form, formlessness, and the realm of emptiness beyond the distinction and opposition of form and the formless. The point of Ti-tsang's final comment is to highlight everyday activity as the primary way of linking the world of form with the higher realms.

The TJL prose commentary (not included in the translation) takes the approach of critiquing and correcting both of the participants in the dialogue. Although the main case seems to suggest that Ti-tsang clearly has the upper hand, the commentary withholds approval. First, the TJL remarks that Hsiu-shan could have said "It's just the same as here" in response to the initial query about Buddhism in the South. Then, according to the TJL, Ti-tsang should have answered, "If so, it's the same here as in the South," rather than somewhat arrogantly asserting the superiority of his own style of practice. Or, Ti-tsang should have simply and humbly said, "I'm busy planting the fields," so as "to avoid Hung-chih [the original compiler of the TJL] listing his crime on the same indictment."

The TJL commentary concludes by valorizing "ancients who would reap and boil chestnuts and rice at the end of a hoe in a broken-legged pot deep in the mountains, content and free of attachment. They are never seeking, peaceful, and serene." In other words, praise is given to the classical, though somewhat idealized, image of the forest ascetic who neither "discusses things" nor "plants the fields"—neither ploughs with the pen nor with the rake, according to the case pointer—but focuses purely on continuing spiritual cultivation.

Dangerous Women: Zen "Grannies" and Nuns

23. Chao-chou Checks Out an Old Woman

Main Case

Each time a monk from Mount Chao-chou asked an old woman, "What is the path to Mount Wu-t'ai?" the woman said, "Go straight ahead." After the monk had taken just a few steps the woman sneered, "A fine monk—and off he goes."

Later, one of the monks told master Chao-chou about what was happening. Chao-chou said, "Wait till I check out the old woman for you." The next day Chao-chou went and asked her the same question posed by the monk. The woman gave him the same answer offered to the other monks.

Chao-chou returned to his assembly and said, "That old woman at the foot of Mount Wu-t'ai—I've checked her out for you."

Prose Commentary

The old woman was only sitting there in her tent, planning her next campaign, but did not realize that she was being shadowed by a spy. Although Chao-chou showed that he could sneak into the enemy camp and outmaneuver its defenses, he did not prove himself to be a great commander-in-chief. Now, tell me, what did Chao-chou check out about the old woman?

Verse Commentary

> The questions were all the same,
> And so were the answers.
> Sand in the rice,
> Thorns in the mud.

Discussion

This kōan, which originally appears in the CCL (Taishō 51:276–278) and other transmission of the lamp records that deal with the life of master Chao-chou, is cited from WMK case 31 (Taishō 48:297) and is also included in TJL case 10 (Taishō 48:323a–323c) and MS case 133 (DZZ 5:133). This is one of several cases in which a man is given his comeuppance by a woman, although it is not entirely clear who emerges as the winner of the encounter.

In Zen literature there are two main scenarios in which women play a key role. One involves elderly laywomen who are usually not schooled in Buddhism and may represent another style of religiosity, such as popular Taoism or shamanism, who outsmart or outwit monks, as in this case and in cases 24 and 26. Another example of this style is the story of Huang-po before he became a disciple of Pai-chang. While traveling, Huango-po asked a woman for food, and she said that he was "insatiable." When he asked how this can be if he has not even eaten yet, she dismissed him and sent him on his way to his eventual master. The other style that valorizes the role of women involves nuns who exist on the periphery of the Zen monastic institution and appear challenging or even threatening to men who must grapple with the question of deferring to the authority of their female counterparts, as in cases 13, 25, and 51.

The current case, as a prime example of the first category, focuses on an old woman sitting at the foot of Mount Wu-t'ai who may be a witch—the

Chinese character is the same term as the more benign "old woman"—or practitioner of some esoteric or occult type of religion. In any case, she is able to turn the tables on a series of visitors from the monastery and seems to attain at least a standoff, if not outright victory, in her encounter with Chao-chou.

This case recalls case 19 in which Chao-chou "checks out" the two hermits. As with that kōan, a translation renders the title as "Chao-chou Sees Through the Old Woman," which implies that he emerges as the winner of the contest, but this is not necessarily supported by what actually transpires in the dialogue. The woman clearly gets the best of the younger monks, who meet her in the foothills on their way to Mount Wu-t'ai. When they ask for directions she gives them the most simplistic response and then laughs at them for taking her words at face value and following her advice. But a literal reading of the dialogue leaves the question of who is victorious in her encounter with Chao-chou wide open: The kōan may affirm the role of Chao-chou as the investigator who has checked out the old woman and perhaps seen her true nature. On the other hand, since he receives the same treatment as the junior monks, it is certainly possible—and this is the approach implied in the second sentence of the prose commentary—to interpret the woman as a brilliant strategist who remains undisturbed and unimpeded by her meeting with the patriarch, and she is able to send him on his way. The verse commentary ironically suggests a draw, with no clear victor emerging.

In addition to the issue of gender, another key element for understanding the case is Zen's relation to Mount Wu-t'ai religiosity. As previously mentioned, visiting Mount Wu-t'ai was forbidden by masters Lin-chi and Yün-men as a site of inauthentic religiosity. Yet Zen monks, hearing of visions of the bodhisattva Manjusri who might appear as a golden lion riding amid multicolored clouds or as a wandering hermit or beggar, continued to make pilgrimages there. In the early stages of his own journeys in pursuit of enlightenment, Chao-chou was once headed on a visit to Mount Wu-t'ai when a master cautioned him with the following verse (Taishō 51:277a):

> What green mountain anywhere is not a place to learn the Way?
> Why bother to hike with your staff all the way to Mount
> Wu-t'ai?
> Even if the Golden Lion (Manjusri) reveals himself in the
> clouds,
> This is not auspicious when looked at with the Dharma-eye.

According to the account in the CCL, Chao-chou reacted by asking, "What is the Dharma-eye?," to which he received no response. It is not clear whether or not he ever completed the trip, although he did end his career as abbot of a temple in the vicinity of Mount Wu-t'ai. But the message of the kōan seems to be ambiguous and indirect regarding the Zen approach to what this site represented. As the verse commentary suggests, Chao-chou and the old woman, as well as the tension about traveling or not traveling to the mountain, all represent concealed dangers like "thorns in the mud."

24. Te-shan and the Woman Selling Rice Cakes

Main Case

Te-shan was traveling to the south in search of the Dharma when he came across a woman on the roadside selling refreshments and asked, "Who are you?" She responded, "I am an old woman selling rice cakes." He said, "I'll take some rice cakes." She said, "Venerable priest, why do you want them?" He said, "I am hungry and need some refreshments [Ch. *tien-hsin*, Jap. *ten-shin*]."

She said, "Venerable priest, what are you carrying in your bag?" He said, "Haven't you heard I am 'King of the *Diamond Sutra*'? I have thoroughly penetrated all of its levels of meaning. Here I have my notes and commentaries on the scripture."

Hearing this the old woman said, "I have one question. Venerable priest, may I ask it?" He said, "Go ahead and ask it." She stated, "I have heard it said that according to the *Diamond Sutra*, past mind is ungraspable [Ch. *hsin-p'u-hua-te*, Jap. *Shinfukatoku*], present mind is ungraspable, and future mind is ungraspable. So, where is the mind [*hsin/shin*] that you wish to refresh [*tien/ten*] with rice cakes? Venerable priest, if you can answer, I will sell you a rice cake. But if, venerable priest, you cannot answer, I will not sell you any rice cake."

Te-shan was struck speechless, and the old woman got up abruptly and left without selling Te-shan a single rice cake.

Discussion

This kōan is cited from the prose commentary section of PYL case 4 (Taishō 48:143b–144c), and it is discussed as the main topic of the KS

"Shinfukatoku" fascicle (DZZ 1:82–86) on the "Ungraspable Mind." This case is another example of an elderly laywoman who makes no claim on transmission or lineal authority, yet is apparently able to outsmart a leading patriarch. As a result of an encounter dialogue, the woman defeats Te-shan at his own game—the study of the seminal Mahayana Buddhist scripture on the doctrine of emptiness, the *Diamond Sutra*—although Dōgen's extensive commentary calls into question the adequacy of her treatment of Te-shan but without giving him full credit, either.

Te-shan appears as the protagonist in case 6 (cited from PYL case 4; the current case is extracted from its section of prose commentary), which deals with his encounter with Kuei-shan. Te-shan was an expert in scriptural exegesis who was known as the "King of the *Diamond Sutra*." He boasted of having written twelve volumes of commentary and of being an unsurpassed lecturer on the methods of scholastic Buddhism. Te-shan began his practice in the north, and it took him years of wandering till he attained enlightenment in the south. Hearing about the style of Southern school (direct, sudden transmission), he traveled to the southern district while carrying in a backpack his collected writings about the sutra, which epitomized the Northern school style. He decided to join up with the assembly of Lung-t'an and was later enlightened by training under this master, as recorded in WMK (case 13).

While taking a rest on the side of the road, Te-shan comes across an old woman selling refreshments. She makes an ingenious philosophical pun because the term for rice cakes, also pronounced "dim sum," literally means "pointing to the mind," which, according to the *Diamond Sutra*, is ungraspable. With Te-shan stunned speechless at the conclusion of their dialogue, the old woman seems the clear winner in a way that is more incontestable than the previous case in which Chao-chou had the last word, although that was delivered not to his challenger but to the monks back in the monastery.

However, Dōgen's commentary tries to reverse the conventional understanding by criticizing the woman as well as Te-shan. Dōgen points out that while Te-shan thought that he was "checking out" the old woman, it turned out that she had checked him out and found him wanting. He challenges Te-shan for not asking in resonse to her query, "I cannot answer your question, what would you say?" But Dōgen then suggests that she should have said, "Venerable priest, if you cannot answer my question, try asking me a question to see if I can answer you." He is quite critical of the old woman as well as those who automatically praise her handling of Te-shan.

According to Dōgen, it is not clear that the woman is enlightened—she is a marginal figure who can challenge Zen monks, but should not be considered the equal of a Zen master. Dōgen seems particularly reluctant to sanction the authority of a laywoman, although in his interpretation of case 25 he praises a nun and attacks monks who deny the abilities of legitimately ordained women.

Dōgen argues that Te-shan should have said, "If you say so, then don't bother to sell me any rice cakes." Or, to be even more effective, he could have turned the tables on the woman by inquiring, "As past mind is ungraspable, present mind is ungraspable, and future mind is ungraspable, where is the mind [*hsin*] that now makes the rice cakes used for refreshment [*tien*]?" Then, the woman would confront Te-shan by saying, "You know only that one cannot refresh the mind with a rice cake. But you do not realize that the mind refreshes the rice cake, or that the mind refreshes [or liberates] the mind." And just as Te-shan is feeling overwhelmed and bewildered she would continue, "Here is one rice cake each for the past ungraspable mind, the present ungraspable mind, and the future ungraspable mind." If he should fail to reach out his hand to take the rice cakes, she should slap him with one of the cakes and say, "You ignorant fool, don't be so absent-minded." Dōgen concludes by arguing, "Therefore, neither the old woman nor Te-shan were able to adequately hear or express the past ungraspable mind, the present ungraspable mind, or the future ungraspable mind." Yet, despite Dōgen's playful, probing critique of the old woman, it seems clear that she has prevailed over the monk with one of the most effective puns in the history of Zen literature that is replete with diverse styles of wordplay.

25. Mo-shan Opens Her Mouth

Main Case

Chih-hsien was sent by his master, Lin-chi, to study with Mo-shan. On their first meeting she asked, "Where have you come from?" Chih-hsien answered, "The Mouth of the Road" (the literal meaning of the name of his village). Mo-shan retorted, "Then why didn't you close your mouth when you came here?" Chih-hsien prostrated himself and became her disciple.

Some time later he challenged her by asking, "What is the Summit of the Mountain [the literal meaning of the name Mo-shan]?" She replied,

"The Summit of the Mountain cannot be seen." "Then who is the person on the mountain?" he demanded. "I am neither a male nor a female form," she responded. "Then," he asked, "why not transfigure into some other form?" "Since I am not a fox spirit, I cannot transfigure."

Once again Chih-hsien bowed and decided to serve as supervisor of Mo-shan's temple garden for three years, proclaiming her teaching the equal of Lin-chi.

Discussion

This kōan, which originally appeared in CCL vol. 11 (Taishō 51:289a), is cited from the KS "Raihaitokuzui" fascicle (DZZ 1:302–315), where it is discussed extensively by Dōgen, and it is also included in abbreviated fashion in Dōgen's EK vol. 9 case 32 (DZZ 4:202). There are also other versions of the narrative in various transmission of the lamp records that have different outcomes and ways of treating the question of whether the monk in the end defers to the authority and superiority of the nun, whose wisdom in expressed in ingenious wordplay.

This case mixes a number of fascinating supernatural and ritual elements involving gender issues and the role of magical, shapeshifting foxes with punning that conveys a message about nonduality. The dialogue focuses on the role of the nun as a teacher of men. She is recommended to Chih-hsien by Lin-chi, which means she is sanctioned by one of the leading patriarchs, an honor that Iron Grindstone Liu is denied by Kuei-shan in case 13. Yet, when Mo-shan opens the dialogue with the standard query, "Where have you come from?," which refers not so much to geography or place as to psychology or state of mind, Chih-hsien replies with a pun on the name of his hometown. Mo-shan responds with a sarcastic put-down resembling the approach of the Zen grannies in the other cases in this section. Chih-hsien tries a comeback by making a pun on Mo-shan's name, and she responds with a denial of any claim to a transcendence of gender differentiation by resorting to an ironic repudiation of fox imagery.

The reference to the fox alludes to a famous story in the *Lotus Sutra* of a Naga princess who is able to change her sexual identity in order to prove her enlightenment, but this ability in the end only highlights her non-human or supernatural status. Mo-shan, on the other hand, seeks to demonstrate that her accomplishments are not based on a display of magical skills. Yet this denial is possible only against the backdrop of wide-spread belief in the powers of shapeshifting animals and spirits. In the end,

Chih-hsien submits to Mo-shan and works for her, at least for a couple of years. In an epilogue to the dialogue he declares, "I was given half a ladle of water by Lin-chi and another half a ladle by Mo-shan. Now that I have drunk a full ladle, I have nothing more to seek further."

Another story recorded in the transmission of the lamp records including the CCL deals with whether a nun should be allowed to enter the Dharma Hall to preach. Here, master T'an-k'ung asks a nun who wants to open the hall to demonstrate a supranormal power to prove herself worthy, and she refrains from doing so though presumably she could have if she had wished. Ironically the refusal to perform puts her in higher regard than an actual demonstration, and she is given entree. But, in general, Zen literature is ambiguous about whether a woman can teach a man if she has not previously taken her teaching from a monk and become legitimate in one of the accepted lineages.

Dōgen devotes a complete fascicle of the *Shōbōgenzō* to the case of Mo-shan and related anecdotes about the role of nuns. While he is critical of some of the Zen grannies who are lay and perhaps occult practitioners, as in his commentaries on cases 24 and 26, he defends Mo-shan, who is ordained, and severely attacks monks who reject the authority of women as "ignorant fools who deceive and delude secular people" and therefore "can never become bodhisattvas." Dōgen comments that he was struck by the "skin, flesh, bones, marrow" transmission story of first patriarch Bodhidharma, who interviewed four people, including a woman, before selecting his successor by transmitting his marrow, and Dōgen supports Mo-shan's authority.

However, several factors call into question whether Dōgen is consistent in his acceptance of a lineal model for women. First, in other fascicles (particularly "Shukke kudoku," written late in his career), he tends to consider nuns unequal to men. Also, even in "Raihaitokuzui," he makes ironic references that may undercut his support for women. For example, he announces that legitimate teachers can be found "whether man or woman, ancient or modern, stone pillars or shapeshifting foxes."

26. Chao-chou Recites the Sutras

Main Case

In the district of Chao-chou, an old woman sent a message to the master with a donation and a request that he recite the entire collection of

Buddhist sutras. Hearing of this, the master stepped down from his seat and walked around the chair one time. Then he said, "I have finished reciting the collection of sutras."

The messenger returned to the old woman and told her what happened with Chao-chou. The old woman said, "I asked Chao-chou to recite the complete collection of sutras. Why did he recite only half the sutras?"

Discussion

This kōan, which appears in transmission of the lamp records on Chao-chou's teachings, is cited from MS case 74 (DZZ 5:164) and it is also discussed briefly in *Ta-hui yü-lu* vol. 9 and more extensively in Dōgen's KS "Kankin" (DZZ 2:320–342). Once again, an old woman turns the tables on Chao-chou, although the outcome of the encounter is somewhat ambiguous. This case, along with anecdotes about similar encounters, were frequently discussed in Zen records. Dōgen examines several versions of the story without offering a clear-cut statement about the result.

The background of the kōan narrative is the longstanding practice of the recitation of the sutras. Many of the most popular sutras, or at least portions of the longer scriptures, were read and chanted as part of the liturgy of Mahayana Buddhism, including Zen. Some of these sutras, especially the *Lotus Sutra*, were considered imbued with magical powers so that copying scripture (sometimes using blood for ink), reciting it, or chanting the title alone could have a ritual efficacy in communing and evoking the presence of the universal Buddha-nature. The entire collection of handwritten sutras, often in scrolls, was so vast that it could never be recited in a single sitting or even an extended period. As a surrogate for reciting the entire collection, a common practice was to view the collection that was usually stored in a special reservoir building located in a temple complex. In some cases, priests and worshipers would circumambulate the sutra building. Many of these practices were conducted within the Zen monastic ritual cycle. But at the same time the Southern school advocated a "special transmission outside the sutras" and even recommended burning or destroying the sutras, at least according to some of its rhetoric.

In this case, Chao-chou upholds the iconoclastic ideal and shows the futility of circumambulation by walking around his chair only one time. However, although his action seems to be a good demonstration of the Zen sense of irreverence and anti-ritualism, it is an inadequate response to the woman's request, which was already an expression of a fundamental absurdity. Therefore, the woman gets the last word in this case, and once again Zen literature preserves a narrative that highlights the wisdom of a female, albeit an anonymous layperson.

But is Chao-chou really in the wrong? In the "Kankin" fascicle, which deals with the role of "Sutra Reading," the conventional interpretation of the case is reversed. Dōgen says that Chao-chou walking around his chair really did represent the whole of the Buddhist sutras, whereas the old woman was merely lost in her concern for the relative number of scriptures recited. At the same time, in contrast to this line of interpretation that is critical of the woman, Dōgen suggests that perhaps the old woman really wanted to see Chao-chou walk around the chair backwards, or in the opposite direction, to expose his appreciation of absurdity.

"Kankin" also contains several other versions of the narrative culled from the transmission of the lamp records. In one version, master Shen-chao of Mount Ta-sui in I-chou also walks around the chair. But this time the old woman is criticized for not saying, "I asked him to recite the entire collection of the sutras. Why did the master worry himself so much?" In another version, master Tung-shan first bows to the messenger who returns the bow, but then he walks around the chair with the officer and asks the officer if he understood. When the messenger replies "no," Tung-shan says, "Why can't you understand that I have read a sutra with you?" In a fourth version, Dōgen relates how his Chinese mentor Ju-ching, who was once asked to read a lengthy sutra and deliver a sermon, drew a big circle in the air with his fly-whisk and said, "Now I have read it for you!" Then he cast away the fly-whisk and descended from the dais.

In the rest of the "Kankin" fascicle, Dōgen spends time outlining and analyzing the precise way the ritual of sutra reading is to be conducted, including minute details about preparing and serving food as well as the time and place for the reading. But he also discusses other dialogues that highlight the futility and absurdity of the ritual. In one example that is particularly intriguing for its irreverent tone, master Yüeh-shan is known for forbidding the recitation of sutras and yet one day is discovered reading a sutra himself. When asked by a disciple why he is doing precisely what he does not allow others he responds, "I am only trying to cover my eyes with the scroll!"

[THREE]

Encountering Supernatural Forces

The question of the significance of encounters with supernatural forces in Zen literature lies at the heart of the two-fold discursive structure of the kōan tradition. On the one hand, Zen writings continually express dismay and disrespect for that which is said to exist beyond the confines of concrete reality by advocating killing the Buddha, damaging the sutras, and rejecting forms of worship. On the other hand, the practice of Zen in the context of East Asian religiosity clearly plays an important role in kōan literature, or perhaps reluctantly allows the infiltration and assimilation of diverse elements of the marvelous. These include alternative states of consciousness such as trance, visions, and dreams, as well as mysterious, magical, or esoteric forms of being such as ghosts, goblins, shapeshifting animals, spirits, gods, and bodhisattvas, whether of Buddhist or non-Buddhist (especially Hindu, Taoist, and Shinto) origins.

Dreams and various otherworldly or other-dimensional realms of experience, play a key role in heightening, bridging, or challenging the enlightenment experience. Dreams in particular function on several levels in Zen discourse. As influenced by early Mahayana Buddhist doctrines of the emptiness of conceptual categories and distinctions in the Madhyamika school, as well as the inseparability of interior and exterior reality in the Yogacara school, dreams are considered to reflect an extreme form of illusion, distortion, misperception, and falsity. This is comparable to seeing a flower in the sky or eating a painted rice cake, conditions that must be refuted and negated in order to attain liberation. At the other end of the experiential spectrum, as influenced by shamanistic trance and related types of visionary experiences in esoteric Buddhism and indigenous religious and literary traditions, dreams represent a higher, transcendental dimension of reality. Dreams are the vehicle for revelations of past and future karma, healing, prophecy, and intuitive connections to earthly patriarchs and celestial beings. However, dreams, as a passageway to inspiration and transcendence, or the daemonic, can also, depending on the context, lead to a domain of the terrifying and occult, or the demonic.

Somewhere between the levels of illusion and transcendence, dreams function as a metaphor for the relativity and evanescence of existence, which is constantly shifting between opposite levels. Zen is very much influenced by Chuang Tzu's notion of the person who awakens from a dream that he is a butterfly and does not know which identity is based on illusion and which on reality, as well as ongoing speculation in Chinese thought about who really is the dreamer and who it is that tells about the dreamer's dream. Some Zen thinkers often used the expression "explaining (or disclosing) a dream within a dream." This served as a way of conveying the inseparability of being lost in delusion and of rising above mundane existence precisely by clarifying the state of self-deception. Explaining a dream within a dream is also referred to as a process of disentangling entangled vines by means of the vines themselves.

Although Zen sought to find the transcendence of illusion in terms of an inner state that was achieved through practice based on self-power, it also incorporated divine entities into monastic rituals, liturgy, and kōan literature. The deities included traditional arhats redefined as Zen gargoyles in addition to bodhisattvas from the Mahayana pantheon, especially Manjusri, who was enshrined in Zen monasteries as the god of wisdom and the emissary for the destruction of ignorance. Zen deities also included gods incorporated from esoteric Hindu-Buddhist movements that were often represented on tantric mandalas, as well as from Taoist and Shinto cults. Zen luminaries, patriarchs, saints, and heroes, including the immortalized Bodhidharma and the "Laughing Buddha" who became identified with the bodhisattva Maitreya, were also elevated to divine status. Another important category of gods in Zen included local tutelary or land deities that oversaw mountains, villages, and other domains, and became associated with monastic compounds and various sacred sites located in remote places. The local gods, once encountered, converted, and assimilated into the Zen institution, enabled the opening of the mountain and offered protection for the temple thereafter. These gods were then enshrined in the compound, usually in a prominent site near the main buildings including the Dharma Hall and the abbot's quarters.

Folklore in Zen was also heavily shaped by magical or shapeshifting animals, especially foxes and snakes assimilated from local folk tales and animistic cults, which were in turn challenged, threatened, and tamed by Zen masters as part of the process of opening mountains. Numerous kōans in the major collections deal with the role of animals, including a castrated water buffalo (MS case 3), a cat cut in half (WMK case 14, PYL case 63–64, TJL case 9, and MS case 181), a hare (PYL case 90), a rhinoceros (PYL case 91), a buffalo (WMK case 38), a dog (WMK case 1 and MS case 8), a snow lion (TJL 26), and an ox icon (EK vol. 9 case 11). However, shapeshifting animals play a special role because they reflect an interaction with liminal forces that represent a mixture of para-human and sub-human qualities that at once encompass good and evil, and angelic and demonic intentions and behavior. As with the local gods and spirits, encounters with magical animals either trigger liberation in a monk or serve as an opportunity for the master to awaken the deity to its true nature as a symbol or representative of the Dharma.

TRANCE, VISIONS, AND DREAMS

27. A Woman Comes Out of Absorption

Main Case

It happened one time in the age of the World Honored One that Manjusri went to where the assembly of Buddhas gathered and found that each one had already returned to his original abode. The only one remaining there was a woman, sitting in a state of total absorption (*samadhi*) near the Buddha's throne.

Manjusri asked Sakyamuni Buddha, "Why can a woman sit near the Buddha when I cannot get such a seat?" Sakyamuni responded, "Why don't you wake the woman up, arouse her from the state of absorption, and ask her yourself?" Manjusri circled the woman three times, lifted her up, and transported her to Brahma heaven, where he summoned all his spiritual powers in order to arouse her.

Sakyamuni said, "Even a hundred thousand Manjusris would not be able to awaken the woman from the state of absorption. But down below, past twelve hundred million lands as innumerable as the sands of the Ganges River, there is a bodhisattva called Dim Light who will be able to arouse her." In a flash, Dim Light rose up from the earth and made prostrations before the World Honored One, who gave him his instructions. Dim Light walked over to the woman and snapped his fingers one time.

The woman was aroused from her state of absorption.

Prose Commentary

That old master Sakyamuni put on quite a show, but it didn't penetrate down to the common folk. Let me ask you, Manjusri is the teacher of the Seven Buddhas, so why couldn't he arouse the woman from her state of absorption? How was it that Dim Light, a novice bodhisattva, was able to do it? If you understand this intimately, you will appreciate the Naga's state of absorption even in the midst of karmic consciousness.

Verse Commentary

> Arousing or not arousing the woman,
> Both bodhisattvas attained freedom,
> One with the head of a god, and the other with the face of a
>   demon,
> Showing gracefulness even in defeat.

Discussion

This kōan, cited from WMK case 42 (Taishō 48:298a–298b), combines a parable about the Buddha and bodhisattvas from an early Mahayana sutra known in Japanese as *Shobutsu yōshūkyō* (Taishō 17:763a) with a passage from CCL vol. 27 about a woman in an extreme state of trance. This is one of a handful of kōans whose primary source is material from outside of the Zen tradition, and the case is replete with supernatural and ritual elements, including divine beings navigating between heavenly realms, meditative trance that borders on obsession, a woman who outperforms male counterparts, and questions of authority in relation to lineage and hierarchy. However, most interpretations of the case strip away the mythological features and reduce the image of the woman interacting with various bodhisattvas to the symbolism of an inner conflict of contemplation versus distraction due to arrogance.

In this kōan there are several instances of Manjusri being embarrassed—one time by the anonymous woman who is permitted to have a seat next to Sakyamuni, whereas the bodhisattva is not given this privilege, another by a much lesser bodhisattva, whose name, rendered here as "Dim Light," suggests darkness, ignorance, and the obfuscation of truth. Manjusri is the patron saint of Zen Buddhist temples because he represents wisdom and the destruction of ignorance, much like Lord Siva in Hinduism. Like other bodhisattvas, there are various depictions of Manjusri in different Buddhist schools or cultural regions. For example, he is shown riding astride a lion amid multicolored clouds on Mount Wu-t'ai (see case 14). He is also sometimes portrayed as a wandering beggar on the slopes of Mount Wu-t'ai. This image was especially prominent in the Kamakura era Japanese Ritsu (Vinaya, Ch. Lu) school, which depicted Manjusri on a mission to save the poor and downtrodden in a troubled and changing society. In Zen iconography, Manjusri is shown carrying a sutra in one hand and the sword of wisdom, used to sever delusions, in the other hand.

In the current case, Manjusri demonstrates miraculous skills in transporting the woman up to Brahma heaven, yet his supranormal powers fail to arouse her. Although women were considered defiled in Buddhism, numerous kōans, including cases 23–26, show that in Zen they were, under certain circumstances and with some restrictions, considered equal or even superior to monks, and here a woman's meditation surpasses the capabilities of the leading bodhisattva. *Samadhi* (absorption or trance) implies the calming or cessation (*samatha*) of all thought-forms leading to ignorance and desire. Along with *vipassyana*, or insight into the conditioned nature of things, *samadhi* is the highest state of meditation or absorption into ultimate reality, but without being accompanied by insight it may result in an extreme or obsessive state of detachment. Zen texts frequently debated the merit of meditation leading to a state of "dead wood" or "cold ashes," and consistently warned against that situation. So, although the anonymous woman outdoes Manjusri, she remains suspect, and that is why the prose commentary refers to her as a Naga, a term generally used for a large, aggressive serpent or dragon, which implies either that she is not really human or not deserving of the respect accorded to male practitioners despite her accomplishments.

The bodhisattva Dim Light represents all those who emerge as heroes despite a lowly status—although, once again, in some constructions Manjusri is a god associated with the downtrodden. Dim Light's role recalls Hui-neng, who rose to prominence and became sixth patriarch even though he was illiterate and stood outside the elite structure of the Zen monastic system. Dim Light, summoned from the lesser realms of existence, can do with a snap of a finger what Manjusri was unable to achieve with all his travels to the higher realms. It seems that Manjusri's apparent greatness was actually a source of oppressiveness. But, the verse commentary, which refers to the obscure bodhisattva as having the "face of a demon," suggests that he must deal gracefully with defeat, just like his rival, the esteemed Manjusri who has the "head of a god." Perhaps the woman was so lost in absorption that it took a demon's face to summon her consciousness.

28. Huang-po's "Gobblers of Dregs"

Pointer

The great capacity of the Buddhas and patriarchs is completely under their control. All the people and gods and myriad beings in heaven and on earth heed their call. Their casual words and phrases astound the crowds and stir the masses. With a single action or gesture they can smash the sufferer's chains and knock off their fetters. In dealing with a situation above and beyond the ordinary, they use methods that are above and beyond the ordinary. Now tell me, What is their secret? If you want to know, consider the following.

Main Case

Huang-po addressed his assembly by saying, "All of you people are gobblers of dregs. If you keep up practicing this way, what will you ever expect to achieve? Do you realize that in all of T'ang China there is not a single genuine teacher of Zen?" Then a monk came forward and said, "But surely there are many who teach disciples and lead assemblies. What do you call those people?"

Huang-po said, "I didn't say that there is no genuine Zen. I just said that there is no genuine Zen teacher."

Discussion

This kōan, cited from PYL case 11 (Taishō 48:151b–152c), also appears in TJL case 53 (Taishō 48:260b–261b). The case expresses a delightful irony about the absence of genuine Zen teachers in China despite the presence of authentic practitioners and assemblies. Huang-po seems to be setting a remarkably high standard that excludes even himself and his own teacher and disciples. His mentor, Pai-chang, was the main disciple of Ma-tsu's Hung-chou branch of the Southern school that advocated encounter dialogues. Huang-po's main disciple was Lin-chi, founder of the main Zen sect in East Asia. The four patriarchs—Ma-tsu, Pai-chang, Huang-po, and Lin-chi—make up the lineage known as the "four houses" (Ch. *ssu-chia*, Jap. *shike*), whose teachings form the core of the kōan tradition. Is there "not a single genuine teacher of Zen" among them?

It is no doubt disingenuous for Huang-po to negate the patriarchs in such a harsh way, and the main aim of the PYL prose commentary (the TJL commentary is somewhat different) is to rehabilitate and highlight the value of his role in the process of lineal transmission. The commentary, based on a hagiographical narrative from the CCL and other transmission of the lamp records, relates several important encounters that Huang-po underwent as a background that is necessary for understanding his ironic put-down in the main case. These included meetings with a supernatural monk as he wandered in search of a true teacher; master Pai-chang, who transmitted the quality of Ma-tsu's method of teaching; a prime minister who he instructed in the essence of Zen; and Emperor Hsüan-tsung, who gave him the title "Crude-Behaving Ascetic."

According to the PYL commentary, Huang-po was seven feet tall with a round lump like a pearl on his forehead that reflected an innate, natural understanding of Zen. One time when he was traveling to Mount T'ien-t'ai, he met a monk along the way, and they chatted and laughed together like they were old friends. Then Huang-po looked him over carefully, for he had a light in his eyes that pierced people and an altogether strange appearance. As they traveled along, they came up a roaring valley stream, and Huang-po put down his staff, took off his hat, and stopped there. The monk said that he would cross over and asked Huang-po to do the same, but the master just said, "No, you go yourself." The monk then gathered up his robes and walked across the waves as if treading along on level ground. He turned back and said, "Come across! Come across!" But Huang-po chastised him by saying, "You self-attainer! If I had known you would be concocting wonders I would have cut you off at the knees!" The term for "self-attainer" implies the status of *pratyeka buddha*, and the word rendered here as "wonders" is also often used in folk tales to describe the marvelous powers of magical beings. The monk sighed and said, "You are a true vessel of the Mahayana teaching," and just as he finished speaking these words he disappeared from view.

Following this supernatural event and his rejection of the monk, Huang-po met Pai-chang, who explained how Ma-tsu once shouted in his ear so loudly that he stayed deaf for three days. When Huang-po asked Pai-chang who would inherit the lineage, Pai-chang said, "I thought you'd be the one to do it," and then he got up and went back to the abbot's quarters. Pai-chang and Huang-po had a complex relation that was based on one-upping one another, as evidenced by the epilogue to case 38 in which Huang-po struck his teacher.

In spite of Pai-chang's prominence as the founder of Zen monastic regulations, it was Huang-po who succeeded in being recognized by government officials. Prime Minister P'ei-hsiu, an important lay disciple also featured in case 48, received Huang-po's teaching in the record *Transmission of the Essentials of the Mind* (Ch. *Ch'uan-hsin fa-yao*, Jap. *Denshin hōyō*). P'ei-hsiu, a Buddhist philosopher in his own right who had studied with Tsung-mi and others, played a crucial role in the publication of Huang-po's text. He also wrote a book that he showed the master, who put it down abruptly without even opening it. In response, P'ei-hsiu offered the following verse using supernatural imagery in praising Huang-po's integrity in refusing to walk across the river with the magical monk:

> I attained the mind seal from the great teacher,
> Who stands seven feet tall, with a round jewel in his forehead,
> One time, he set down his staff and stayed for ten years by the
>   River Shu,
> But eventually his coracle came floating across to the banks of
>   the Chang,
> Eight thousand dragons and elephants follow in his mighty
>   footsteps,
> Ten thousand blooming flowers support his excellent cause,
> I hope to become one of his disciples,
> But I do not yet know to whom he will entrust his teaching.

Huang-po gave no indication of whether he approved, but offered the following verse:

> A mind like the boundlessness of the ocean,
> A mouth that spews red lotuses to nurse the sick,

I have a pair of hands with nothing to do,
And never take in a foolish follower.

Finally, Huang-po also served as a mentor to Hsüan-tsung some time before he became emperor. Hsüan-tsung played a crucial role in the history of Zen because when he ascended to the throne in 847 he restored Buddhism after several years of severe prohibitions instigated by his nephew Wu-tsung. When training under Pai-chang while Huang-po was still serving as rector of the monastery, Hsüan-tsung questioned why Huang-po bowed before statues of the Buddha when he believed that enlightenment could only be found within. Huang-po slapped Hsüan-tsung, who called him crude, and Huang-po responded with the line evoked later by P'u-hua in his encounter with Lin-chi, "Why talk about crude and fine when trying to express the Buddha Dharma?" (see case 16).

29. Sermon from the Third Seat

Main Case

Master Yang-shan had a dream that he went to the abode of Maitreya and was seated in the third seat. A senior monk struck the gavel and said, "Today is the turn for the one sitting in the third seat to explain the Dharma."

Yang-shan stood up and struck the gavel, saying, "The perfection of wisdom is beyond the four truths and surpasses the hundred negations. Heed this truth!"

Prose Commentary

Now tell me, did Yang-shan preach the Dharma, or not? If he opens his mouth he misses the point, and if he keeps his mouth shut he loses out. Whether he opens his mouth or not, he is still 108,000 miles from the truth.

Verse Commentary

On a clear day and under a blue sky,
He spins a tale about a dream within a dream,
What a strange and marvelous story,
Fooling everyone in the assembly!

Discussion

This kōan, cited from WMK case 25 (Taishō 48:296a), is also included in TJL case 90 (Taishō 48:285b–286a) as well as one of the main transmission of the lamp records, the *Wu-teng hui-yüan* vol. 9 (although it does not appear in the CCL, which treats Yang-shan's biography in vol. 11). The other versions of the case in TJL and *Wu-teng hui-yüan* refer to Yang-shan occupying the "second seat." Either way, the first seat in the Dharma Hall is reserved for the head monk next to the master (in this case, Maitreya), which is largely a ceremonial role, and the second or third seat is a place of distinction for the monk who is being called upon to deliver a sermon during a convocation or to teach others in a special way. In the section of the LL that deals with Lin-chi's travels to attain enlightenment, another master offers praise for the young monk by saying, "See to it that this gentleman is seated in the third seat," that is, a place of honor nearby the abbot and before the assembly.

This case is filled with mythological elements that revolve around master Yang-shan's dream of appearing in Maitreya's congregation. The role of the supernatural in an anecdote about Yang-shan seems particularly anomalous. Yang-shan was the foremost disciple of Kuei-shan, an important follower of Pai-chang, who continued the Zen tradition of fathering his own lineage, as seen in case 6. This branch, known as the Kuei-Yang house, was the first lineage to develop as a semi-autonomous (although short-lived), institutional network in the Southern school following Ma-tsu. The Kuei-Yang house was especially known for an emphasis on iconoclasm and subjectivity. Kuei-shan characterized his approach as "Patriarchal Zen" because of its focus on a realization experienced by concrete, individual persons, in contrast to the focus of the "Tathagata Zen" approach based on abstract theory or doctrine expressed in the sutras or other writings that enunciate the doctrine of Buddha-nature.

Kuei-shan's style of teaching highlighted the psychological double bind method that is alluded to in the prose commentary on this case, which refers to the story of a man hung from a tree. As he barely holds his grip, a passerby walking underneath the tree calls up and asks why Bodhidharma came from the west. The man is told that if he does not answer the question he will have failed the passerby and if he does answer he will lose his life. "At such a time," he is asked, "how will you answer the question?" Yang-shan also continued the iconoclastic tradition of his mentor by rejecting conventional linguistic or artistic symbols of ultimate reality, as in case 49.

But, in the current case, Yang-shan undergoes a significant oneiric experience that places him near Maitreya, the future Buddha, and thereby undercuts, or perhaps complements, his image as an irreverent iconoclast. His response to being put on the spot is to deliver a brief but vigorous defense of the transcendence of language. While the dream sequence can be understood demythologically as having only a psychological or symbolic meaning, it also shows the importance of alternative states of awareness and communing with deities and divinities in early Zen, thus recalling a Zen saying cited in the TJL commentary, "With holy ones, dreams and wakefulness make one and the same stream."

The WMK verse begins with a depiction of concrete reality, albeit in idealized fashion, but the second line refers to the process of disentangling oneself from entangling dreams. Where does one state leave off and the other begin, and how does this issue relativize an understanding of the distinction yet inseparability of dream and wakening, or illusion and reality? The third line of the verse commentary evokes supernatural imagery by referring to the "strange and marvelous," although the final line suggests that Yang-shan was deceiving people, perhaps as a technique of using skillful means to offer instruction. This resembles the *Lotus Sutra* parable in which a guide conjures an illusory city as an oasis for travelers to help them overcome fatigue and discouragement and inspire them to conquer their fears and press to reach a goal of genuine peace and harmony.

According to the version of the case in the *Wu-teng hui-yüan*, after Yang-shan awakens he explains the dream to his master, who confirms his enlightenment and attainment of the highest rank. In response to this show of approval, Yang-shan bows. This epilogue to the mythical encounter was excised from the WMK version, perhaps in order to leave open-ended the question of whether there really was such a dream. Perhaps it was a dream within a dream. After all, Yang-shan remains "108,000 miles from the truth," according to the prose commentary, which evokes the traditional Buddhist notion that there are 108 defilements in the realm of samsara.

30. Kuei-shan Turns His Face to the Wall

Main Case

Kuei-shan was lying down one day when he was approached by Yang-shan with a question. The master, still lying down, turned his back to Yang-shan. Yang-shan asked, "Why do you behave like that with one of your disciples?" As the master started to stand up, Yang-shan went to leave the room. The master called out, and Yang-shan turned his head. The master said, "Let me tell you about a dream. Please listen." Yang-shan lowered his head and listened to the master's dream. The master said, "Please interpret the dream for me." Yang-shan took a bowl of water and a towel to the master. The master scrubbed his face, and then sat for a while.

Then Hsiang-yen came into the room. The master said, "Just now Yang-shan demonstrated a supreme ability in supranormal powers. This ability is not like that of the Hinayanists." Hsiang-yen said, "I was in the other room, but I clearly perceived this." The master said, "Now it's your turn to interpret." Hsiang-yen made a cup of tea and brought it to the master.

Then the master said, "You two disciples have supranormal powers that are beyond the abilities of Sariputra and Maudgalyayana."

Discussion

This kōan, which was originally contained in CCL vol. 9 (Taishō 51:265c) and other transmission of the lamp records such as the *Tsung-men t'ung-yao chi* vol. 4 and *Tsung-men lien-teng hui-yao* vol. 7, is cited from MS case 61 (DZZ 5:158), and it is also discussed extensively in Dōgen's KS "Jinzū" fascicle (DZZ 1:392–402). This, like case 26, is another rather obscure kōan that became the basis for a lengthy discussion in the *Shōbōgenzō*.

While Yang-shan's dream in case 29 is fanciful and mythical, the dream of Kuei-shan that Yang-shan is asked to interpret becomes the basis for a possible intuitive, occult connection between master and disciple who are especially known for their strong emotional attachment as the core members of the Kuei-Yang house or lineage. The content and nature of the dream itself is never disclosed, and this heightens the sense of mystery and uncertainty surrounding the oneiric experience as well as Yang's interpretation of it.

The ritual background of the case is the procedure referred to in Zen as "entering the abbot's room," which was first mentioned in Pai-chang's monastic rules text and became institutionalized in later codes of conduct. According to Pai-chang's rules, the temple abbot, who resides in a ten-foot-square room behind the Dharma Hall, delivers two formal sermons a day in the main hall which are attended by the leaders and rank-and-file of the full assembly. The abbot also invites back to his quarters individuals or small groups of followers who receive special instruction. In some cases, the abbot selects disciples who are ready for advanced training or require a specific clarification of doctrine, and in other cases the monks request the meeting in order to pose a question that has been troubling them. In this case, Yang-shan has entered the abbot's room with a query and feels rebuffed by the uncharacteristically impolite response.

When Kuei-shan calls him back to the room and tells of the dream, Yang-shan is challenged to reveal his intuitive abilities. If Yang-shan is able to interpret the teacher's dream, then he will have demonstrated the supranormal power of reading other minds. The case is somewhat unclear about the outcome of the encounter. When Yang-shan brings Kuei-shan a washbowl and towel, this can be seen as a concrete action that implies a dismissal of the whole idea of intuition and mindreading, and the master's approving comment that Yang-shan has surpassed the powers of Hinayanists is so much tongue-in-cheek irony. The encounter with Hsiang-yen, who suggests that he intuitively knew about the encounter of Kuei-shan and Yang-shan while he was waiting in another room, reinforces the irony. Hsiang-yen brings a cup of tea, and Kuei-shan escalates his praise so that the towel and the tea demonstrate that the disciples have surpassed two of the Buddha's closest followers.

On the other hand, it is clear that the challenge and responses, however ironic, occur in the context of a tradition in which it was taken for granted that masters and disciples enjoyed a distinctive intuitive bond. In some of the more prominent examples, second patriarch Hui-k'o was led to find Bodhidharma by the vision of a spirit, Chü-chih established his connection with the master who taught him the One Finger method through a dream, and Dōgen was led to discover his mentor in China by a dream that took place at a time of disillusionment when he was on the verge of returning prematurely to Japan. Yet, in KS "Jinzū," Dōgen offers a thoroughly demythological interpretation of the current case by arguing that the so-called supranormal powers are minor abilities compared to the genuine mystical insight of a disciple receiving transmission into the teachings of his master.

Another case dealing with the issue of intuitive connections can also be interpreted as ambiguous about confirming or negating the efficacy of supernaturalism. According to "Tung-shan Visits Nan-yüan," cited from the TSL (Taishō 47:520c), as Tung-shan walked into the Dharma Hall Nan-yüan greeted him by saying, "You and I have already met." Tung-shan left the hall. But the very next day he returned to the Dharma Hall and said to Nan-yüan, "Yesterday, I received Venerable Nan-yüan's kindness. However, I do not know where it was that I met you previously." Nan-yüan replied, "Between mind and mind there is no interval. They all flow together into the great ocean of the true Buddha-nature." Nan-yüan's comment perhaps admits that talk of mindreading powers is disingenuous, and Tung-shan responds ironically, "I almost fell for what you said!"

SPIRITS, GODS, AND BODHISATTVAS

31. P'u-chi Subdues the Hearth God

Main Case

On Mount Sung, there was an anonymous monk known as "Hearth-busting" Tou whose manner of speaking and practicing was unfathomable. He became a recluse in the deep mountain forests, where in one of the valleys there was a shrine that was considered to have great spiritual power. Inside the hall of the shrine stood a hearth that was used by people from near and far for sacrificing innumerable animals. The lives of many animals were lost at this altar.

One day master P'u-chi entered the shrine with an attendant monk and smashed the hearth three times with his staff while saying, "O Hearth, you are composed of mud and bricks. From where does your spiritual power arise, that you should cause lives to be sacrificed?" Again he struck the hearth three times, until it collapsed.

Shortly after this, a tall man dressed in blue robes appeared. He bowed down to the master, who said, "Who are you?" The man said, "I am the spirit of the hearth in the shrine, and for a long time have been suffering from an affliction. Today I was released from this fate and freed from all doubts while listening to you explain the teaching of the Unborn, O venerable priest. The reason I am here is to express my gratitude to you." The master said, "This is due to your original nature, and not to anything I said."

The spirit bowed down again, and disappeared.

Discussion

This case is cited from a passage in CCL vol. 4 (Taishō 51:232c–233a), and deals with the notion of bondage to and release from karmic affliction in a way that recalls shamanistic influences on Buddhist morality tale literature. In particular, P'u-chi's actions toward the hearth deity resemble the techniques for the exorcism of troublesome or demonic forces that have possessed a particular person or location. The exorcism leads to a recovery and redemption by the true nature of whatever spirit has been affected by the possessing force. The victim is able to acknowledge and make a confession of its transgressions or sins, and is thus liberated from karmic bondage that was caused or reflected by the possessing force. This account of a Northern school master encountering and overcoming a force of possession is based on the doctrine of the Unborn, or the emptiness of conceptual categories and the conventional polarity of life and death. The truth of the unborn undermines the power of the hearth that had been demanding animal sacrifices. The anti-supernatural message is delivered in a supernatural context. After all, the hearth consists only of mud and bricks, and yet it does contain a spirit that has been agonizing over its spiritual affliction.

In another version of this record, there is an enhanced supernatural element in that the hearth collapses on its own, not through the physical effort exerted by P'u-chi striking the bricks. In either case, this record of exorcism, involving a master who was extremely successful in attracting followers in the early history of Zen and was also one of most popular heroes in secular folklore in China, sets the pattern for Pai-chang's encounter and elimination of the magical fox in case 38. In that kōan Pai-chang pronounces the doctrine of the efficacy of karmic causality that liberates the spirit of a monk from bondage to a vulpine possession it had been suffering for hundreds of lifetimes.

Like Shen-hsiu, the main patriarch of the Northern school, P'u-chi was probably best known for subjugating snakes and transforming their power into an energy that aids and protects the Dharma. In the pattern of these folktales, which evoke the image of a snake either as a malevolent spirit to be pacified or as the force that reveals the presence of a spring or some other natural resource that will make possible the foundation of a monastery, a threatening snake appears and remains at first unmoved when confronted by P'u-chi. But the next day, the Zen master finds a treasure hidden at the foot of a tree or some other location that he uses to build a temple.

In another famous account of P'u-chi's exorcistic exploits, the master scolded a monk about failing to take care of his begging bowl, the most important possession of novices in training, which in fact had accidentally been broken by another careless monk. Overcome by fear of retribution, the owner died. P'u-chi warned all the monks in the assembly to remain in their rooms, and that night a large snake came to visit the temple. The snake was a wrathful apparition that was actually a reincarnation of the dead monk coming for revenge. P'u-chi appeased the snake with a sermon on karmic retribution, and foretold the former monk's favorable rebirth as a precocious girl in the family of an aristocratic and devout Buddhist family.

32. Nan-chüan Is Greeted by the Earth-Deity

Main Case

Nan-ch'üan happened to be traveling through a vegetable garden when the monk charged with stewarding the garden came prepared to greet him. Nan-ch'üan said, "I usually travel without being noticed. How is it that you were prepared to receive me?" The monk replied, "Because last night the earth-deity [or protector-spirit of the monastery compound] informed me you would be coming by."

Nan-ch'üan said, "I must be lacking in the power of spiritual cultivation. That is the only explanation for why the earth-deity saw me." The monk said, "But you have already attained great wisdom. I do not understand why the earth-deity could have seen you coming."

Nan-ch'üan thought, "I'd better go and make an offering of rice to the earth-deity."

Verse Commentary

> He once traveled freely, his presence unnoticed by others;
> He could not be distinguished from a god or demon;
> But finally caught, he confessed that he had lost his spiritual
>   power,
> Though in the beginning his comings and goings were far from
>   any crowd.

Discussion

This kōan, originally contained in several of the transmission of the lamp records including CCL vol. 8 (Taishō 51:257c), is cited from EK vol. 9 case 63 (DZZ 4:224). This case also appears in the record of master Hung-chih (Taishō 48:34b), the original compiler of the cases that appear in the TJL collection. It is also included in MS case 19 (DZZ 5:134), and is discussed extensively in Dōgen's KS "Gyōji," part I (DZZ 1:145–170).

The central theme of many hagiographal writings that is articulated in a number of encounter dialogues is the contest between the supranormal powers of Zen Buddhist masters that is derived from meditation and the supernatural powers of animistic spirits attributable to their non-human status. This is part of a long-standing assimilative pattern expressed in early Buddhist *jataka* and *avadana* literature whereby Buddhas and bodhisattvas are skillful in subduing and converting local gods, often referred to as Naga (serpents, dragons, reptiles), by demonstrating superior power based on compassionate activity, sustained ascetic discipline, or the performance of miracles and wonders. In China the role of the Naga is taken up by "anomalous" or "strange" (*kuai*) phenomena, including foxes, tigers, and snakes, as well as local, autochthonic earth deities. The spirits are often converted to Buddhism and perform the function of preaching the Dharma as well as protecting the monastery compound. Yet they may retain an independent attitude that can conflict with or challenge Buddhist masters. A strategy of a number of kōans is the transmutation of the local gods by a meditator or ascetic, sunk in profound *samadhi* or wielding the psychic powers of meditation, which was also a standard motif of Buddhist morality tales.

This case, which recalls a story about Nan-ch'üan's encounter with an earth spirit, reflects the notion found throughout Buddhist hagiographical literature of the encounter between a master and local spirits, celestial beings, or demons who have jurisdiction over a particular geographical or spatial domain, such as a mountain, valley, village, or field. Prior to attaining full realization the impending master both makes and receives offerings from the local gods, many of whom come to be enshrined in the Zen monastic compound, but once perfected he escapes from ever being seen or known by the otherworldly entities because his powers surpass their abilities. If the master loses his aura of invisibility and is subsequently seen by a field god whose role is the protection of that portion of the monastic compound, this is taken as a sign of a spiritual failure that highlights the need to continue the master's training and appease the deity through prayer or offerings. According to the current case, Nan-ch'üan is surprised as he enters a vegetable patch, where he usually goes unnoticed, when he is greeted by a novice who says that the field god had notified him of the master's imminent arrival. Nan-ch'üan now must make an offering to the deity before resuming his discipline.

The key to understanding the discursive function of the case, whether mythological or demythological, lies in the context in which it is cited and interpreted. For example, when used in transmission of the lamp texts such as the CCL, it contributes to the genealogy of the master by establishing the authenticity, or lack, of his credentials. The case is also mentioned in Dōgen's "Gyōji" fascicle, the closest his *Shōbōgenzō* writings come to the transmission records genre. He retells the history of his lineage in light of the doctrine of "sustained zazen practice" (*gyōji*), which has the spiritual power to support Buddhas and sentient beings, heaven and earth, self and other. Early in the fascicle, Dōgen refers to masters Ching-ching and I-chang as being notable because they cannot be perceived by the native gods. Then he contrasts Nan-ch'üan, who has been spotted, with Hung-chih, before whom a local deity is literally stopped in its tracks. The god's feet will not budge, recalling the "immovable robe" in the legend of Hui-neng's escape in case 46.

On the one hand, Dōgen seems to be scoring a sectarian point on behalf of Hung-chih, a predecessor of his mentor Ju-ching, while denigrating a master from a rival Rinzai lineage. Up to this stage, Dōgen is operating within, though at the same time refashioning, the standard mythological framework. But he then rationalizes demythology by commenting that the real meaning of being seen or not seen lies not in supranormal power in the literal sense, but in the perpetuation of authentic discipline. This requires an ongoing process of detachment from, or casting off, conventional pursuits. Yet even Dōgen's turn to an anti-supernatural interpretation reveals an assumption of the efficacy of the indigenous spirit world. His verse commentary in the EK version is basically noncommittal—but certainly does not deny—the issue of supernaturalism.

33. The Tea Ceremony at Chao-ch'ing

Main Case

Governor Yen went to Chao-ch'ing temple for the tea ceremony. When Elder Lang held up the tea kettle for Ming-chao, he overturned the kettle. Seeing this the governor asked Lang, "What is it that is under the kettle?" Lang said, "It's the god of the hearth." The governor said, "If it's the god of the hearth that is dwelling there, then how was the tea kettle overturned?" Lang said, "You can serve as an official for a thousand days, but in a single instant you can lose everything." Governor Yen swung his sleeves and left the room.

Later, master Ming-chao said, "Elder Lang, you've been taking your rice at Chao-ch'ing temple for a long time. But you still go off, north of the Yangtze River, to gather wood." Lang said, "What about you, teacher?" Ming-chao said, "The hearth god took the advantage."

[Hsüeh-tou commented: "If I'd been there, I would have just kicked over the hearth!"]

Verse Commentary (by Hsüeh-tou)

> The question was a burst of fresh air,
> The response was hardly appropriate,
> Alas, the One-Eyed Dragon of Ming-chao
> At first did not bare his fangs and claws.
> Once the fangs and claws were unsheathed,
> Thunder and lightning!
> Surging waves
> Rage all about!

Discussion

This kōan, cited from PYL case 48 (Taishō 48:183c–184c), deals with the encounter between national and religious patriarchal systems, or between the Zen institution and the Court, as well as the convergence and conflict between the ritual requirements of monastery life and supernatural forces that may or may not be lurking in the compound. These themes are set in a context that emphasizes the relation between the Northern versus Southern styles of religious training.

The case narrative opens with a tea ceremony prepared for the district governor, who had appointed Chao-ch'ing abbot and frequently patronized his temple. Apparently the master is absent or unavailable, and Elder Lang, the vice-abbot, is serving tea instead. He is accompanied by Ming-chao, known as the One-Eyed Dragon as mentioned in the verse commentary (see also case 14), who later in his career became the leader of another temple. The tea ceremony was an extremely important function of Zen temples, and the procedures and etiquette were described in intricate detail in the main monastic manuals, such as the *Ch'an-yüan ch'ing-kuei* of 1103. Tea ceremonies prepared for government dignitaries were a way for temples to entertain and return favors for their most important patrons and supporters. The performance of the ceremony required great attention to detail, planning, and comportment at every stage in order to create a comfortable and harmonious atmosphere for the guest of honor who might be considering a donation or some other form of support for the temple. Through the performance of the ceremony, monks were able to demonstrate in a compelling way their spiritual attainment and continuing commitment to contemplative mindfulness and concentration. However, when, in the current case, the kettle is turned over by Lang, it could be taken as a sign of a break in concentration and serenity that may have a disastrous implication by interfering with the guest's appreciation of the aesthetic setting of the monastery.

The governor's question about what lies under the hearth provides Lang an opportunity to shirk responsibility and blame his error on a mischievous or troublesome supernatural force. The context for this segment of the dialogue is the belief that the gods are highly localized and specialized, with some having jurisdiction only over a specific location or domain, such as a garden, latrine, kitchen, or hearth. Yet, in a turn of rhetoric that goes against the grain of Zen iconoclasm, the governor considers the god a protector spirit that most likely would have prevented, rather than caused, the accident with the tea kettle. But Lang makes a sarcastic, dismissive comment indicating disdain for supernatural beliefs, and the governor leaves in a huff. This part of the encounter captures some of the aura of Bodhidharma's willingness to thumb his nose at the emperor in PYL case 1. But, the intent seems reversed, in that the court official has snubbed the Zen master. In that sense, the court system asserts its judgment and dominance over the Zen monastic system, which is subject to the wishes and whims of its donors and patrons.

The second encounter in the kōan between Lang and Ming-chao, which functions as an epilogue to the main part of the narrative, makes use of several successive put-downs that are capped off by the interjection of Hsüeh-tou, the original compiler and commentator on all of the PYL cases that were further edited and commented on by Yüan-wu. First, Ming-chao charges that Lang had gone "north of the Yangtze River to gather wood," meaning that he was susceptible to the tendencies of the Northern school, including its acceptance of the supernatural. Lang offers a feeble retort, and Ming-chao argues that the hearth god was the one who had seized the opportunity to turn the tables on the vice abbot. Hsüeh-tou remarks that he would have taken an action like Kuei-shan, who kicked over a water pitcher when challenged by the geomancer Ssu-ma in case 6. The verse commentary begins by favoring the governor, whose question seemed like a burst of fresh air. It concludes by emphasizing that Ming-chao had not gone far enough in his critique of Lang's approach to the issue of the supernatural in his mishandling of the tea ceremony.

34. Hu-kuo's Three Embarrassments

Pointer

One who doesn't wear a stitch of clothing is truly a heretic; one who doesn't chew a grain of rice must pay homage before the horrid face of the king of ghosts. Even if you dwell in the realm of the sacred, you still may have to take a leap off the top of a pole. Is there any place to go to conceal the shame?

Main Case

A monk asked Hu-kuo, "What happened when a crane stood on a withered pine?" Hu-kuo said, "It was surely an embarrassment to the ground below." The monk asked, "What happened when a drip of water became a speck of ice?" Hu-kuo said, "It was surely an embarrassment once the sun came out."

The monk next asked, "What happened to the two benefactor spirits who protect the Dharma by guarding the temple gate when it was the time of the proscription of the Buddhist Order [in the 840s]?" Hu-kuo said, "It was surely an embarrassment for both of the spirits!"

Verse Commentary

> The mature man is dignified but his temples are not yet gray,
> The young man who is not motivated will not be enfeoffed,
> I think back to the whole lineage in its purity,
> And to refusing to water an ox in the same stream where ears
>   were being washed.

Discussion

This kōan, cited from TJL case 28 (Taishō 48:245a–246a), highlights the role (or, in this case, the lack of role) played by the guardian spirits of monasteries in commenting on the single most important political event that affected Zen and all other forms of Buddhism in China in the ninth century. Nearly all Buddhist temples had two guardian deities, usually fierce-looking spirits who could intimidate and ward off the approach of demons enshrined in a preliminary gateway for the path leading to the main entrance, or "mountain gate," of the temple.

The prose commentary section of the TJL is devoted largely to discussing the political implications of the case, and the verse commentary can also be read for its allegorical meaning. In the mid-840s Emperor Wu-tsung, whose debilitating ailments were being treated by a Rasputin-like Taoist priest who convinced the ruler that the key to his suffering was the presence of foreign cults, undertook the greatest purge in the history of Chinese Buddhism. Buddhism had previously been affected by the whims of imperial leadership, even just a century before, but Wu-tsung's was the most devastating persecution. All other foreign religions were also affected, and that included a number of faiths that had migrated to China through Silk Road trafficking and missionary activities, including Christianity, Islam, Judaism, and Zoroastrianism. These religions were for the most part effectively eliminated from functioning in China, although there is evidence, including the writings of travelers such as Marco Polo in the thirteenth century, that some of them remained in operation despite the ban.

Buddhism, which was considered a foreign religion since it was imported from India, was also greatly impacted because it was perceived by authorities to be an escapist, antisocial ideology that enriched an elite class of clerics. According to the TJL prose commentary and other sources, thousands of temples were shuttered and hundreds of thousands of monks and nuns were returned to lay life. In addition, other aspects of the Buddhist institutional network, including libraries, icons, and ritual objects, were severely damaged or destroyed. The first two questions in the main case referring to a crane that does not rest on a dead tree and the flow of water that has become frozen and rigid highlight the debilitated condition of the Buddhist institution. Yet the persecution of Buddhism was lifted by Hsüan-tsung (a student of Huang-po, discussed in case 28) shortly after Wu-tsung's death, and this was marked by a resurgence of interest. As the TJL prose commentary notes, "In discussing the suppression of Buddhism in terms of the question of the role of the spirits, we have to consider that Wu-tsung's petty persecution led to Hsüan-tsung's great revival, during which there came to be three times as many temples as before the persecution."

As might be expected, the TJL gives a demythogical interpretation of the significance of the protector spirits. It argues, "The powers of the protector spirits are not within the grasp of those who are ordinary or vain. However, if we look at this issue from the perspective of a patchrobed monk, the Dharma Gate has no ups and downs, so what is the point of speaking of the comings and goings of spirits? That's why Hu-kuo said, 'An embarrassment for both of the spirits guarding the temple gate!'" The commentary suggests that the embarrassment lies in speaking of the role of the spirits, and not, as a literal reading of the main case suggests, in the failure of the spirits to save the Dharma at the time of the purge.

The pointer of the case warns against the excesses of ascetic practice that might lend a rationale to the imperial critique of Buddhism as antisocial. Yet the concluding portion of the prose commentary, along with the final lines of the verse commentary, make it clear that the purity of practice despite the vicissitudes of political intrigue and turmoil is what must be valued. "According to the *Historical Records*," the TJL reports, "Hsü-yü was a recluse on Mount Chi, who took his food from the mountain and drank water from the mighty mountain stream. Emperor Yao (24–23 centuries B.C.) wanted to abdicate his throne to the recluse. But when Hsü-yü heard of this, he went to the river and washed his ears. Chao-fu, who was watering his ox there, asked him, "People usually wash their faces, but you just washed your ears?" Hsü-yü said, "I heard Emperor Yao is going to ask me to be the chief of the nine provinces, so I am washing out this and that." Chao-fu said, "The trees of Yu-hsiang grow in the high mountains where even the carpenters do not go. If you want to escape secular society, why not withdraw deep into the mountains? Now you are wandering in the world of people, seeking for fame and fortune. If I go down to the river to let my ox drink, I fear it may defile the ox's mouth." So he led the ox to another, purer spot upstream where it could water.

35. Yün-chü and the Spirits

Main Case

Yün-chü built a hut on Mount San-feng. Days went by and he did not show up in the refectory. Master Tung-shan went to the hut and asked him, "Why haven't you come by for meals for the past few days?" Yün-chü replied, "Because every day, of their own accord, the heavenly spirits come and bring me food." The master said, "I always thought you were an exceptional person. But why do you still hold onto such views? You'd better come and visit my quarters this evening."

Later that evening, Yün-chü arrived at the master's quarters. When Tung-shan saw the hermit coming he called out, "There's the hermit," and Yün-chü called back. The master said, "Don't think of good, and don't think of evil. Now, tell me, what is it?"

Yün-chü returned to his hut and resumed his practice of peaceful meditation. From this time on, the heavenly spirits were unable to spot him, and after three days they stopped appearing altogether.

Discussion

This kōan, which originally appears in CCL vol. 17 and *Tsung-men t'ung-yao chi* vol. 8, is cited from the TSL (Taishō 47:513b). In most other cases cited in this and other chapters of the book, the appearance of supernatural forces marks the intrusion of otherworldly spirits that must be subjugated, banished, or exorcised, though perhaps with the potential to have their inner nature converted through the act of repentance and an awareness of the fundamental condition of emptiness into the status of a practitioner or protector of the Dharma. In this case, however, the supernatural forces are not hostile or demonic but represent heavenly spirits that tend to the everyday needs of the hermit. But, as in case 4 on Ox Head school founder Niu-t'ou, who is similarly served by celestial powers, even the beneficial appearance of supernaturalism must be overcome and eliminated from the iconoclastic Zen standpoint of "killing the Buddha."

Yün-chü was an important master in the Tung-shan lineage who developed a branch that continued the Tung-shan school into the seventeenth century. As in case 19, in which Chao-chou checks out the hermits who were advanced in Zen practice, Tung-shan visits Yün-chü's hut when he realizes that the hermit has been missing from the monastic round of activities for a long period. Short-term retreats were required as part of the training, but Tung-shan's concern is that a prolonged absence signals a problematic situation. When Yün-chü responds with an assertion of the efficacy of the guardian spirits, Tung-shan insists that he pay a visit to the abbot's quarters for special instruction.

Upon the arrival of Yün-chü, Tung-shan says that "the hermit" is coming, which calls into question Yün-chü's status—his excessive attachment to the spirit world indicates that he has become irregular and roguish.

Tung-shan then delivers a simple but pointed exposition of the primordial nature of emptiness that exists ontologically (rather than chronologically) prior to good and evil, which recalls the encounter between Hui-neng and his rival in case 46. After this, the spirits no longer attend to Yün-chü—not because they have given up, but due to the fact that, as in case 32, a genuinely attained master can no longer be seen by supernatural entities. The Zen master's own supranormal powers derived from a state of serene contemplation surpasses their more limited abilities, and this renders Yün-chü invisible so that the celestial spirits have nothing to behold.

36. The World Honored One Ascends the High Seat

Pointer

A single lute string is plucked and he can name the whole tune. Such a person is hard to find even if you search for a thousand years. Like a hawk chasing a hare, the race goes to the swiftest. He expresses the universe of discourse in a single word, and condenses a thousand great worlds into a speck of dust. Is there anyone who can live the same way and die the same way, penetrating each and every hole and crevice? Now consider this.

Main Case

One day the World Honored One took the high seat to preach the Dharma. Manjusri struck the gavel and said, "Clearly understand the Dharma of the King of Dharma. The Dharma of the King of Dharma is just like this."

Then the World Honored One got down off his seat.

Prose Commentary (selection by Yüan-wu)

This took place before the World Honored One had raised the flower. From the beginning at Deer Park to the end at Hiranyavati River, how many times did he need to use the jeweled sword of the Diamond King? At this particular time, if there had been someone in the assembly with the true spirit of a patchrobed monk and with a supreme understanding, then it would have been possible to later avoid the sticky situation of having to raise the flower.

Verse Commentary

> Among the assembly of great sages, had there been someone
> with true knowledge,
> The decree of the King of Dharma would not have been like
> this,
> If there had been a Man of Saindhava among them,
> It would not have been necessary for Manjusri even to strike the
> gavel.

Discussion

This kōan, originally contained in CCL vol. II (Taishō 51:283b) and other transmission of the lamp records, is cited from PYL case 92 (Taishō 48:216b–216c). It is also included in TJL case 1 (Taishō 48:227c–228b), MS case 141 (DZZ 5:200), and the kōan collection of master Ta-hui. In addition, this case is discussed extensively in Dōgen's KS "Osaku sendaba" fascicle (DZZ 2:253–258).

The dialogue in the main case involves the World Honored One, or the Primordial Buddha, and the bodhisattva of delusion-destroying wisdom, Manjusri. The dialogue takes place in a mythical era prior to the time of the origin of Zen. According to another mythical account—in a sermon of a much later though equally legendary era—Zen Buddhism originated when Sakyamuni Buddha silently held up a flower before the assembly and only Mahakasyapa in the audience smiled as a sign that he grasped its symbolic significance. The PYL commentary's disingenuous blasphemy argues that the "sticky situation of Sakyamuni's having to raise the flower" could have been avoided if an authentic monk had understood clearly the full meaning of Manjusri's tautological words and the World Honored One's perplexing behavior. "The World Honored One took the high seat and then immediately got down," the PYL points out. "He had not yet explained his view of the Dharma, so why did Manjusri strike the gavel so quickly? He made the World Honored One's sermon seem foolish. But who really did the foolish thing?"

All of the discussions in the major kōan collections, including the PYL, TJL, and *Shōbōgenzō* commentaries, stress the role of "Saindhava," which originally stemmed from early Hindu mythology that was appropriated by Buddhist sutras. The PYL indicates that according to the *Nirvana Sutra*,

"The term 'Saindhava' refers to four different things: the first is salt, the second is water, the third is a bowl, and the fourth is a horse. There was a wise attendant who well understood the four meanings. If the king wanted to wash and was in need of Saindhava, then the attendant would bring him water; when he asked for Saindhava while eating, the attendant served salt; when he was finished the meal, the attendant offered Saindhava by bringing him a bowl to drink hot water; and when he wanted to go out of the palace, the attendant offered him Saindhava by rounding up a horse. The attendant was able to respond to the king's intentions before they were even expressed. He was a very clever fellow to be able to act in this way."

Therefore, Saindhava refers to an intuitive connection between master and disciple, but the commentaries caution against understanding this in a literal or facile way. The PYL mentions another kōan: When a monk asked Hsiang-yen, "What is the king asking for Saindhava?," Hsiang-yen said, "Come over here," and the monk went. Hsiang-yen said, "Don't be such a fool!" The monk later asked Chao-chou, "What is the king asking for Saindhava?" Chao-chou got off his meditation seat, bent over, and folded his hands." Dōgen cites this account and also tells the irreverent story of Nan-ch'üan, who saw his disciple coming and decided to up the ante about Saindhava by commanding him, "The pitcher is an object. It contains some water. Bring the water over to this old priest without moving the object." But the monk brought the pitcher to the master and poured water all over him. Dōgen distances himself from the ritual implications and comments exclusively on the metaphysical significance of this act, "We must study the water in the pitcher and the pitcher in the water. Was it the water that was being moved, or was it the pitcher that was being moved?"

MAGICAL ANIMALS

37. A Snake Appears in the Relic Box

Main Case

A monk was always carrying around with great reverence a golden image of the Buddha and other relics. Even when in the assembly hall or dormitory, he constantly burned incense to them and showed his respect with prostrations and offerings. One day the Zen master said, "The Buddha image and relics that you are worshiping will be of no use to you later." The monk disagreed.

The master continued, "This is the handiwork of demons. You must get rid of these items at once." The monk grew indignant and started walking off. The master called after him, "Open your box and look inside." When the upset monk stopped and looked in the box, he found a poisonous snake coiled inside.

Discussion

This kōan, cited from SZ vol. 2 record 1 (DZZ 7:64), was extracted by Dōgen from the *Hsü kao-seng chuan,* the second great monk biography text compiled by Tao-hsüan in the seventh century. The narrative culminates in a compelling element of melodrama and surprise when the true identity of the snake is revealed to the monk. This is similar to other cases highlighting the intrusion of the supernatural in the life of a Zen practitioner that provides a necessary instruction leading to a breakthrough from some impasse rooted in ignorance and attachment. Examples of this pattern include Chü-chih's One Finger Zen that was learned from a bodhisattva appearing in a dream and reinforced by his severing the disciple's finger in case 51, Hui-neng's immovable robe that shocks his rival in case 46, or Pai-chang's exorcism of the wild fox appearing as a monk in case 38. All of these cases evoke the quality of morality tale literature known by the Japanese term, *setsuwa bungaku.*

In this genre of Buddhist-influenced folklore, a person is transformed and enlightened by learning a crucial moral lesson through a heightened moment of encounter with otherworldly forces. These forces manifest at a crucial moment or key turning point and reveal an important truth that cuts through illusion and alters the person's perspective forever. The supernatural forces that play a key role in *setsuwa bungaku* often include magical animals that have a shapeshifting ability, especially snakes and foxes, which represent a seduction, temptation, or betrayal that heightens the sense of illusion until this comes to a breaking point that allows the truth to be revealed in a compelling fashion. Snakes and foxes are double-edged swords in that they represent the forces of protection and redemption as well as seduction and delusion.

Therefore, the literary structure of morality tale literature is strikingly parallel to the function of kōans in which there is frequently an experience of a breakthrough to another dimension of spirituality. Often referred to by the Japanese term *satori,* this breakthrough may be triggered by otherworldly intervention or by a wordplay, pun, or some type of rhetorical flourish. In cases 1–3 and 31, dealing with the masters of the Northern school, the supernatural and demonic forces are overcome through an appeal to the doctrine of emptiness that undercuts their power. In the current case, the strategy is somewhat reversed as the supernatural appearance of the snake is evoked, deliberately yet ironically, to defeat an attachment to a ritual that has become merely superstitious. This approach to the question of overcoming illusion is an example of "using poison to counteract poison," to cite a prominent Zen saying about the function of kōans.

This case also has important implications for understanding the role of rituals in Zen, especially in regard to worship of the Buddha in various halls and rooms in the monastic compound. In Chinese Buddhist schools other than Zen, the key temple building was the Buddha Hall, which housed gold statues of Sakyamuni and various Buddhas that were the central focal point for devotional practices. Additional images of the Buddha were placed in various locations throughout the compound. The basic aim in the development of the Zen school's approach to religious training was a transition from devotion and worship to meditation and contemplation, and from venerating images of the Buddha as an otherworldly symbol of enlightenment to respecting and honoring the temple abbot or master as a concrete, here-and-now, this-worldly appearance of a "living Buddha." These transitions also involved a shift from the Buddha Hall as the primary site in the monastery to the Dharma Hall, where the master delivered his daily round of sermons. The rules attributed to Pai-chang call for eliminating the Buddha Hall from the Zen monastic compound and replacing it with the Dharma Hall alone.

Dōgen's commentary in the *Shōbōgenzō zuimonki* is rather even-handed, however. His own temple, Eiheiji, had both a Buddha Hall and a Dharma Hall. Dōgen is by no means entirely dismissive of worshiping images and relics, which he admits have value in representing the power of the Buddha and delivering the devotee from the effects of evil karma. Yet he also argues, "Expecting enlightenment by worshiping icons is an error that leads you into the hands of demons and poisonous snakes."

38. Pai-chang and the Wild Fox

Main Case

Whenever Zen master Pai-chang gave a lecture, an old man came to hear him expound the Dharma along with the assembly of monks. When the assembly left the Dharma Hall, the old man also left. One day, however, he stayed behind. Pai-chang asked, "Who is this standing here before me?"

The old man responded, "I am really a non-human being. A long time ago, in the age of Buddha Kashyapa, I was abbot of this very temple. But the change happened when a disciple asked me, 'Does even a person of great cultivation fall into causality, or not?' I answered, 'Such a person does not fall into causality.' For five hundred lifetimes after that, I have been transfigured into a wild fox body. Now, master, may I ask you to express a turning word that will turn my words around and release me from this wild fox transfiguration."

The old man then asked, "Does even a person of great cultivation fall into causality, or not?" The master answered, "Such a person does not obscure causality." On hearing these words, the old man experienced a great awakening. He bowed and said, "I am now released from the wild fox transfiguration, and my fox corpse is already lying behind the gates of the temple compound. Master, may I dare to request that you bury it with the rites accorded a deceased monk?"

The master instructed the monk in charge of rules to strike the clapper and announce to the assembly that a monk's burial would be taking place after the midday meal. The monks were puzzled and wondered, "Who could this be, as we are all healthy and no one has been sick in the Nirvana Hall?" After the meal, the master led the assembly behind the temple gates where he used his staff to uncover the carcass of a wild fox lying under a large rock. The fox corpse was cremated in accord with the regulations for Buddhist funeral rites.

That evening, during his sermon in the Dharma Hall, Pai-chang told the congregation the whole story concerning the debate about causality. Thereupon Huang-po asked, "The old man was transfigured into a wild fox for five hundred lifetimes because he used an incorrect turning word. Suppose his turning word had not been incorrect, then what would have happened?" The master replied, "Come up here and I'll explain it to you." After hesitating, Huang-po approached Pai-chang and slapped him. The master, clapping his hands and laughing, exclaimed, "I thought it was only the barbarian who had a red beard, but here is another red-bearded barbarian!"

Prose Commentary

"Not falling into causality"—why was he transfigured into a wild fox? "Not obscuring causality"—why was he released from the fox body? If you can see this with a single eye you will understand how the former abbot of Pai-chang monastery cultivated his five hundred lifetimes of transfiguration.

Verse Commentary

> Not falling, not obscuring,
> Two sides of the same coin.
> Not obscuring, not falling,
> Hundreds of thousands of entanglements.

Discussion

This kōan, cited from WMK case 2 (Taishō 48:293a–293b), appears in a variety of transmission of the lamp records, including the *T'ien-sheng kuang-teng lu* (HTC 135:656b–657a, the earliest but slightly different version), *Tsung-men t'ung-yao chi, Tsung-men lien-teng hui-yao,* and *Wu-teng hui-yüan*. In addition, the case is included in the recorded sayings of Pai-chang, the *Pai-chang yü-lu,* several kōan collections including TJL case 8 (Taishō 48:231c–232b) and MS case 102 (DZZ 5:178–180), as well as two fascicles of Dōgen's KS, "Daishugyō" (DZZ 2:185–195) and "Jinshin inga" (DZZ 2:387–394).

This case is remarkably rich in supernatural and ritual elements that convey a message about the necessity in Zen to adhere to monastic rules and resist the tendency to allow philosophical nonduality to become a rationale for antinomian behavior. The narrative involves the multifaceted encounter between Pai-chang and a mysterious visitor to the Dharma Hall. Pai-chang, the foremost disciple of Ma-tsu, was known for his strict adherence to the notion of "a day without work is a day without eating." He is greeted by the guest who confesses, "I am not really a human being," or, in another rendering, "I am really a non-human." The term *fei-jen* (Jap. *hinin*) is the translation of the Sanskrit for all other-than-human creatures, *amanusya,* including gods, ghosts, and animals, and in East Asia the term also refers to a shapeshifter or magical animal, especially foxes or snakes, and also is used as an epithet for outcasts and marginal groups. The non-human claims to have lived in the mythical era of Kashyapa, the sixth of seven primordial Buddhas culminating in Sakyamuni, who is also considered the first patriarch in Zen mythology. The monk/fox thus represents the forces of disruption and chaos that are plaguing Zen and need to be vetted and eliminated.

The "person of great cultivation" refers to a realized master who continues to practice meditation diligently after the attainment of enlightenment and must continue to deal with the effects of karma. Causality (Ch. *yin-kuo*, Jap. *inga*) is the Chinese translation of the Sanskrit *hetu-phala*, which refers to the universal principle of the necessary relation between original or root cause and end result. In Sino–Japanese Buddhism this terms also implies the moral process of karmic determination and retribution, whereby a good cause begets a good result and an evil cause begets an evil result. The "turning word," as cited in numerous other texts including the LL and the records of Hung-chih, refers to the use of a terse utterance—a phrase or even a single word—that can inspire a revolution in one's thinking which results in an experience of liberation. Here it functions as an exorcism of the intruding fox spirit. "Not falling into causality" could be turned into a positive construction such as "becomes free from causality," and is set up here in polarized contrast with "not obscuring causality" or "remains bound to causality."

In the Zen monastic system, the monk in charge of rules for the samgha was one of six main officers who would strike an octagonal anvil with a hammer signifying an event about to take place in the institution. The Nirvana Hall refers to the infirmary, and the name makes an association between *nirvana* as the termination of mundane existence and illness/death as the end of life. The discussion of the burial of the fox highlights the importance of funeral rites in Zen monastic life as codified in the main rules texts. Huang-po is labeled by Pai-chang the "red-bearded barbarian," a term that was used to slander foreigners but in Zen rhetoric became a duplicitous insult cum praise of the bearded Bodhidharma, the twenty-eighth Zen patriarch and first in China who "came from the west (India)." The word for barbarian (Ch. *hu*, Jap. *ko*) is a homophone for fox, and the TJL version refers to Huang-po as a "red-bearded fox."

The WMK prose and verse commentary establishes a line of interpretation based on nonduality that was championed by dozens of interpreters. The single main exception was Dōgen's "Jinshin inga" fascicle. The main case clearly states that the position of not falling into causality is ethically deficient and led to the monk's endless rebirths as a fox, which dovetails with the image of Pai-chang as an upholder of the precepts. Yet the WMK argues from the uncompromising standpoint of nonduality that the opposites of not falling and not obscuring causality are "two sides of the same coin," or in other renderings "odd and even are on one die" or "two winning numbers, one roll of the dice." This paradoxical view seems consistent with the notion of universal oneness but may be problematic in terms of limiting the ability to make ethical choices, when judgments and distinctions must be weighed carefully and decisions made convincingly. In other words, the nondual approach may give license, even without intending this, to an antinomian tendency to bypass ethical decision-making in the name of the transcendence of all worldly distinctions. However, by suggesting in the prose commentary that there was a "cultivation" or enjoyment of the fox incarnations, and by referring in the verse commentary to thousands of "entanglements," the WMK indicates an awareness of the complexity of the issue: neither the paradoxical/antinomian view nor the karmic/causality view is correct.

In the "Daishugyō" fascicle of the *Shōbōgenzō*, written early in his career, Dōgen upholds the nondual interpretive perspective. But later in his career, after returning from a trip to Kamakura where he saw Zen being used to justify the samurai warrior code, Dōgen became much more puritanical in his ethical convictions, as seen in his punishment of the rogue monk Gemmyō in case 55. At that point, he rewrote "Daishugyō" as the fascicle "Jinshin inga" on "Deep Faith in Causality," which argues that "the single greatest limitation in Sung China" is an adherence to the nondualistic and potentially antinomian standpoint. Dōgen's advocacy of the distinction between causality and non-causality has been the keynote of a recent social reform movement known as "Critical Buddhism" (*Hihan Bukkyō*) that stresses the need for Zen to overcome its involvement in nationalism, militarism, social discrimination, and other deficient trends. According to Critical Buddhism, these tendencies stem from traditional interpretations of the fox kōan, which maintain that causality and non-causality, as well as good and evil, are "two sides of the same coin."

39. Ta-kuang Does a Dance

Main Case

A monk asked Ta-kuang, "What did Ch'ang-ch'ing really mean when he said, 'Let us give joyful thanks for the midday meal'?"[1] Ta-kuang did a dance.[2] The monk bowed.[3]

Ta-kuang said, "What have you seen, that you have bowed?"[4] The monk did a dance.[5] Ta-kuang said, "You wild fox spirit."[6]

Notes (by Yüan-wu)

1. The light shines in once more. This lacquer tub casts doubt, but if he doesn't ask he will never learn.
2. Do not deceive people like this. He acts in the same way as Chin-niu did before him.
3. He too acts like this, correctly, although I am sure he will be misunderstood.
4. Push him to the limit; it is important to be discriminating.
5. He draws a cat by following a model. But since he misunderstands so much, he is still playing amid the shadows.
6. Such kindness is difficult to requite. This is just what the thirty-three patriarchs have transmitted.

Prose Commentary (selections by Yüan-wu)

The twenty-eight patriarchs in India and the six patriarchs in China only transmitted just these words; but do you people realize what it all comes down to? If you do know, then you will avoid falling into the errors of this monk; but if you do not know, then, like him, you will be nothing other than a wild fox spirit.

There are those who say that Ta-kuang grabbed and twisted the monk's nostrils in order to reprimand him; but if this were actually the case, what would be the point? Ta-kuang was very adept in helping disciples along the path of understanding the words and phrases of other masters. In general, a teacher of the Zen school must be able to pull out the nails, draw out the pegs, remove the sticking points, and untie the bonds. That results in a liberated awareness.

Ta-kuang did a dance, the monk bowed, and in the end the monk also did a dance and Ta-kuang called him "You wild fox spirit!" This did not transform the monk, who still did not get the real point. If you just do a dance, mimicking the master in this way, you will never reach a conclusion. Ta-kuang said, "You wild fox spirit"—these are words to release the monk Chin-niu, and they are not obscure or unusual. That is why it is said, "He studies the living word, not the dead word." Hsüeh-tou also likes to use the saying, "You wild fox spirit!" That is the basis on which he produces his verse. But tell me, is the expression "wild fox spirit" the same as or different from, "Tsang's head is white; Hai's head is black," "This lacquer tub!", or

"Good monk!"? Just tell me, are these the same or different? Do you know? You will encounter this same question everywhere you go.

Verse Commentary (by Hsüeh-tou)

> The first arrow hit lightly, but the second arrow went deep;
> Who says autumn leaves are nothing other than yellow?
> If the waves of Ts'ao-ch'i [sixth patriarch Hui-neng] were like this,
> Then people would be unsettled and never find peace.

Discussion

This kōan, cited from PYL case 93 (Taishō 48:217a–217b), evokes PYL case 74, in which master Chin-niu is said to dance in the Monks' Hall while serving rice before the statues of the bodhisattvas, and Ch'ang-ch'ing remarks that he is "giving joyful thanks for the midday meal." Also, the line near the end of the prose commentary, "Tsang's head is white; Hai's head is black," is based on a passage in PYL case 73. The playful references to the monk being a wild fox reflect an ambivalent, ironic use of supernatural imagery.

The main case revolves around a typical negative reference to supernatural entities, but the commentary reverses this implication and in the end introduces a positive meaning. In the case, Ta-kuang asks about the significance of another master's utterance and he responds, not with words, but by dancing while the disciple, in turn, bows. When Ta-kuang queries the disciple to test whether the bowing reflects a genuine understanding of the significance of the dance, the monk himself dances in a way that apparently imitates the original action without expressing any insight. Ta-kuang scornfully retorts, "You wild fox spirit!," highlighting the empty pretense, fakery or mere show of the disciple's dancing, which is a pale shadow of the master's genuinely spontaneous nonverbal gesture. Here, the epithet, like the similar term "fox drool" used in many kōans, is intended to expose and cut off the ignorance of the "lacquer tub," or a stubborn monk who is incapable of seeing the real meaning and can only superficially mimic the master's actions.

Yet in the prose commentary section of the PYL, the meaning of the key term changes drastically as it is associated with the doctrines of the two levels of truth and the pedagogical instrument of skillful means. An additional layer of commentary (not translated here) points out that the World Honored One (Sakyamuni Buddha) explained timely, provisional doctrines throughout his lifetime as talks that "put an end to the crying of children," an allusion to Ma-tsu's explanation of an instructional method by which he gave situationally appropriate yet contradictory answers to the same question. Ma-tsu used this as the rationale for why he said, "This very mind itself is Buddha," but when the crying stopped he articulated the opposite teaching, "No mind, no Buddha" (these teachings are the focal points of WMK cases 30 and 33, respectively). Furthermore, Yüan-wu's commentary on the exchange uses the fox image in the positive sense of characterizing Ta-kuang, who offered confusing but essentially beneficial instruction, "'This wild fox!'—Ta-kuang just wanted to transmute the other's active discriminating consciousness; within the process there are provisional and real, there are also illumination and function. Only thus can you see the grasp of the patchrobed monk there. If you can understand, you'll be like a tiger with folded wings."

In the section of notes on the main case, Yüan-wu criticizes Ta-kuang's original dancing as "deceiving people" and he applauds the monk's dance as "correct" behavior. But then he scolds the monk for "playing amid the shadows" and praises Ta-kuang's "kindness" in using the term "wild fox," not merely to scold, but as a "turning word" that transmutes the monk's ignorance into wisdom. The term "thirty-three patriarchs" at the end of the section of notes refers to the formula for the transmission from Sakyamuni to first Chinese patriarch Bodhidharma, the twenty-eighth Indian patriarch, and then to sixth patriarch Hui-neng in China.

40. Hsüeh-feng and the Turtle-Nosed Snake

Pointer

The Dharma-realm is vast as the limitless universe and as fine as the dust of an atom. Grasping and releasing are not caused by another, and enfolding and unfolding occur of their own accord. To cut the bonds and be released from entanglements, you must have a direct experience unimpeded by the sound of words. Then you will be able to remain still even in a tidal wave and stand tall like a cliff that is a mile high. Now, tell me, who dwells in such a realm? To test yourself, examine the following case.

Main Case

During a sermon to the assembly Hsüeh-feng said, "There is a turtle-nosed snake on South Mountain. All of you should go and take a good look at it." Ch'ang-ch'ing said, "Right here, there is one among us has already lost his life."

Some time later a monk related this encounter to Hsüan-sha, who said, "Only brother Leng (Ch'ang-ch'ing) could give such an answer. But I feel differently." The monk asked, "How do you feel about it, teacher?" Hsüan-sha said, "Why bother talking about South Mountain at all?"

Hearing this, Yün-men threw down his staff in front of Hsüeh-feng and then made a gesture as if he himself were afraid of the snake.

Verse Commentary (with capping phrases by Yüan-wu)

> Elephant Bone Cliff is so high that no one can reach it,
> *A thousand or ten thousand seek but do not find. It's beyond this realm.*
> Those who do get there must be master snake handlers.
> *It takes a spirit to know a spirit, and a thief to know a thief. What's the point of gathering in crowds? But you must be part of the group to be known.*
> Master Leng (Ch'ang-ch'ing) and Master Pei (Hsüan-sha) couldn't make it,
> *They were caught in the same crime, and were released at the same time.*
> How many have lost their lives in this way!
> *A crime can't be judged twice; that's the rule even for commoners.*
> Yün-men can make it,
> *He's made it somewhat. This old man only has a single eye. He is a clever one.*
> The others are searching in the weeds.
> *What's the point of groveling about in the weeds? Is the snake there? Strike!*
> South, north, east, west—it's nowhere to be found,
> *Is it there, is it there? Your eyes can't see.*
> Suddenly Yün-men throws down his staff,
> *Look! Gaze higher! Strike!*
> It lands right in front of Hsüeh-feng, and opens its mouth.

It gives and it receives by itself. It swallows a thousand or ten thousand, but what is gained? No one on earth can find it.

The wide-open mouth strikes like a flash of lightning,

A double kōan, after all. Fortunately, there is a final word.

If you try to raise your eyebrows to see, you'll still miss it.

It's already gone. Search high and low for such a person, but you won't find one anywhere. And by the way, where is the snake?

Right now it's in hiding on Ju Peak.

Where can it be? Even the great Hsüeh-tou acts like he's been snared. Today, I myself have been bitten.

People come, one by one, looking carefully,

They're all blind! Don't look under his feet, look right where you are, under your own feet. It won't do any good to try shooting it with an arrow.

Master Hsüeh-tou called out in a loud voice, "Look right under your feet!"

He draws his bow after the thief has already fled. Second time, third time. Don't keep saying the same thing over and over again.

Discussion

This kōan, cited from PYL case 22 (Taishō 48:162b–164a), is also included in TJL case 24 (Taishō 48:242c–243b) and recalls TJL case 59 on "Ch'ing-lin's Dead Snake." The translation includes capping phrases on the verse commentary. Supernatural imagery involving snakes and spirits is evoked throughout the kōan, which creates an atmosphere of the dangerous and threatening as well as of the need for developing strategies and making judgments. Although the imagery is used in an ironic, tongue-in-cheek fashion that supports a demythological interpretation, it is clear that the pervasiveness of supernatural references is based on a context of belief in the magical, shapeshifting powers of snakes and other forces.

The main case contains three highly compressed encounter dialogues: one between Hsüeh-feng and Ch'ang-ch'ing, a disciple in the assembly who responds to the master's sermon concerning the turtle-nosed snake on South Mountain; another between Hsüan-sha and an anonymous monk who reports on the previous encounter and solicits a reaction from the master; and the third, which violates the order from a sequential standpoint, involving Yün-men's demonstrative response to Hsüeh-feng in which he uses his staff that is also known for transforming into a dragon in case 42. This power is evoked in the capping phrases on the verse commentary.

The "turtle-nosed snake" is a double-edged image used repeatedly in Zen literature. It conjures the image of an aged, twisted-looking venomous serpent that swallowed up all the Buddhas and patriarchs, who emerged from the ordeal as poisonous snakes. This can be interpreted to mean that the masters underwent a "great death" experience that enabled them to enhance their skills in prevailing over rivals in encounters or Dharma-combat. "South Mountain" may simply refer to a peak lying south of the monastery, or it may have broader implications for the Southern school approach to dialogues where the venom (or "poison to counteract poison") is cultivated. Ch'ang-ch'ing, Hsüan-sha, and Yün-men all respond to Hsüeh-feng's emphasis on the snake located on South Mountain either by showing an ironic, exaggerated sense of concern and fear or an indifference and transcendence of the snake's power.

This irony is reinforced by the PYL capping verse on the first sentence of the main case: "If you see something strange as not being strange, then its strangeness disappears all by itself; how very strange! This can't help but cause people to doubt." The PYL capping phrase on the reference to "snake handlers" rendered above, "It takes a spirit to know a spirit, and a thief to know a thief" is echoed by a similar passage in the TJL: "It takes a fox to know a fox, a dog to know a dog." The sense of irony is further enhanced by the "art of war" and legalese rhetoric in the PYL capping phrases that refer to being caught and judged for crimes and also comment on the deficient strategy of Hsüeh-tou being like "drawing the bow after the thief has already fled."

Another kōan that evokes magical animals in a similarly ironic way is "The Hermit of T'ung-feng Makes a Tiger's Roar," cited from PYL case 85 (Taishō 48:210b–211b). According to the case pointer that eulogizes the ascetic practices of patchrobed monks, "Holding the world fast so that not a speck of dust leaks out and all people in the world throw down their weapons and quiet their tongues—this is the calling of the patchrobed monk. The light emanating from his forehead illuminates the four quarters of the world—this is the function of the diamond eye of the patchrobed monk. To touch iron turns it into gold, and to touch gold turns it into iron, to suddenly take hold and to suddenly let go—this is the activity of the staff of the patchrobed monk. To stop in their tracks the chattering of tongues throughout the world, so that they are as quiet as if three thousand miles away—this is the force of the spirit of the patchrobed monk."

The main case begins with a monk who visited the master of T'ung-feng's hermitage and asked, "What if, on this very mountain peak, you were to encounter a tiger? What would you do?" The hermit roared like a tiger, and the monk then made a gesture of fright. The hermit made a hearty laugh and the monk said, "You old thief!" The hermit said, "What can you do to me?" and the monk stopped short. The verse commentary on PYL case 85 continues the rhetorical strategy:

> The tiger has fine stripes,
> But it's missing fangs and claws,
> Haven't you heard about the meeting on Mount Ta-hsiung?
> The vast sounds and light they emitted still fills the earth,
> People of great capacity see this,
> They take the tiger by the tail and grab it by the whiskers.

The line about Mount Ta-hsiung alludes to a famous incident in which master Pai-chang referred to Huang-po as a tiger after the disciple returned from a hermitage on Ta-hsuing Peak that was particularly known for being prowled by both magical animals and mysterious hermits.

Despite the irony, Zen masters knew that they needed to eliminate the presence of troublesome or threatening animals or spirits. One of the devices used by Zen masters to exorcise spiritual intruders was discussion or wordplay that evoked emptiness. But they also summoned the power of important symbols such as sticks, staffs, and robes, to challenge and offset the forces of disruption, as will be seen in the following chapter.

FOUR

Wielding Symbols of Authority and Transmission

The monastic life of Zen Buddhism seems to be based on simplicity and naturalism that fosters a strict de-emphasis on rituals and the vast array of symbols that are crucial for carrying out rites, ceremonies, and festivals. The transition in Zen (previously mentioned in discussions of the impact of Pai-chang's monastic rules text) from highlighting the role of the Buddha Hall to the Dharma Hall epitomizes the way Zen set limits on the role of symbols in its approach to religious training. The Buddha Hall housed ornate gold statues of Sakyamuni and other Buddhas, whereas the Dharma Hall was the site for the abbot or master as a "living Buddha" to present daily sermons to the assembly. Compared with other schools in East Asia that stressed symbols used in rituals of devotion and prayer in the Buddha Hall, Zen iconoclasm represented an approach that tended to eliminate the need for symbols.

At the same time, both complementing and conflicting with this approach, Zen has always relied heavily on a small but crucial handful of symbols in representing, demonstrating, or evoking the teachings of masters and their styles of training disciples. Despite its reliance on the rhetoric of nonduality, Zen operates on the basis of one fundamental yet all-important distinction that determines its use of symbols: the difference between enlightenment and unenlightenment, which is concretized and personalized in the roles of masters and disciples. This dichotomy has been perpetuated through the transmission of a lineage from a founder or patriarch of a house or branch, or from the leader of one generation, to the anointed successor for the next generation. According to the history of Zen as portrayed in the transmission of the lamp records, the most significant and exciting events were the establishment of a master's authority that was tested through encounters and challenges by a variety of rivals or disciples, as well as the selection of the inheritor of the lineage's mantle.

Skeptics may argue that the hagiographical records idealized, romanticized, and exaggerated the claims of authority, or that the fixation of the Zen institution with the process of choosing successors was often based on corrupt or deviant tendencies such as financial or political considerations, rather than the purity of religious training and spiritual understanding. Nevertheless, kōan literature is replete with references to a variety of symbols that often take on a magical, supernatural significance over and above their role in delineating the rituals of authority and transmission.

One class of Zen symbols, including sticks, staffs, fly-whisks, and fans, involves utensils wielded by monastery abbots as indicators of their authority or as part of their way of testing the lineal legitimacy of hermits or other irregular practitioners. Masters almost always carried a staff or fly-whisk when they delivered their sermons, which they raised up, threw down, or used to draw a circle in the air or in some other physically demonstrative, dramatic fashion. Many of these symbols were incorporated into Zen ritualism from indigenous shamanistic or Taoist techniques in China, such as the fly-whisk, which derived from a shaman's purification device. According to Zen lore expressed in numerous kōan cases, especially those highlighting the role of master Yün-men, Zen devices can possess or reflect the supranormal powers of their owners. Also, staffs are sometimes carried into the temple gates by a hermit who tries to evoke the power of the symbol as a means of challenging the authority of the abbot or proclaiming the integrity of his own style of practice.

Another important Zen symbol that stemmed from early Buddhist monastic practice was the robe passed from master to disciple as part of the process of transmission. Early Zen records indicated that Bodhidharma's original robe was in the hands of latter-day patriarchs. This claim became crucial in the contest between Hui-neng and his Northern school rival, when he was declared the sixth patriarch and established the dominance of the Southern school. In addition, Zen used portraits or other icons as ceremonial objects for honoring and venerating former or deceased masters by their line of disciples. The portrait was a representation of the former master placed on his "high seat" during memorial services in lieu of his presence. This technique was borrowed from the way the imperial court commemorated deceased emperors by attaching a symbol of their presence to the thrones. Finally, Zen also used diverse written and verbal symbols, such as circles and mantras that were often infused with supernatural meaning as influenced by the function of spells in esoteric Buddhism or indigenous Chinese religions.

Zen literature contains so many examples of kōans referring to the use and power of staffs, fly-whisks, robes, and so on that this chapter on symbols could easily be the longest in terms of the number of cases. However, the cases selected have been limited to the most important, representative examples. Citations of several interesting but relatively minor cases have been integrated into the discussion sections for some of the kōans.

Symbols of Authority

41. Chih-men's "I Have This Power"

Main Case

Master Chih-men was returning to the temple after traveling alone in the mountains. The head priest, Yün-men, led a group of members of the assembly out on the path to look for him. They came upon Chih-men wandering on the road, and Yün-men said, "O priest, your travels along the steep mountain crags must not have been easy."

Chih-men picked up his walking staff and proclaimed, "I possess the full power of this stick." Then Yün-men walked up to him, grabbed the staff away forcefully, and threw it aside. Chih-men fell down as if the energy was draining out of his body. A group of priests ran up and helped him get back on his feet.

Chih-men picked up the staff and started running off. Then he said to an attendant who came up after him, "I possess the full power of this stick."

Discussion

This kōan is cited from Dōgen's MS case 238 (DZZ:250-252), although it is not mentioned in his main text, the KS *Shōbōgenzō*, and it also appears in the early recorded sayings text, the *Huang-lung yü-lu* (Taishō 47:638c), as well as several of the transmission of the lamp records, including *Tsung-men t'ung-yao chi* vol. 10 and *Tsung-men lien-teng hui-yao* vol. 26.

This case highlights the importance of the Zen walking staff in asserting the authority of a master or evaluating the comportment of a hermit and determining through an encounter dialogue the validity of his claim to legitimacy as an authentic Buddhist practitioner. According to Zen tradition, all masters spent time wandering in the mountains in a solitary retreat to perfect their skills of contemplation. These travels could take place at various times, including prior to enlightenment when the potential master, while still a student, was making a pilgrimage to different temples in search of an authentic teacher. Or the journeying might take place after the attainment of enlightenment in order to renew a master's spiritual understanding and commitment.

The master was expected at some point during his mountain journeys to bring back a stick or staff at least six feet tall that was taken from the fallen branch of a tree. This practice was no doubt a throwback to pre-Buddhist shamanistic practices rooted in Chinese folk religions. In Zen practice, the staff was considered a symbol of the master's supreme state of spiritual awareness in that he had achieved a profound sense of communion with nature and yet tamed the environment in transforming natural elements into an expression of the Dharma. In many instances, supernatural powers were attributed to the staff itself, and similar claims were made for other Zen utensils, including fans and fly-whisks. The powers of the staff could be seen either as the basis for or as a reflection of the supranormal powers that were a by-product of the master's attainment of enlightenment.

In the current case, there is a clear and direct link between the powers of the staff and the degree of attainment of the master returning from his pilgrimage in the mountains. Chih-men was a second generation disciple of Yün-men, who was particularly known for his own use of magical staffs and fans (as will be seen in cases 42 and 43). Chih-men became famous as a poet whose main disciple was Hsüeh-tou, the original compiler and verse commentator on the cases in the PYL. Chih-men's return from his travels seems to have been anticipated by Yün-men, which may imply an esoteric connection between disciple and master, who intuitively knows the whereabouts of his followers in both a literal and metaphorical sense.

Chih-men's claim about possessing the full power of the stick can be read demythologically as a sign of his attachment—perhaps to ego, or an image of self-importance—that became an obstacle preventing him from realizing the true meaning of enlightenment. His master, Yün-men, who once had his leg broken by a teacher who dismissed him from the temple and threw him out the gate that he slammed shut abruptly, calls Chih-men's bluff. Yet Chih-men, exposed and embarrassed by the incident, does not relent or repent. In a demythological interpretation, the image of the energy "draining out of his body" indicates a deficiency of spiritual awareness.

However, it is clear that this encounter could take place only in a context in which supernatural attributes for sticks and staffs were commonplace, and practitioners were frequently tested not only for their own abilities but for the degree of attainment represented by their prized utensils. The stick serves to illustrate that an object, rather than a monk, can be powerful. The master said he possessed the power of the stick. So, to prove that he was wrong, Yün-men took the staff and showed that the pilgrim could not stand without it, thereby demonstrating the extent of belief in the staff's power.

42. Yün-men's Staff Changes into a Dragon

Pointer

There is originally no distinction between Buddhas and sentient beings. How can there be a distinction between mountains and rivers and the self? Why, then, should they be separated into polarized categories? Even if you are well-trained in Zen kōan cases and can handle them with great facility, it will not be possible to let go. But if you do not let go, the entire world cannot be grasped. Now tell me, what does it mean to be well-trained in Zen kōans? Examine the following.

Main Case

Yün-men held up his staff before the assembly and said, "This staff has changed into a dragon and swallowed the entire universe. Mountains, rivers, and the great earth are nowhere to be found!"

Verse Commentary (by Hsüeh-tou)

> The staff swallows the universe,
> But don't talk idly about peach blossoms floating on the waters.
> For those whose tails have been cut off, there is no use in
>   grasping at the clouds and mist,

Those who are worn thin can still hold on to their courage and
   spunk.
My verse is finished,
But have you been listening, or not?
Cast off all your worries and doubts,
Relinquish all your mixed-up confusion.
Seventy-two blows would be letting you off easy,
Even one hundred and fifty wouldn't be sufficient—
Hsüeh-tou suddenly came down from his seat waving his staff, and
   the entire assembly dispersed without a moment's hesitation.

Discussion

This kōan is cited from PYL case 60 (Taishō 48:192b–193a), and it also
appears in YY record 197 (Taishō 47:558b). It is one of at least half a dozen
cases in the record of Yün-men that make fantastic claims about the powers
of the sticks, staffs, and fly-whisks that the master wields in the Dharma Hall
while giving a sermon before the assembly. For example, in other sermons he
commented, "The whole universe is on top of the staff," and "The entire
Buddhist canon is right on the tip of this staff." He also was reported to have
said one time, "If you are able to know this staff, your life's study will be
complete." Another time, while holding up his staff, Yün-men remarked,
"The entire universe is shaking all at once." In addition, he claimed, "This
fly-whisk is perfect light, formless form." There are also many other
instances of Yün-men picking up and throwing down or making some other
incorporation of his staff or fly-whisk during a sermon. This was a technique
commonly used in Zen sermons to provide a dramatic, though indirect and
inconclusive, comment on a topic that had been discussed during a master's
presentation in a somewhat more direct or logical fashion. Ironically, the
illogical gesture helped reinforce the logic of Zen.

   Hsüeh-tou's verse commentary begins by referring not to the transformation of the staff into a dragon but only to the second claim, "The staff swallows up the universe," yet Yüan-wu's capping phrase turns this into irony by
asking rhetorically, "What is he talking about? The staff is only used for
beating dogs." The line in the verse about peach blossoms is an allusion to
the Dragon Gate Falls on the Yellow River, which is also evoked in PYL case
7. This refers to a legend of an emperor who harnessed the river by cutting
into the high cliffs to let the river through, and so a three-terraced falls called
the Dragon Gate was created. Every spring, it is said, the crimson petals of

peach blossoms flutter down onto the waters, and hundreds of fish gather below the falls. The energetic ones leap the falls, and their tails are scorched by lightning and transformed into dragons. Seizing onto the very clouds and mist, they ascend to heaven. But those who fail to make the leap fall back on the rocks below and die, their gills exposed to the sun. The ascent of the carp was a metaphor for passing very severe government examinations, as only the strongest could ascend and become dragons rising to heaven. In Zen, this image represented overcoming challenges to attaining enlightenment. Also, Yüan-wu's capping phrase on the final line in the verse, which refers to Hsüeh-tou scaring the assembly with his staff, indicates that Hsüeh-tou "has the head of a dragon but the tail of a snake."

Another kōan, "Huang-po's Single Staff," cited from MS case 91 (DZZ 5:172) and also included in the *Lang-yen yü-lu*, makes a similar use of the symbolism of the staff. According to this case, Huang-po said while giving instructions to the assembly, "The ancient Venerables of all directions are all located on the tip of my staff," and one of the monks prostrated himself. Some time later, this monk went to the place where Ta-shu was staying and told him about what Huang-po had said. Master Ta-shu remarked, "Huang-po may have said that, but has he actually met all the Venerables in the ten directions?" The monk returned to Huang-po and told him about Ta-shu's comment. Huang-po reaffirmed his position: "What I previously said has already become famous throughout the world."

Some time later master Lang-yen remarked, "Ta-shu seemed to have excellent perception but he was really blind. The single staff of Huang-po could not be broken even if everyone in the world chewed on it." In other words, Lang-yen is skeptical of Ta-shu's critique of Huang-po. However, in EK vol. 1 record 12 (DZZ 3:10), in his characteristic approach of rewriting encounter dialogues the way he feels they could or should have developed, Dōgen challenged and suggested reversing Lang-yen's critical comments. Agreeing with Ta-shu, Dōgen asked, "Why didn't Lang-yen say, 'Huang-po's staff can be broken as soon as everyone in the world sets about trying to break it'?"

43. Kan-feng's Single Route

Main Case

A monk asked master Kan-feng, "The Bhagavats of the ten directions all take a single route to nirvana. I wonder where this single road lies?" Kan-feng raised his staff, drew a line in the air, and said, "It lies right here!"

The monk later asked Yün-men for additional instruction. Yün-men held up his fan and said, "This fan has leaped up into the Thirty-Third Heaven and bumped right into the nose of Indra, the celestial ruler. When the carp of the Eastern Sea were given a blow, it rained down in buckets. Do you understand?"

Prose Commentary

One person goes down to the bottom of the deepest sea and raises a cloud of sand and dust. Another person goes to the top of the highest mountain peak and stirs up waves that touch the heavens. Holding still or letting go, each uses a single hand to set up a way of getting to the source. They are like two children racing like mad from opposite directions who bump into one another. In the whole world, there is hardly anyone who is of the same stature. But from the standpoint of the True Eye, even these two great masters did not yet know the real meaning of the route to nirvana.

Verse Commentary

> You haven't even taken a step, yet you've already arrived,
> Before moving your tongue, you've already finished explaining,
> Even if you feel you're on top of the game at every move,
> You must realize that no matter what, there's always a way up
>   from a higher place.

Discussion

This kōan is cited from WMK case 48 (Taishō 48:299a), and it also appears in YY record 158 (T 47:555a) as well as *Wu-teng hui-yüan* vol. 13. Once again, Yün-men, who challenged Chih-men's supernatural claims about his staff in case 41 and was known for the irreverent utterance that the Buddha is nothing more than "a dried shit-stick" in WMK case 21, waxes utterly fantastic about the powers of one of his utensils or symbols of authority. While in many cases a master's straightforward, concrete exposition or demonstration with a staff or fly-whisk makes an ironic comment that serves as a corrective to pretensions about supernaturalism, in this case it is Yün-men's supernatural claim about his fan that serves as the antidote to Kan-feng's apparent down-to-earth remarks made with his staff.

The question posed to Kan-feng presupposes that there must be a single direct path to nirvana taken by the Bhagavats, a term for deities alluding to early Indian Hindu–Buddhist cosmology that is also evoked more explicitly by Yün-men's fanciful remarks. Kan-feng's demonstrative response attempts to defeat the presupposition in two ways: by drawing a line in the air with his staff he indicates that the question is merely an abstraction, and by saying that the route "lies right here" he suggests that concrete, everyday practice is the key to enlightenment.

However, the response of Yün-men, who once uttered the injunction "Every day is a good day!," moves the issue in the other direction, beyond the abstract and straight to the supernatural. Indeed, Yün-men's appeal to supernatural elements of celestial realms and the rulership of Lord Indra clearly outdoes the argument made by Kan-feng stressing the realm of the concrete. Yün-men's comments, like the verse commentary on case 42, refer to the mythical carp that becomes a dragon and ascends to heaven despite a stormy wind and torrential rain. This image can be interpreted as referring to the challenging process of attaining enlightenment. But the WMK prose commentary ironically suggests that neither Kan-feng nor Yün-men have a complete, thoroughgoing understanding.

Another prominent use of the image of a fan as a key to understanding the way to attain enlightenment is Pao-ch'e's "There is No Place the Wind Does Not Circulate," cited from MS case 123 (DZZ 5:194). This kōan, which also appears in *Tsung-men t'ung-yao chi* vol. 3 and *Tsung-men lien-teng hui-yao* vol. 4, is commented on by Dōgen at the conclusion of the KS "Genjōkōan" (DZZ 1:2–7) fascicle, the first section in most editions of the *Shōbōgenzō*. In this case, one day when master Pao-ch'e of Mount Ma-ku was fanning himself a monk asked, "The nature of wind abides everywhere, and there is no place it does not circulate. Master, for what reason, then, do you sit there fanning yourself?" Pao-ch'e replied, "You only know the principle that the nature of air abides everywhere, but you do not know the meaning of the idea that there is no place it does not circulate." The monk asked, "What is the principle that there is no place it does not circulate?" Pao-ch'e just sat there fanning himself. The monk prostrated himself before the master. Pao-ch'e then said disparagingly, "If the manner of teaching of a Zen master is ineffective, even if should offer a thousand explanations, it would not be useful instruction."

According to Dōgen's strictly anti-supernatural commentary, Pao-ch'e's use of the fan makes an important metaphysical argument about the unity and inseparability of time and change, stability and instability, continuity and ephemerality in the practice of meditation: "The true experience of the Buddha Dharma, the vital path of the true transmission, is like this. If you say that you do not need to fan yourself because the nature of wind is ever abiding and you can feel the wind without the need for fanning, you will not understand the nature of wind or the meaning of permanence. It is because the nature of the wind is permanent that the wind of the Buddha's house brings forth the gold of the earth and makes fragrant the cream of the long river." The "gold of the earth," for Dōgen, refers to the rewards of continuous zazen training—which, like the fan, helps keep the wind, or the constancy of Buddha-nature, ever circulating.

44. The Hermit of Lotus Flower Peak Holds Up His Staff

Main Case (with capping phrases by Yüan-wu)

The hermit of Lotus Flower Peak held up his staff before the assembly and said,

> *Look! He has an eye on his forehead. This is a nest for people of these times.*

"Why is it that the ancients got this far, but did not stay there?"

> *You can't drive a stake into empty space. As a provisional teaching he manifested an illusory city.*

No one in the assembly could answer.

> *A thousand, ten thousand, as numerous as hemp and millet. It's a shame how little they've attained. But the falcon is sitting on the roost.*

So the hermit himself replied, "Because they weren't capable of staying the course."

> *If you take the route, you'll be traveling for a fortnight. Even if you seem capable, it won't do any good. Are there really none at all?*

Then the hermit asked another question, "What's it like at the end?"

> *A thousand people, ten thousand people are sitting right here. Among a thousand or even ten thousand people, there will be just one who understands.*

And again he gave the response,

> "Carrying a staff over the shoulder,
> Paying no heed to anyone else,

Going straight into the myriad peaks,
I keep on going and going."
He deserves thirty blows, because he's still like someone carrying a
board across his shoulder. But if you seem to catch a glimpse of his face
on the back of his head, don't go following after him.

Discussion

This kōan, cited from PYL case 25 (Taishō 48:165c–166c), refers to a hermit who apparently was in the lineage of Yün-men. The location of his mountain is unclear. Lotus Flower Peak probably refers to a part of the network of temples connected with the T'ient-t'ai school in eastern, Chekiang province that was based on the teachings of the *Lotus Sutra*, but some commentaries indicate that it may have been in the vicinity of the cluster of the five peaks of Mount Wu-t'ai in northern, Shansi province.

While many interpretations of this case assume that the hermit was the abbot of a temple who was addressing his own assembly, because of his anonymity and the vagueness of the location it seems more likely that at the time of this encounter, he was an irregular practitioner who charged into the monastery to challenge the leadership. It is said that for over twenty years of practice, as soon as the hermit of Lotus Flower Peak saw a monk coming he would hold up his staff and ask questions to which no one could respond, and the PYL prose commentary remarks, "the hermit's feet still aren't touching the ground." The hermit's staff is the key to his claim for legitimacy and authority over and above the mainstream institutional structure. As he says, "Carrying a staff over the shoulder,/I pay no heed to anyone else," which suggests that it is the challenge of the staff that proves difficult and unanswerable rather than the questions that he asks, and this is what causes the other monks to remain perplexed and silent.

The PYL prose commentary reinforces the hermit's irregular status by celebrating the role of ascetics in a passage that includes an emphasis on Confucian-style filial piety directed toward the lineal patriarchy. "After the ascetic practitioners had attained the Way," it says, "the ancients would dwell in thatched huts or stone grottoes, boiling the roots of wild greens in broken-legged pots, passing the days. Not seeking fame or fortune, they lived in accord with conditions. They would offer a turning word, hoping to repay their gratitude to the benevolence of the Buddhas and Patriarchs and transmit the Buddha Mind Seal." On the importance of staffs the PYL adds, "Master Shan-tao of the Stone Grotto, when he suffered the great persecution [of 845], used to take his staff and show it to the assembly while saying, 'All the Buddhas of the past are thus, all the Buddhas of the future are thus, all the Buddhas of the present are thus.'" Yet, the capping phrase commentary that begins by praising the hermit's construction of an "illusory city," which alludes to a provisional, pedagogical technique advocated by the *Lotus Sutra*, concludes that the hermit still "deserves thirty blows." The hermit "carries a board across his shoulder," a Zen put-down indicating that the person suffers from a blind side or a hopelessly limited, one-dimensional perspective (see case 7).

In another kōan about the use of a staff, "Ma-ku Carrying His Ring-Staff," cited from PYL case 31 (Taishō 48:170a–171a) and TJL case 16 (Taishō 48:156a–157a), a hermit uses the ring-staff to challenge two prominent masters. Ma-ku and the masters were all disciples of Ma-tsu, with Ma-ku being the most junior of the group. The ring-staff is a special utensil used by traveling monks that was adorned with six or twelve rings at the top symbolizing either the six realms of samsara (gods, titans, hungry ghosts, denizens of hell, animals, and humans) or the twelve links of the causal chain of dependent origination (ignorance, action, consciousness, form, sense, touch, pleasure, love, attachment, existence, birth, and death). The jingling sounds of the rings are a constant reminder that the itinerant monk is immersed in the condition of suffering, as well as the possibility for transmuting the six realms or twelve links into gateways to enlightenment.

The PYL case pointer opens with an emphasis on double-bind theory that is reinforced by the interaction in the main case: "Move and a shadow appears; become aware and ice forms. Yet if you do not move or are not aware, you still can't avoid entering into a wild fox den. If you can penetrate thoroughly, without so much as a hair causing obstruction, then it is like a dragon finding water or a tiger taking off for the mountains. Release, and the bricks and pebbles will emit light; hold steady, and even real gold loses its luster. The public records of the ancients could not help but be vague and indirect, but tell me, what were they trying to explain?"

According to the main case, Ma-ku carried his ring-staff and went off to see Ch'ang-ch'ing. He circled the meditation seat three times, shook his staff one time, and stood there upright. Ch'ang-ch'ing said, "That's it! That's it!" (To this Hsüeh-tou added a word, "No!") Ma-ku also went to see Nan-ch'üan. He circled the meditation seat three times, shook his staff one time, and stood there upright. Nan-ch'üan said, "That's not it! That's not it!" (To this Hsüeh-tou added a word, "No!") Ma-ku then said, "Ch'ang-ch'ing said, 'That's it!' Why do you say, "That's not it!'?" Nan-ch'üan replied, "Ch'ang-ch'ing is right; it is you who are not right. You are blown about by the force of the wind. In the end this will lead to reversal and decline." Although the case itself seems to critique Ma-ku and assert the superiority of his seniors, the TJL verse commentary says that when Nan-ch'üan and Ch'ang-ch'ing hear the shaking of Ma-ku's ring staff, "They feel like they are seeing ghosts right in front of their skulls."

45. Ch'ing-yüan Raises His Fly-Whisk

Main Case

Master Ch'ing-yüan asked Shih-t'ou, "Where did you come from?," and Shih-t'ou said, "From Mount Ts'ao-ch'i." Picking up his fly-whisk, Ch'ing-yüan said, "Is there anything like this on Mount Ts'ao-ch'i?" Shih-t'ou said, "No, not on Mount Ts'ao-ch'i. Not even in India." Ch'ing-yüan said, "But you've never been to India, have you?"

Shih-t'ou responded, "If I go to India, the fly-whisk will be there." Ch'ing-yüan said, "What you are saying is not in accord with the Way." Shih-t'ou said, "Please express for me just half a word that is in accord with the Way. Don't leave me completely alone to do it." Ch'ing-yüan said, "It's not that I refuse to express it. I can do this, but if I do it for you, then in the future no one will understand what you say."

Verse Commentary (two verses)

> Shih-t'ou stands at the crossroads with Ch'ing-yüan, seen from
>   inside and out,
> A shuttered window is no different than one that is wide open,
> From a realm beyond air, water, or wind,
> The stone-headed man, Shih-t'ou, has glimpsed the great realm.
>
> Ch'ing-yüan never really knew how to hold up the fly-whisk,
> Nor did he experience the Way or learn how to express it,
> Shih-t'ou's "express for me just half a word in accord with the
>   Way. Don't leave me completely alone to do it,"
> Means there is no penetration of the Way without some words
>   from each master.

Discussion

This kōan is cited from EK vol. 9 case 18 (DZZ 4:102–104), and it also appears in Dōgen's MS case 1 (DZZ 5:126), although it is alluded to only indirectly in the *Shōbōgenzō*. Shih-t'ou, the founder of one of the main lines of Zen, was a second-generation follower of Hui-neng whose most prominent disciple was Yüeh-shan. After attaining enlightenment through studying under the auspices of Ch'ing-yüan, Shih-t'ou, whose name literally means "stone-headed" as mentioned in the first verse commentary, took up residence in a small hut on a large flat rock. He spent twenty-three years in his secluded mountain hut, meditating and instructing a small but thriving flock of disciples.

This case is one of several accounts of the first encounter between Shih-t'ou and his teacher that records their discussion about Mount Ts'ao-ch'i, one of the most famous and respected summits among the many mountains revered in Zen because it was the place where Hui-neng preached. According to another dialogue, when Shih-t'ou visited Ch'ing-yüan the master asked where he was coming from and Shih-t'ou responded, "Mount Ts'ao-ch'i." Then Ch'ing-yüan asked what he had brought with him, and Shih-t'ou said, "That which had never been lost even before I went to Mount Ts'ao-ch'i." Ch'ing-yüan asked why he went to the mountain at all and Shih-t'ou said, "If I had not gone to Mount Ts'ao-ch'i, how could I have realized that it had never been lost?"

In the current case, Ch'ing-yüan challenges Shih-t'ou by raising his fly-whisk, an ornate horsehair utensil borrowed from shamanistic purification devices that is carried by Zen masters in the Dharma Hall as a primary symbol of their legitimacy and authority. By holding up the fly-whisk, Ch'ing-yüan may simply be saying that his temple style is better than the other one, but this is done in a way that evokes the context of numerous claims about the supranormal powers of the device. Shih-t'ou responds by highlighting supernaturalism in his comment on the fly-whisk appearing magically in India. That is, he draws the supernatural context from the background and places it at the heart of the discussion. This compels Ch'ing-yüan to put him in his place, but the verse commentaries, as usual, take a neutral stance on the question of the victor of the encounter.

There are numerous kōans in which the use of the fly-whisk is deliberately given a demythological interpretation that ironically reinforces the significance of the supernatural context and the twofold discursive structure of kōan literature. A prominent example is "Pai-chang Visits Ma-tsu Once Again," cited from EK vol. 9 case 82 (DZZ 4:238–240) and also appearing in MS case 54 (DZZ 5:152), CCL vol. 6 (Taishō 51:249c), *Yüan-wu yü-lu* vol. 18 (Taishō 47:798b), and *Ta-hui yü-lu* vol. 9 (Taishō 57:848c). In this case, Pai-chang paid one of several visits to Ma-tsu, and the master raised his fly-whisk. Pai-chang asked, "Will you make use of this, or will you cast it aside?" Ma-tsu put the fly-whisk back down. Pai-chang just stood around for a while, and then Ma-tsu said, "From now on, when you open up your mouth, what will you say to instruct others?" Pai-chang picked up and held his fly-whisk straight up. Ma-tsu asked, "Will you make use of it, or cast it aside?" Pai-chang put it back down. At this Ma-tsu gave out a loud shout. Some time later Pai-chang confessed to his main disciple, Huang-po, "There was a time that Ma-tsu shouted at me so loudly that my ears were ringing and I couldn't hear a thing for three whole days." According to the verse commentary,

> Pai-chang all of a sudden awakened to the formless truth,
> But who knows if he understood it each and every time the fly-
> whisk was raised; By some mistake he went home and was
> offered a poisonous brew,
> By the ancestor of old who was known to furrow up his brows.

Another example is "Lo-han Raises His Fly-whisk," cited from MS case 229 (DZZ 5:246) and several transmission of the lamp records including CCL vol. 12 (Taishō 51: 371c), *Tsung-men t'ung-yao chi* vol. 10, and *Tsung-men lien-teng hui-yao* vol. 16. According to this case, when Master Lo-han saw a monk approaching, he immediately raised a fly-whisk and showed it to the priest. The monk then bowed and prostrated himself. Lo-han asked, "What have you seen that made you want to prostrate yourself like that?" The monk said, "I am showing thanks for the master's instruction." Lo-han struck the monk and reprimanded him by saying, "When you saw me hold up the fly-whisk you prostrated yourself as a way of giving thanks for my instruction. But why is it that when you see me sweeping the ground or floor every day you don't prostrate yourself as a way of giving thanks for my instruction?" Lo-han explains that a disciple should not be intimidated by the ritual authority of the fly-whisk but should see it as relative to other examples of concrete, everyday activity.

In "Lin-chi Raises His Fly-whisk," cited from MS case 255 (DZZ 5:258), CCL vol. 21 (Taishō 51:436b), *Tsung-men t'ung-yao chi* vol. 5, and *Yüan-wu yü-lu* vol. 19 (Taishō 47:801b), the same iconoclastic message is delivered in a straightforward, unambiguous manner, although the hagiographical element involves an exaggeration of the degree of irreverence in the master's attitude: "Master Lin-chi, watching a priest walking toward him, raised his fly-whisk. The priest bowed and prostrated himself, and Lin-chi immediately struck him."

TRANSMISSION SYMBOLS

46. Hui-neng's Immovable Robe

Main Case

The Sixth Patriarch Hui-neng was once pursued by the monk, Ming, all the way to a ridge on Mount Ta-yü. When the patriarch saw Ming approaching, he cast the robe and begging bowl he was carrying on a rock and said, "This robe represents faith. It should not be fought over. I'll leave it here for you to take it away."

Ming tried to pick up the robe but it was as immovable as a mountain. Trembling with fear, Ming cried out, "I came to learn the Dharma, not to take away the robe. Please instruct me." The Sixth Patriarch said, "Without thinking of what is good and without thinking of what is evil, right now at this very moment what is the original face of monk Ming?"

Hearing these words, Ming experienced a great enlightenment. His whole body was drenched in sweat. Weeping, he bowed and asked, "Aside from the esoteric words with their esoteric meaning that you have just revealed to me, is there any other, even more profound teaching you can teach me?" The Sixth Patriarch replied, "What I have just explained is not an esoteric teaching. The deeper meaning you are looking for is to be found nowhere else than right within you."

Ming said, "Although while studying under the Fifth Patriarch at Huang-mei I participated along with the rest of the assembly, I was never able to see my original self. Now, thanks to your instruction that directed me to a true inner realization, I am like one who has drunk water and can tell for himself whether it is cold or warm. You, my lay brother, are my real teacher!" The patriarch said, "If you are so awakened, then both you and I have the Fifth Patriarch as our teacher. Take care to cultivate your attainment."

Prose Commentary

The Sixth Patriarch could be said to have risen to the occasion to help someone out, showing all the kindness of a grandmother. It is as though he peeled a fresh lychee, removed its seed and then put it into your mouth, so that all you have to do is swallow it.

Verse Commentary

> It cannot be described, and it cannot be drawn,
> Since it cannot be praised in full, stop fumbling around,
> The original face cannot remain hidden,
> When the whole world collapses, it remains unharmed.

Discussion

This kōan, cited from WMK case 23 (Taishō 48:295c–296a), features one of the most important and dramatic events that supposedly took place at a crucial turning point in the early history of Zen when there was a struggle for succession to the fifth patriarch, and a transition from the Northern school to the dominance of the Southern school based on the teachings of sixth patriarch Hui-neng as recorded in the classic Zen text, the *Platform Sutra*. The dramatic impact of the case rests fully on the ritual significance and supernatural claims of the two key symbols of lineal transmission, the robe and the begging bowl.

According to Zen tradition, these specific items belonged to first patriarch Bodhidharma and were handed down each and every generation to the successive string of patriarchs. The meaning of the tools, however, is rooted in the earliest days of Buddhist monasticism when the robe and bowl were the only possessions of itinerant monks. Throughout the history of Buddhism there was considerable debate about the color, substance, and quality of the robe used by monastics and ascetics. In China, an important issue was whether it was appropriate to produce robes of silk rather than the traditional coarser material, and whether a master could or should accept a robe of finer design and color that was donated or assigned by imperial authorities. Zen literature often praises "patchrobed monks," which recalls the ideal of *dhutanga* practitioners, who were supposed to piece together a robe from discarded garments and rags found near graveyards or by the roadside.

In this case, the robe has a magical quality when it proves to be "immovable as a mountain" to the monk who pursues Hui-neng and experiences a conversion. Shaken and repentant he beseeches the master, as does the fox/monk in case 38, to offer instruction, which convinces Ming to remain a loyal follower of Hui-neng who is about to take over leadership of the entire sect. As in case 41 on Chih-men's staff, the kōan expresses a direct link between the physical and spiritual state of the practitioner and his use of a symbol, or between the powers of the robe and the mental as well the bodily prowess of monk Ming.

The background of the case, as discussed in the biographical section of the *Platform Sutra*, concerns Hui-neng's rapid rise to eminence in the institutional structure of Zen. At that time, Shen-hsiu was the likely heir of fifth patriarch Hung-jen, and therefore he expected to receive the robe and bowl. During a poetry contest planned by Hung-jen to anoint his successor, Shen-hsiu submitted a four-line verse that compared the body to the Bodhi Tree and the mind to a clear mirror that needs to be constantly wiped clean so that no dust could alight on it. Hui-neng, who was a young, inexperienced monk from an impoverished, uneducated family, realized the limitations in Shen-hsiu's verse that relied too heavily on metaphors for original enlightenment. He submitted his own verse that asserted the priority of emptiness and eliminated the use of metaphorical expression:

> Bodhi fundamentally has no tree,
> The mirror is without a stand;
> Originally there is nothing at all,
> So where can the dust collect?"

Hung-jen declared Hui-neng the winner of the contest. But realizing that the other monks would be jealous of the precocious novice, he encouraged and helped Hui-neng flee the monastery in order to spend some time polishing his realization before he would return and be accepted by the assembly as the true heir to the transmission. However, as soon as the other monks heard what happened, they took up a chase led by Ming, a former military general who finds Hui-neng at the ridge of Mount Ta-yü, which stands between northern and southern China. Ming told him, "We cannot tolerate that an illiterate rube such as you inherits the robe and bowl. Give them to me at once, without causing any trouble." Echoing his verse, Hui-neng instructs Ming in the nature of fundamental reality, or the original, pure Self prior to the realm of differentiation and discrimination between good and evil, right and wrong, this and that, or other aspects of polarity.

This case marks the transition of authority in Zen to the Southern school, but its rhetorical style is based on the Northern school emphasis on encounters with magic and supernaturalism as the key to learning a lesson about emptiness and nonduality. Another kōan, cited from WMK case 16 (Taishō 48:295a), "Putting On the Robe When the Bell Sounds," uses the image of the robe to question the role of ritual propriety in the conduct of monastic rules and ceremonies. According to this brief case Yün-men said, "The world is so vast and so wide. Why do we put on a formal, seven-piece robe at the sound of the bell?" The verse commentary transmutes the case's central question into an expression of the typical Zen double-bind situation:

> When you understand, then all things are one,
> When you do not understand, there is only endless multiplicity
>   and differentiation,
> When you do not understand, then all things are one,
> When you understand, there is only endless multiplicity and
>   differentiation.

However, the key to this case is the ritual significance of the robe, which must be made of material and worn in a way that is appropriate to both the ideal values and practical decorum of the Zen monastic system.

47. Tung-shan Makes Offerings Before the Image

Pointer

It cannot be portrayed, and it cannot be drawn. P'u-hua turned the tables, and Lung-ya just revealed half of his body. In the end, who is it that is in this condition?

Main Case

As Tung-shan was making offerings before the image of Yün-yen, he told once again the story from an earlier time about the question of depicting the master's image. A monk approached and asked, "When Yün-yen said, 'It is just like this,' what did that mean?" Tung-shan replied, "At that time,

I wasn't sure if I understood my late teacher." The monk said, "Did Yün-yen himself know whether the image is reality, or not?"

Tung-shan said, "If he didn't know, how could he have said this? If he did know, why would he have said this?"

Discussion

This kōan, cited from TJL case 49 (Taishō 48:258a–258c), is based on an earlier dialogue between Tung-shan and Yün-yen that highlights the ritual significance of the images of masters, such as portraits, statues, and other kinds of icons, including mummies, which were used to commemorate deceased abbots and patriarchs.

The most common style of image used in Zen monastic life was a portrait of the master sitting cross-legged on a chair, holding either a fly-whisk or a bamboo staff, or with his hands forming the meditation mudra. But other kinds of portraits were popularly used, such as busts, portraits enclosed in a circle, or portraits of the master either standing or in a natural setting such as with animals. Portraits of deceased abbots were often placed in the master's high seat or throne in a fashion that was probably influenced by imperial ceremonies of dedication or memorials for deceased emperors, but they were also hung on the wall of a temple in a central part of the Dharma Hall. While conventional interpretations see these images as replicas or substitutes for the dead figures, it is more likely that they were not merely momentos or reminders, but magical devices that had a reality in that they embodied and transmitted the charismatic power of the master. Often, the master's body parts, such as hair, were attached to the portrait to serve as relics that helped empower and animate the image. This practice was influenced by the eye-opening ceremony used in many schools of Theravada and Mahayana Buddhism, in which the painting or placing of an eye on an icon or image is considered to bring it to life, while removing or shutting the eye renders it powerless.

The background of this case—"the story from an earlier time"—is a previous encounter depicted in the prose commentary section of the TJL. When Tung-shan was about to take leave of his master, Yün-yen said that it would be difficult for them to meet again and Tung-shan responded that it would be "difficult not to meet," implying an esoteric, intuitive connection between teacher and disciple. Then he asked, "A long time from now, after your death, when someone asks me to describe what you were really like, what should I say?" After a pause Yün-yen said, "Just like this." Tung-shan was pondering the meaning of Yün-yen's expression when the master told him, "You are responsible for resolving the great matter, so you must investigate it thoroughly." Tung-shan left abruptly without responding. Some time later, as he was crossing a river he saw his reflection in the water and for the first time had a thoroughgoing breakthrough to enlightenment.

The main case presupposes the ritual significance of the master's image and turns the question of its efficacy into a double-bind formula. According to Tung-shan, whether or not Yün-yen understood the meaning of his own image and the question of its reality, he could not or should not have spoken about it directly or indirectly—it is beyond words and forms of expression. The impact of the double bind evoked by the case, then, is not necessarily iconoclastic, but it remains neutral and leaves open the issue of the supernatural significance of the image as an actual embodiment of the deceased master.

Another kōan, "Yüeh-shan Washing the Buddha Image," cited from MS case 86 (DZZ 5:168) and also included in several recorded sayings texts including those by Huang-lung (Taishō 47:630b) and Yüan-wu (Taishō 47:792a), takes a more overtly iconoclastic position on the use of images. According to this case, a priest in a cotton robe lived in the order of master Yüeh-shan and became head monk of the Buddha Hall. While they were washing an image of Buddha one day, Yüeh-shan asked the monk, "Can you only wash this image over here? What about the image that is over there?" The monk said, "Please bring here that image from over there," and Yüeh-shan was rendered speechless. Apparently, Yüeh-shan's silence suggests that the image "over there" does not represent or embody the true Buddha, which is not an object either here or there, for the genuine meaning of Buddha lies entirely within the subjectivity of the practitioner.

48. Prime Minister P'ei-hsiu Replies, "Yes"

Main Case

One time Master Huang-po left his flock and entered another temple as a regular monk. He joined in the labor with the other members of the assembly and was sweeping up in the main halls of the temple when Prime Minister P'ei-hsiu came one day and burned incense. The head priest received the minister. The minister saw a portrait hanging on the wall of the temple and asked, "Whose picture is this?" The priest responded, "This is a picture of the temple abbot." The minister said, "I see his picture, now

I'd like to meet him. Where can I find him?," but no one in the assembly could answer him.

The minister asked, "Aren't there any men of zazen in this temple?" The priest said, "There is a monk who came here recently and joined in our labors. He seems to be a man of zazen." The minister said, "How about if you invite him here so I can ask him the question?" The priest found Huang-po right away and brought him over to meet the minister. The minister said, "Just now I asked a question and there wasn't anyone here who could give me an answer. Now I'd like to ask you the same question and have you give me one word that will change my life."

Huang-po said, "Prime Minister, please go ahead and ask me the question." The minister repeated his previous question. Huang-po called out loudly, "Mr. Prime Minister!" The minister looked over and said, "Yes." Huang-po said, "Where can I find you?"

The minister was enlightened just like that, as if he had received a pearl from the knot in Gautama Buddha's hair. Then he said, "You are truly a worthy priest." And he continued to come to practice at the temple.

Verse Commentary

> The man gazes at the wall and the wall gazes at the man,
> Each seeks the answer to the question, "Where can I find you?"
> Just as they open their mouths to share a laugh,
> The plum blossom secretly erupts on the snow-filled branch.

Discussion

This kōan is cited from Dōgen's EK vol. 9 case 48 (DZZ 4:212–214) and it is included in his MS case 9 (DZZ 5:130), although—like several other cases from these texts that are discussed in this volume—it is not dealt with in Dōgen's *Shōbōgenzō*. The case also appears in CCL vol. 12 (Taishō 51:293a) and several transmission of the lamp records, including *T'ien-sheng kuang-teng lu* vol. 8 and *Tsung-men lien-teng hui-yao* vol. 8.

In this kōan case, a Zen portrait hanging on the wall and a question about the whereabouts of the master it represents transmutes into a quest for identifying a true man of zazen. Huang-po, who apparently has gone on retreat from his own temple on Mount Huang-po where he serves as abbot, performs chores unpretentiously in the new monastery like he is one of the regular monks. This impresses others in the assembly who do not seem to be aware of his esteemed status, and they present him to the minister as exemplary of a man of zazen. Huang-po's handling of the encounter dialogue by asking the probing question, "Where can I find you?" leads Prime Minister P'ei-hsiu, who became a very important lay follower of Huang-po, to an enlightenment experience, symbolized by the late winter plum blossoms depicted in the verse commentary.

One of the interesting features of the narrative is the reaction of the monks to the minister's inquiry about the portrait. P'ei-hsiu asks who the portrait represents, and he is told it is the abbot. Yet, when he asks to meet the abbot, the person portrayed in the picture he finds so fascinating, "no one in the assembly could answer him." When the minister changes the question slightly to ask if there aren't any men of zazen in the temple, then they are able to bring him to meet Huang-po. But he is not the abbot—at least, not for this temple—so in a sense the basic question about the abbot still goes unanswered.

Why does this simple question seem so perplexing and confusing? Why cannot the monks give the minister a response? There are several possibilities. The most likely scenario is that the portrait shows the venerated, deceased abbot of the temple. Although he is still referred to as abbot in a way that implies that he is alive, the monks assume the minister understands that he is not available for a meeting and they are disconcerted and dismayed by his breach of propriety and etiquette. They are not quite sure how to salvage an awkward situation. Another possibility is that the question highlights their sense of uncertainty about the true leader of the temple, given the presence of Huang-po. Perhaps the abbot is still alive because it some cases a portrait would be commissioned in mid-career, but the monks are no longer so confident in his leadership in light of the authentic, disciplined training methods of the visitor who they likely suspect is an abbot elsewhere. Either way, the kōan highlights the ritual importance of portraits as a key Zen symbol while showing the gap that often separates image and reality, or the painting of a rice cake and real refreshment. The case narrative also illustrates the first encounter between Huang-po and P'ei-hsiu, who eventually renounced the world of civil service and played a crucial role in spreading and disseminating the master's teachings by editing, publishing, and writing a preface for his main text.

Another kōan, "Ti-tsang Offers a Meal to Hsüan-sha," cited from MS case 25 (DZZ 5:138) and also included in *Tsung-men t'ung-yao chi* vol. 10 and *Tsung-men lien-teng yao-chi* vol. 26, expresses an ironic affirmation of the importance of the image of a deceased master that is supposed to be animated and "alive" with the presence of his spirit. In this case, the master of Ti-tsang temple prepared dinner for the anniversary of the death of his teacher, master Hsüan-sha. He invited another master as a guest to share the meal with him that evening. The visiting master looked over at the customary place where the symbol of the teacher's spirit would have been kept. But he saw nothing. After a while he asked Ti-tsang, "Don't you have a symbol of your teacher?" Ti-tsang bowed down with joined hands and said, "Look!" The visitor said, "From the beginning there has never been any image of Hsüan-sha." Ti-tsang said, "You have completely missed the form of Hsüan-sha!" Ti-tsang thereby affirms the power of imagery, though perhaps not as an actual external painting but an interior realization.

49. Yang-shan's "Just About Enough"

Main Case

A monk asked Yang-shan, "Do you know the written characters, or not?" Yang-shan answered, "I know them well enough." The monk then walked in a circle around him one time to the right and said, "Which character is this?" Yang-shan drew a cross on the ground.

The monk then walked in a circle around him one time to the left and said, "Which character is this?" Yang-shan changed the cross into the mystic symbol of good fortune (swastika). The monk drew a circle and raised it up with his hands like a titan holding up the sun and moon, and he said, "Which character is this?" Yang-shan then drew a circle around the swastika.

The monk then took on a pose just like the appearance of Rucika. Yang-shan said, "That's right! You do that so well!"

Verse Comments (with capping phrases by Wan-sung)

> The void of the circle of the Way never reaches its limit,
> *Like snow on the river,*
> The characters on the seal of emptiness are not yet formed.
> *Don't try to carve them.*
> The marvelous wheel of heaven and the globe of earth,
> *Holding on to the scales,*
> Subtly practicing the literary and cultural arts.

These functions are complete.
Letting go and holding on,
Mu-chou still lives,
Standing alone and traveling everywhere.
Lao-tsu is born again.
The pivot is mysteriously activated, and thunder rolls in the clear blue sky,
You can't hold on,
The eye takes in violet light, seeing stars in broad daylight.
To the light shining over the four corners of the world.

Discussion

This kōan is cited from TJL case 77 (Taishō 48:204b–205a), and also appears in the transmission of the lamp record, the *Wu-teng hui-yüan*. In this case, the encounter between master and disciple involves a verbal repartee not about supernaturalism and emptiness but the use of visual symbols, especially the circle and related geometrical patterns such as the cross and the swastika. This was traditionally a mystic symbol of infinity in Buddhism that is still used today to designate Buddhism on the cover or the frontispiece of books or as the locator of a temple on a map of East Asia.

Yang-shan was particularly known for his use of circles in transmitting enlightenment, and circles were also used extensively by his contemporary Tung-shan, who developed a system of "five ranks" that was illustrated by patterns of full, half, and new moons (darkened, half-darkened, and empty circles). According to traditional accounts, Yang-shan was enlightened by receiving knowledge of ninety-seven circles that had specific information written in characters and other kinds of markings placed inside that gave the circles a particular meaning and esoteric significance. Circular symbols in the form of mandalas occur throughout Buddhist history and also have a resonance with the practice of circumambulation by monks walking around a Buddha icon. In China, the use of circles was reinforced by the powerful poetic image of the moon as well as yin-yang symbolism (note the references to Lao-tsu in the capping verse commentary). Yang-shan's emphasis on circles is seen in another dialogue (Taishō 51:383b), in which the master had his eyes closed and a monk came and stood quietly beside him. Yang-shan opened his eyes and drew a circle on the ground, and inside it he wrote the character for water, leaving the monk speechless.

However, Yang-shan was also skeptical and critical of an over-reliance on the circular symbol as a form of divination or sorcery. In another anecdote (Taishō 48:283), he asked a monk what he knew beside Buddhism and the monk responded by saying the techniques of the I Ching. The master lifted his fan and asked, "Tell me which of the sixty-four hexagrams this one is," and the monk could not reply. The master roared, "It is the great potentiality of thunder and lightning transformed into the destruction of earth and fire!"

In the current case, Yang-shan is challenged by a monk, who tries literally to walk circles around him, and he responds by drawing first a cross and then a swastika. The monk attempts to appear mighty, but then Yang-shan turns the tables by drawing a circle. But perhaps the monk draws even in the encounter—"the pivot is mysteriously activated," according to the verse commentary—by appearing like Rucika, the last of the 1,000 Buddhas of the present era, according to Buddhist mythology, who would appear at the time of a world conflagration with the precious jewel of *vaidurya* (lapis lazuli).

In a similar vein, the kōan "Yün-men Casts A Spell," cited from YY record 77 (Taishō 47:549c) and also evoked in record 82 (Taishō 47:550a), that deals with the topic of Yün-men's "sword," involves the ironic use of a spell for fending off spirits. In this case, a question was asked, "What happens when one realizes that the triple world is mind only and all phenomena are nothing but products of consciousness?" The master replied, "It is like rolling the body up and hiding it in one's mouth." "What happens to the body?" The master said, "Su-lu, su-lu," a *dharani*-like collection of syllables perhaps borrowed from indigenous shamanistic incantations.

This approach is reinforced by "Chao-chou and the Stone Symbol," cited from CCL vol. 10 (Taishō 51:277a). In the master's cloister there was a stone symbol, possibly an amulet or some magical image, perhaps with an esoteric *dharani* inscribed on it, that was broken off by the wind. A monk asked, "Does this make the magical symbol holy, or does it make it profane?" The monk was apparently serious about trying to understand the supernatural significance of the broken image. But the master said, "It does not make it either holy or profane." The monk asked, "What does it make it?," and Cha-chou said in a dismissive, offhanded way, "It makes it fallen down."

The irreverent attitude in these kōans recalls another kind of dialogue reflecting ambiguity and uncertainty about the source and meaning of symbols rather than confident iconoclasm, that is recorded in the *Tzurezuregusa* by the thirteenth-century Japanese Buddhist monk Kenkō (trans. Donald Keene, *Essays in Idleness*, Tokyo: Charles E. Tuttle, 1967, p. 201):

> When I turned eight years old I asked my father, "What sort of thing is a Buddha?" My father said, "A Buddha is what a man becomes." I asked then, "How does a man become a Buddha?" My father replied, "By following the teachings of Buddha." "Then, who taught the Buddha to teach?" He again replied, "He followed the teachings of the Buddha before him." I asked again, "What kind of Buddha was the first Buddha who began to teach?" At this my father laughed and answered, "I suppose he fell from the sky or else he sprang up out of the earth." My father told other people, "He drove me into a corner, and I was stuck for an answer." But he was amused.

FIVE

Confessional Experiences

Giving Life and

Controlling Death

Confession has had an implicit connection with liberation in nearly all major world religions. The history of Buddhist monasticism is particularly rich in examples of confessional experiences that lead practitioners from ignorance and attachment to wisdom and enlightenment. Encountering death and the afterlife is a related experience that can also result in spiritual liberation.

A centerpiece of the early Buddhist monastic tradition was the ordination ceremony that involved administering 250 precepts to guide all aspects of the monks' ethical and practical behavior. To reinforce the significance of a continuing commitment to the practice of the precepts, the tradition required a fortnightly confessional rite. On these occasions, monks acknowledged and repented for transgressions to fellow monks, recited and reflected on the precepts, and received punishments such as temporary banishment or even permanent expulsion for more serious offenses. The four major offenses covered taking life (including the life of supernatural beings), stealing, sexual misconduct (again, including with a supernatural entity), and misusing one of the supranormal powers. Also, once a year at the end of the three-month rainy season retreat, the monks undertook an additional confessional ceremony.

Yet another aspect of the approach to confession and repentance was found in one of the popular genres of early Buddhist literature, the *jataka* stories. These tales that were contained in one of the first collections of folklore in world literature tell of the ways in which the Buddha, in manifold incarnations prior to his historical manifestation as Sakyamuni, appeared in various animal or supernatural forms in order to teach moral lessons. The *jatakas* include accounts of prostitutes, hunters, and thieves, as well as troublesome Nagas, demons, spirits, and sprites, coming into contact with a representative or a symbol of the Dharma, weeping for their misdeeds or sins, and—through the act of converting and following the precepts—finding redemption and becoming enlightened.

Zen appears to advocate a very different standpoint that has dispensed with the need for a ritual approach to confession. As one of the schools of Mahayana Buddhism, it followed the bodhisattva vows of forty-eight precepts, which were more general affirmations of compassion than specific codes of conduct. The *Platform Sutra*, attributed to sixth patriarch Hui-neng, stressed the importance of meditation on emptiness or "formless repentance," rather than repentance for particular misdeeds or "form repentance." Furthermore, Dōgen streamlined the precepts as expressed in the *Shōbōgenzō* "Jukai" fascicle to an essential sixteen vows. The shift in emphasis in Zen in favor of formless repentance was based on the philosophy of nonduality. However, one consequence was a tendency to lose sight of the traditional focus on the ethical quality of the precepts and risk entry into a realm of antinomian behavior. At the same time, as is the case with many other issues, there is a fundamental gap between the iconoclastic rhetoric of anti-ritualism in prominent examples of Zen literature and the actual practice in Zen monastic life. Generally, Zen monasteries in China and Japan have adhered to all of the traditional precepts, in addition to the Mahayana vows, along with various kinds of monthly and yearly repentance rites.

Therefore, despite the apparent rejection of repentance in the *Platform Sutra*, Zen monastic training was consistent with the long-standing Buddhist practices of confessing and maintaining discipline through receiving punishments that included the most severe retribution of banishment from the samgha or monastic community. Zen furthermore enhanced the emphasis on confession by adapting many kinds of practice that were part of the Chinese religious milieu. For example, Zen masters often integrated into the monastic practice of regular confessional ceremonies motifs that borrowed from shamanistic exorcism techniques involving the connection between eradicating evil through ritual and healing. In addition, Zen embraced a trend that was popular in Chinese Buddhist monk biographies of extolling extreme examples of self-mutilation and self-sacrifice, including severing a finger or a limb and ritual suicide, as a means of repentance. Self-sacrifice was often seen as a logical extension of extreme ascetic training.

Also, Zen accepted the traditional Buddhist fascination and preoccupation with death and the afterlife as a key to the attainment of enlightenment. In early Buddhist practice, contemplation of corpses and meditation conducted around cremation grounds and cemeteries, especially for trainees in *dhutanga* austerities, was a common way of experiencing the meaning of suffering and impermanence. Buddhism maintained that true nirvana, or parinirvana, was possible only after death and liberation from the final shackles of bondage to fleshly attachments and desire. In addition, Zen followed the custom whereby the cremated remains of monks who had manifested supranormal abilities were said to have left relics or *sarira* with miraculous powers that were stored in stupas and worshiped by devotees.

The approach toward deceased monks in China also assimilated elements of ancestor veneration as well as Taoist immortalism. For example, monks who died in an untimely or troubled way became ghosts that haunted the living and required a ritual of exorcism until their problems were resolved. However, saints, who were able to control the timing of their death and face it without fear or pain while seated in zazen meditation, were in some cases preserved and mummified when they expired. Or, the saints were considered to maintain "flesh-bodies" that stayed in a prolonged state of meditation without decay or, on the contrary, vanished from their coffin without a trace.

Furthermore, Chinese Buddhism in general, and Zen in particular, allowed that priests became very much involved in mortuary rites, including performing funerals, burials, and memorial services. As a key part of this process, priests made rounds of condolence calls to bereaved families, and these occasions were used as an opportunity to connect the death of a layman with a discussion of the metaphysical and supernatural implications of the relation between life and death.

REPENTANCE AND SELF-MUTILATION

50. Chih-yen Converts a Hunter

Main Case

Master Chih-yen was sitting in concentration that attained a state of deep absorption (*samadhi*) while he was living in a mountain hermitage, when suddenly the valley stream overflowed its banks. The master remained calm and composed with a steady, unmoving mind, and the flood quickly receded of its own accord.

A hunter who came by while this was happening was so impressed by the effects of the master's composure that he decided to reform his previous misdeeds, and as a result he lived a lifetime of practicing virtuous behavior.

Discussion

This anecdote, cited from CCL vol. 4 (Taishō 51:228b), is a primary example of Ox Head school literature reflecting an encounter and demonstration of superior spiritual skills by a hermit that had a great impact on the formal development of the kōan tradition in the Southern school. Like the Northern school, the Ox Head school was heavily influenced by the kinds of marvelous practices reflected in the pan-sectarian hagiographical materials of monk biography texts. However, both the Northern and Ox Head schools began to make a transition to the Southern Zen style of encounter dialogue.

In this case, there is an encounter between a master and a hunter that leads to a profound change of heart on the latter's part, but no dialogue transpires. In that sense, the passage functions on a more mythological level than other examples from the Northern and Ox Head schools (including cases 1, 2, and 31), which revolve around a dialogue between a master and a supernatural being, such as a mountain god, trickster, or hearth deity; as well as cases 3 and 4, in which the dialogue involves a challenge and contest between two masters, with a less advanced master striving to prove his ability to one of the leading patriarchs by eliminating any reliance on supernaturalism. In the current case, the trigger mechanism for spiritual transformation is not a verbal exchange or repartee between two parties, but a quasi-supernatural demonstration of contemplative skills that greatly impresses the hunter.

The clear and concise emphasis on the experience of repentance in the CCL passage resembles an important genre of East Asian Buddhist morality tale literature or *setsuwa bungaku*. *Setsuwa bungaku* is a combination of pre-Buddhist folklore concerning demons, ghosts, and spirits with *jataka* tales about the impact of the Buddha's teachings on the lives of ordinary people. The aim is to show that Buddhist symbols, scriptures, saints, or rituals can overcome or exorcise demonic forces and lead the righteous to an experience of repentance and redemption.

The *setsuwa bungaku* materials often feature dramatic and mysterious narrative elements that are lacking in this passage. On the other hand, the story of the hunter's conversion sends an important message about how the power of Zen meditation reverses the effects of a flood based on the calm composure and serenity of the monk's contemplation. In another CCL anecdote about Chih-yen, two men who had belonged to the master's retinue hear of his flight from the world and come into the deep mountain recesses to find him. "Have you gone mad?," they asked, and he responded, "My madness is to be enlightened, while yours is to remain involved with worldly affairs." The two men gained enlightenment, and went away sighing with satisfaction and remorse for having ever doubted the master.

According to the CCL, Chih-yen's death was accompanied by miraculous signs. In transmission of the lamp literature dealing with the Ox Head school, the typical imagery for the death of a master includes an auspicious cloud that appears and covers the temple while heavenly music is heard throughout the region. Also, a tremendous storm erupts and trees are blown over, and animals weep as the mountain torrents stop running for days. After the cremation of the master, his followers find numerous *sarira* amid the pyre, and so they refuse to leave the mountain although the emerald forests turn white as a sign of grieving by all the elements of the natural environment.

51. Chü-chih's One Finger Zen

Main Case

Whenever master Chü-chih was asked a question, he would simply hold up one finger. One time a visitor to the temple asked Chü-chih's attendant about his master's teachings. The boy also just held up one finger. When Chü-chih heard about this, he cut off the boy's finger. The boy, screaming in pain, began to run away, but Chü-chih called him back. When the boy turned around, Chü-chih held up one finger. The boy experienced enlightenment.

Years later, when Chü-chih was about to die, he instructed the assembly, "I attained One Finger Zen from my teacher, T'ien-lung, and have used it all my life without exhausting it. Do you understand?" So saying, he passed away holding up one finger.

Prose Commentary

The enlightenment of Chü-chih and the attendant are not based on the finger. If you really see through this, then you'll have skewered Tien-lung, Chü-chih, the boy, and you yourself all on one sharp stick.

Verse Commentary

> Chü-chih made a fool of old Tien-lung,
> By testing a boy with his sharp knife —
> Like a Great Spirit raising its hands, and without much effort,
> Splitting into two the mighty peaks of Flower Mountain.

Discussion

This kōan, which originally appeared in CCL vol. 11 (Taishō 51:288b), is cited with prose and verse commentary from WMK case 3 (Taishō 48:292b), and it is also included in the other major classic kōan collections, including PYL case 19 (Taishō 48:159a–160a), TJL case 84 (Taishō 48:280c–281c), and MS case 245 (DZZ 5:254), as well as a variety of other sources including the records of masters Fen-yang, Hung-chih, and Ta-hui (two versions). The version in the PYL and TJL is reduced to a single line, "Whenever any question was asked, Master Chü-chih would simply hold up one finger," but these collections also contain extended prose commentary that includes a complex narrative with a variety of supernatural and ritual elements. The WMK main case, on the other hand, is considerably longer, but the sections of commentary allude only indirectly to the hagiographical narrative through passing references to Chü-chih's teacher, Tien-lung.

This case seems to be a primary example of Zen irreverence and iconoclasm with the severing of the finger symbolizing the pruning of all ignorance, delusions, passions, and attachment, including (or especially) an attachment to the teaching style of one's mentor. This message is reinforced by the irony that Chü-chih remains consistent about his One Finger pedagogy even when the boy is screaming in pain and the master is approaching his own death. However, an understanding of the iconoclastic dimension of discourse changes when the case is considered in light of the pervasive role of violent self-mutilation and self-sacrifice in Chinese Buddhist monasticism that influenced Zen. Also, the supernatural narrative in the

PYL prose commentary depicts a nun carrying a pilgrim's staff, a revelatory dream inspiring a vision of a local protector spirit, and the incarnation of a bodhisattva.

Chü-chih was an obscure figure, not well known beyond this case, except as a master of incantions from the *Saptakotibuddhamatr Dharani*. The source for his name was the sound of the Sanskrit term *koti* in the title of the dharani. Staying for a prolonged period in a mountain hermitage, he was approached one rainy night by a nun wearing robes and a broad rain hat and carrying the large carved staff indicative of a Zen wanderer. She walked around Chü-chih's meditation seat three times and challenged him to speak before she would take off her hat. When he failed to respond, she offered to stay the night, but only if he gave an answer. Failing again, Chü-chih felt inadequate and vowed to go on a pilgrimage to study the Dharma, but that night a spirit told him in a dream that a bodhisattva was to appear. The next day, Tien-lung arrived and taught him the One Finger method.

Therefore, the holding up and detaching of the finger can only be understood in terms of encounters with a woman and supernatural entities. But is Chü-chih justified in his violent approach to the boy? The WMK verse commentary suggests that Chü-chih surpasses his teacher and in his effortlessness reminds us of a god who once split a mountain to allow the Yangtze River to pass through. This recalls Lin-chi's praise for the effortless pedagogy of his mentor, Huang-po. However, according to the TJL prose commentary, Hsüan-sha said that he would have broken Chü-chih's finger, both as part of the boy's grudge and "to renew the world's energy," and a capping phrase on the main case remarks of Chü-chih's gesture in a critical though tongue-in-cheek fashion: "Why did he expend so much energy?"

On the other hand, the verse commentary by Hsüeh-tou in the PYL praises Chü-chih:

> I admire old Chü-chih for his appropriate teaching,
> Who else is like him throughout time and space?
> He cast down a piece of driftwood onto the ocean,
> Letting the blind turtle bob up and down while clinging to it.

The final lines make an allusion to a story in the *Lotus Sutra* and elsewhere of a huge turtle living in the deep blue sea with one eye in the middle of its belly. One day a log with a hole in it came floating by and the turtle was able to put its eye to the hole and look upward to see the sun. The message is that there is a chance in a million to be born as a human, hear the

Buddha's teaching, and attain enlightenment, and Chü-chih's One Finger Zen provided the unique opportunity for this realization.

52. Nalakuvara Broke His Bones and Tore His Flesh

Main Case

One day Master T'ou-tzu was asked by a priest, "Prince Nalakuvakara reciprocated his father's benelovence by breaking his bones, and he reciprocated his mother's benevolence by tearing apart his flesh. In reflecting on the condition of the prince, how can we understand the meaning of his original body?"

T'ou-tzu responded by throwing away the staff he had been holding.

Discussion

This kōan, which originally appears in CCL vol. 15 (Taishō 51:319c) and is cited from MS case 160 (DZZ 5:210), is one of numerous relatively unusual or obscure case records that Dōgen selected from the transmission of the lamp sources for inclusion in his MS kōan collection. The MS, or *Shōbōgenzō* in Chinese (also known as the 300-case *Shōbōgenzō* or *Shōbōgenzō sanbyakusoku*) does not contain commentary and was probably compiled at an early stage in Dōgen's career (1235) as part of his preparation for the composition of the KS, or *Shōbōgenzō* in Japanese, that contains extended prose commentary on dozens of cases (although this case is not included in the KS).

The case can be read as an example of the master's disapproval and disdain for both the actions of the prince and the disciple's question. T'ou-tzu, who was a little-known Ts'ao-tung school master, meets one extreme form of behavior—the prince's violent form of grieving—with another extreme gesture, throwing down the staff, which actually was such a common demonstrative act in Zen records that it had become ritualized. The gesture repudiates the monk's question, which seems to presuppose a dichotomy between spiritual essence or "original body" (Ch. *pen-lai hsin*, Jap. *honrai shin*) and physical existence in a way that violates the Zen approach to nonduality.

However, the case can be understood differently when seen in terms of the popularity of self-mutilation as well as the complex relation between Zen and the family system of mainstream Chinese society, which emphasized the veneration of ancestors. Zen, as a monastic religion, was an institution outside of, or even in conflict with, the conventional social order that was based on the family hierarchical structure. But part of the success of Zen in the competitive religious environment (in which Confucianism had long been the dominant tradition) lay in crafting a lineal structure based on the family model that provided monks with an alternative or surrogate family, rather than demanding a rejection of family values altogether. While Zen practitioners continued to mourn for their own parents and relatives, there was a transfer of affection and loyalty so that filial piety toward the abbot or master replaced the father and veneration of the patriarchs replaced the ancestors.

Prince Nalakuvara was one of the sons of a mythical emperor well known in Japanese folklore as Bishamonten, or Guardian of the North, who was charged with the theurgical function of protecting the imperial domain by summoning the power of the Buddha Dharma. His act of violence represents a combination of the extreme self-sacrificial ("sacrifice" means to make sacred) attitude of monks who express devotion to the Buddha with the filial rites of Confucian society. It is possible that the master's discarding of the staff expresses disapproval of the monk's question for misunderstanding the significance of the prince's actions.

Another kōan cited from YY record 48 (Taishō 47:547b–c), "Yün-men's View of Repentance," conveys the reverse side of the issue of violence and confession. According to this case, "Someone asked, 'If one kills one's father and mother, one can repent in front of the Buddha. Where does one repent if one kills the Buddhas and the patriarchs?'" Yün-men replied, "It is clear!" The term "clear" can mean at once "dew," "tears," or "exposed," and it suggests an ambivalent view that at once expresses remorse/regret/repentance and a transcendental indifference that supports the withdrawal, as an overcoming of attachments, of filial devotion even—or especially— toward the Buddha as the surrogate or spiritual replacement for one's ancestors.

53. Bodhidharma Pacifies the Mind

Main Cases

As Bodhidharma sat in zazen meditation while facing a wall, Hui-k'o, his would-be successor who eventually became the Second Patriarch, stood out in the snow and cut off his arm. He said, "Your disciple's mind is not

yet at peace. I beg you, my teacher, please bring peace to my mind." Bodhidharma said, "Bring me your mind, and I will bring peace to it for you."

The successor said, "I have looked for my mind, but it is not graspable."
Bodhidharma said, "There, I have brought peace to your mind for you."

Prose Commentary

The broken-toothed old foreigner came to China by sailing hundreds of
thousands of miles across the sea. This can be referred to as "stirring waves
without wind." By the end he transmitted enlightenment to a single disciple, who was deficient at the root, anyway. What a shame! But even
Hsieh-shan-lang could not make out the four characters [written on a Chinese coin].

Verse Commentary

> Coming from the West, directly pointing
> To the great matter of transmission,
> The one causing such a stir amid the Zen forest
> Is, after all, none other than you.

Discussion

This kōan, cited from WMK case 41 (Taishō 48:298a), appears in nearly all
the transmission of the lamp records, with some minor but significant variations, so that it is one of the most famous stories of the most important
and intriguing of the Zen patriarchs. As in case 51, the violent sacrifice here
can be read entirely as a metaphor or symbol of the severing of attachments
and the attainment of a standpoint of aloofness and indifference. However,
the supernatural and ritual elements of natural signatures and self-mutilation form a necessary backdrop for understanding the wordplay that liberates the second patriarch.

Bodhidharma is considered the leading iconoclast of Zen, whose ability
is the center of endless mythology. It is not clear whether there was such a
historical personage or whether the image of the foreign teacher represents
a composite of the long line of South and Central Asian missionaries who
transmitted Buddhism to China in the first half of the first millennium.
There is a fascinating paradox in that Zen discourse highlights a romanti-
cization and idealization precisely about Bodhidharma's ability to

demythologize. A primary example is cited in PYL case 1, on the episode in which Bodhidharma tells Emperor Wu that there is "no merit" in the act of constructing temples, monuments, and stupas and that there is "nothing sacred" in the "vast emptiness" of the universe. When asked by the Emperor, "Who is encountering me," Bodhidharma replied, "I don't know." Other examples of the Bodhidharma legend are the account of his aristocratic birth in a brahmin family which he renounced to follow the path of Buddhism, travel to China by crossing the Yangtze River on a single reed, meditation by gazing at the wall of a cave for nine years so that his limbs withered and fell off (as celebrated by limbless Daruma dolls in popular Japanese religion), and removal of his eyelids as self-punishment for sleeping during meditation (which, when discarded, took root in the soil and grew as tea leaves).

The monk Hui-k'o, who was to later become second patriarch and whose given name was Shen-kuang, was an itinerant practitioner who was longing for instruction in meditation. He heard of Bodhidharma's reputation for "wall gazing" contemplation from a spirit that recommended he go and find the master in his cave. In another version, Hui-k'o's head began aching as if it had been cut in half and a miraculous voice told him that his bones were changing and reforming, so that his face looked as if five peaks had risen on it. His teacher interpreted this as an omen that he must travel south and should seek out Bodhidharma at Shao lin temple.

Hui-k'o approached the fifth patriarch in the dead of winter—the snowfall provides a signature for his trials and tribulations—and stood unmoving for days while the first patriarch ignored his presence. Then Hui-k'o cuts himself (in some versions, he severs his hand while the blood trickles a thin line of red onto the virgin snow). Bodhidharma's attitude of indifference heightens Hui-k'o's anguish and frustration so that he is ripe for the message that the mind is not a literal object to be grasped and therefore is fundamentally neither peaceful nor restless, neither serene nor disturbed, but empty of objectivity and eminently dynamic and flexible. Without Hui-k'o's persistence the transmission of the Zen path may never have been completed. But, at the same time, the demand for self-mutilation as a necessary sacrifice in the process of training may well have been a requirement demanded by early Zen training.

Yet the WMK prose and verse commentaries both show that Zen is eager to ridicule and satirize its most prized leaders in a rhetorical strategy of disingenuous blasphemy. Bodhidharma, the foreigner or the "red-bearded barbarian" in the epilogue to case 38, is lambasted as toothless and clueless, and is compared to Hsieh-shan-lang, a folkloric fisherman who could not read or write. He is the one to blame for "causing such a stir" by creating as well as inciting the Zen assembly.

54. Hui-k'o Absolves Sin

Main Case

A layman approached second patriarch Hui-k'o and said, "I would like to become your disciple, but I am very ill. Please absolve me of my sin." Hui-k'o said, "Bring me your sin, and I will absolve you of it."

After a while the lay devotee said, "I have looked for my sin, but it is not graspable." Hui-k'o said, "There, I have absolved you of your sin. You must now take refuge in the Buddha, Dharma, and Samgha."

Verse Commentary

> Sins more numerable than the heavenly bodies,
> The state of sin no different than the heavens.
> If the lay devotee can see this realm,
> A refreshing breeze will lead him on the path.

Discussion

This kōan, originally contained in CCL vol. 3 (Taishō 51:310c), is cited from Dōgen's EK vol. 9 case 5 (DZZ 4:184–186) and is also included in DK vol. 30 (Taishō 82:378c–379a). The DK is a kind of latter-day transmission of the lamp text by Keizan, the second leading patriarch in the history of Sōtō Zen Buddhism in Japan.

This case dealing with the transmission in early Zen from the second to the third patriarch Seng-ts'an is obviously patterned after the preceding case (53) on the transmission from the first to the second patriarch. But the main theme shifts from putting a mind at peace in order to attain liberation to repenting for sins in order to attain healing from illness. Just as case 53 alludes to the practice of self-mutilation, the current case necessarily involves the issue of repentance as a spiritual process and its relation to physical healing. The phrase "absolve me of my sin" could also be translated as "repent my sin for me," although it is not clear whether the emphasis in the kōan is on a self-power or other-power approach to the issue of healing.

In any case, Hui-k'o, having learned his lesson well from his master, is now able to apply the teaching in his instructional role based on inventive word-play about the ungraspability of something like mind or sin that seems objectifiable but is fundamentally intangible and empty of own-being.

According to the narrative background that originally appeared in the CCL, Hui-k'o was searching for the person who would become the third patriarch when a layman over forty years old suddenly arrived. He did not announce his name but behaved with perfect etiquette and asked for healing through redemption from sin. The healing starts by identifying the source of physical illness as something spiritual. In the kōan the illness seems to be relatively simple like rheumatism, but another passage in the DK says that the disease plaguing Seng-ts'an in his first meeting with Hui-k'o was leprosy, which implies that a miraculous cure through faith healing took place. After this incident, Seng-ts'an said that for the first time he understood that the nature of sin lies neither inside nor outside of man, nor between the two. Similarly, the mind and the teaching of the Buddha are nondual.

This case reflects the *Platform Sutra* teaching of formless repentance, which implies that no specific transgression or misdeed needs to be recounted or regretted because all transgressions are fundamentally empty. In terms of healing, the affliction is not attributed to a specific cause or wrongdoing. Nor is the third patriarch required to disclose all his sins. Rather, he learns about the nature of sin from a confessor who is able to expiate them and affect a cure for the penitent. Although the content of the teaching is the Zen notion that the body–mind dichotomy is illusory because mind and reality are "thus," the process of instruction and cure resembles Taoist faith healing achieved through shamanistic trance and exorcism as much as Buddhist ceremonial confession.

According to the CCL, after transmitting the robe and the Dharma Hui-k'o told Seng-ts'an, "Having received my teaching, you should live in the depths of the mountain and not go on a mission journey for a calamity may take place in this country." This prediction stated that although the matter of the third patriarch's understanding was fortunate, its form or the social conditions surrounding it was unfortunate. This provided an impetus to keep Zen primarily a monastic movement in the mountains rather than in an urban and thus politicized environment. It may have also foreshadowed subsequent periods of the suppressions of Buddhism that took place during the T'ang dynasty. Following the transmission, however, it is said that Hui-k'o went into drinking shops or entered the premises of butchers, sometimes sharing in the town gossip or engaging in manual work. When asked whether there was an ethical inconsistency in this kind of activity he replied, "I am attuning my mind with various environments. What business is it of yours?"

55. Dōgen Disciplines Monk Gemmyō

Main Case

Dōgen wanted to rectify the abnormal system of government. During his visit to Kamakura he advised Hōjō Tokiyori, the new military ruler, to restore the imperial regime to the throne. As the proposal was not obeyed, he left at once and retired to Eiheiji Temple, which he had built in the province of Echizen.

This deepened the respect of the ruler, who persuaded one of Dōgen's pupils to take the document of a generous grant of land to his teacher. The priest, Gemmyō, gladly did so. When he heard that Gemmyō had accepted the offer, Dōgen was so enraged that he at once drove his pupil away. He ordered the chair the priest sat on destroyed, the ground under the chair dug three feet deep and the earth thrown away.

After this incident Dōgen was admired more than ever, and Zen practice became popular among the people.

Discussion

This passage parphrased from the KZK, pp. 63–64, also appears in other traditional records of Dōgen's life and is usually documented as being related from the perspective of the standpoint of the remorseful ghost of the offending priest, Gemmyō. Probably the two main features of Dōgen's hagiography in the late period of his life are the Gemmyō incident and an emphasis on the role of *rakan* (or Arhat) veneration in his approach to lay religiosity. Both of these features contain important supernatural and ritual elements.

This episode took place toward the end of Dōgen's career, around 1248, when he returned from a visit to the temporary capital city in Kamakura, just south of the area that later became Tokyo, to his own temple, Eiheiji, in Echizen (present day Fukui) province in the mountains of northwestern Japan. Apparently the new shogun, Hōjō Tokiyori, offered Dōgen the abbacy of Kenchōji temple, which would soon become the leading institution in the Five Mountains (*gozan*) Rinzai sect monastic institution. But Dōgen refused, apparently because he disapproved of the samurai warrior culture that subverted Buddhist values for the sake of militancy. Dōgen tried to convince the shōgun to restore the throne's rule rather than create a new military regime. The ruler considered this an act of great integrity, and he then offered Dōgen a large portion of land for a new temple. But the Zen master decided instead to retire to Eiheiji. Dōgen was particularly disturbed when his disciple betrayed the integrity of his sect. Gemmyō was one of several disciples who became followers of Dōgen's new Sōtō Zen sect after being members of the Daruma-shū, the original Zen sect in Japan that began in the late twelfth century. The Daruma-shū was severely criticized and proscribed by the government because it did not adhere to the traditional Buddhist precepts.

This account closely resembles the call for swift, severe punishment of unruly troublemakers and deceivers through public humiliation and in some cases expulsion and excommunication in the rules text attributed to Pai-chang, the *Ch'an-men kuei-shih* (Taishō 51:251a):

> Anyone who makes a false claim of membership or is insincere or deceitful in his practice and abuses his office, or anyone who breaks the rules or otherwise stirs up trouble among the dedicated members of the monastic community, will be punished by the Rector, who is to remove the imposter's possessions from the Monks Hall and to expel and excommunicate him from the compound. This severe discipline serves as a warning to other monks of the humiliation and disgrace that will ensue should a similar offense be committed.

Pai-chang's rules text is based on — but goes beyond in several ways — the traditional Buddhist Vinaya code in terms of what is considered a banishable offense. There are four main reasons for the severity of the punishment: it leaves the rank-and-file uncompromised; it keeps Zen's reputation for purity in practice from being besmirched; it avoids public litigation; and it prevents news of the affair from spreading to other temples. In short, this approach makes clear that Zen is not an unorthodox, subversive "wild fox" cult that succumbs to a violation of morality based on ignoring or not falling into causality. Zen is grounded on a rigorous ethic of not neglecting or not obscuring causality that could be effective in taming deficient moral tendencies for the sake of the greater social good. Of course, the main factor underlying the last three rules is a concern with the way the sect appears to outsiders.

In both the *Ch'an-men kuei-shih* and the case of the Gemmyō ostracism, there is little room for caring for the transformation of the offender. The legalist approach of the rules text and of Dōgen's dismissal of his impetuous student has the merit of preserving a sense of purity by firmly avoiding evil or reprehensible behavior. But it expresses little or no concern for the dynamics of repentance and redemption, or the process of transforming transgressions into meritorious or praiseworthy behavior. Thus, there appears to be a shortcoming in Zen in coming to terms with the issue of making amends for and redeeming transgressions. However, this emphasis must be seen in the context of the overall intent of Zen discourse, as expressed in hagiographical literature about the exploits of the eminent T'ang patriarchs, on maintaining creativity and ingenuity precisely by cultivating a wild, "crazy" approach to Zen (Ch. *kuang-ch'an*, Jap. *kyōzen*) manifested in "strange words and extraordinary deeds" (Ch. *ch'i-yü ch'i-hsing*, Jap. *kigen kikō*). Zen masters, celebrated for their "divine madness," should know well when to follow rules and when to bend or break them at their own discretion so as to enhance rather than violate the spirit that generated the rules.

Death, Relics, and Ghosts

56. A Woman's True Soul?

Main Case

Fifth Patriarch Hung-ren asked a monk, "Ch'ien's soul was divided into two parts. Which one was the true soul?"

Prose Commentary

If you understand the true meaning of this case, you will know that coming out of a shell and going back in a shell is like a traveler lodging at an inn. If you do not understand it, don't rush about blindly. When earth, water, fire, and wind disintegrate all at once, you will be like a lobster fallen into a pot of boiling water, frantically thrashing about with its arms and legs. At that time, don't say I didn't warn you.

Verse Commentary

> Clouds and moon fuse into a single pale shade,
> Valleys and mountains, so distinct.
> Hundreds of thousands of blessings—
> Is this oneness or differentiation?

Discussion

This kōan, cited from WMK case 35 (Taishō 48:297b), is a main example of a case reliant on images and symbols absorbed directly from lay folk beliefs in supernatural powers, including bilocation and trance, although in asking which manifestation is the true Ch'ien the case is usually interpreted exclusively in terms of the issue of nonduality. The philosophical topic is how a person or object can be divided into component parts, such as body and soul, when they all constitute an indivisible collective unity. And yet universality is not one-sidedly asserted, since that might conceal the distinctiveness of particular manifestations. The WMK verse commentary establishes identity and difference in the first two lines and concludes with an ironic rhetorical question that scrupulously avoids a commitment to either view as an exclusive side of the polarity. This commentary recalls a dialogue cited in Dōgen's *Shōbōgenzō* "Busshō" fascicle (DZZ 1:42) about a monk who once asked master Ching-ts'en of Mt. Chang-sha, "When an earthworm is cut in half the two parts both move. I wonder which of them has the Buddha-nature?" The master responded, "Stop your illusory thinking." The disciple pressed, "But how do you explain their movement [into four elements]?" Dōgen's extended commentary denies a commitment to either view: "The earthworm was neither originally one nor did it become two when it was cut in half. Close attention should be paid to the meaning of the words 'one' and 'two.'"

While the current case functions on an abstract philosophical level when understood as a scholastic exercise, it is important to recognize that the case is clearly based on a famous T'ang ghost tale recorded in the *Li-hun chi* (Jap. *Rikonki*), expressing the theme of duty versus passion (or *giri* versus *ninjō*, which later became such an important influence on Tokugawa era Japanese literature). The folktale uses supernatural elements, such as a spirit journey, in the story of a young woman appearing to her parents, who have resisted her wedding plans, to be sick and lifeless when she is separated for five years from the man she loves. The spirit of Ch'ien manifests in a physical form when she is saddened by her parents' proposal for an arranged marriage. Her alienated soul runs off with her lover, while her former self spends the time in a sickbed, unable to move. Early in the story Ch'ien's father promises her hand in an arranged marriage, which distresses her childhood sweetheart, who is her cousin, whom the father once jokingly suggested should marry his daughter. The young man, on hearing the news, decided to flee the village, and as he was leaving in his boat he made out a shadowy figure on the shore chasing after him. He and Ch'ien went off to a remote area and were married, but five years later they decided to return home out of a sense of duty to her family. The father is at first incredulous because his daughter has been terribly ill, but he realizes that the "other Ch'ien" has run off with her lover and spent the time in a secret marriage. Ch'ien is reunited with her tormented soul that was present in a body lying motionless in bed the entire duration of her flight. Everyone, now purged of feelings of guilt and deception, is able to experience a sense of harmony and fulfilled responsibilities. As in the case of Chuang Tzu's "butterfly dream," Ch'ien admits that she herself cannot tell which is her real identity—the person sick in bed or the one who has been married.

Looking at the kōan from the standpoint of the folklore dimension indicates that the simple though profound philosophical issue of nonduality is considerably amplified by an emphasis on the disturbing emotional experiences of the main characters. These highlight the tensions involved in the crossing over of a variety of borders, including social boundaries such as security and alienation, or family and outcast status, as well as metaphysical boundaries such as self and other, life and death, or human and ghostly realms. The folklore dimension reinforces and enhances rather than delimits or conflicts with the scholastic level of discourse. Yet Ch'ien's final declaration about the unsettling and irreconcilable issue of her personal identity suggests that the philosophical debate concerning universality versus particularity remains an enigma.

A connection between the philosophical issues and foklore elements is indicated in another verse dealing with the imagery of death that is suggested by the narrative's reference to Ch'ien's double identity (in Zenkei Shibayama, *Zen Comments on the Mumonkan* [New York: Mentor, 1973], p. 257):

> Peach branches and reeds in front,
> Paper money after the funeral cart,

O disciples of the old foreigner,
You will not enter into the realm of the dead.

The first two lines refer to customs for keeping away demons in traditional funeral processions, indicating that the mythical issue of where the dead soul resides and how it returns to life is intertwined with the demythological issue of how to attain nirvana. The third line is a frequently used ironic self-criticism of Zen monks, disciples of the first patriarch Bodhidharma who brought the transmission to China from India. The final line suggests that the central philosophical question about the permeability of boundaries separating pairs of opposites such as life and death has a paradoxical conclusion. The boundaries are at once navigable and impenetrable: life is inseparable from death and yet life is distinctively life and death is distinctively death; universality and particularity, oneness and manyness are ever intertwined. The conclusion in the form of a challenge moves the kōan beyond mere intellectual abstraction and dares the Zen disciple to attain the degree of insight of folk heroine Ch'ien, who in a sense rode in the funeral cart—or perhaps she escaped this fate—to and from the land of the dead (or enlightenment).

57. P'u-hua Passes Away

Main Case

One day P'u-hua went around the streets of the town, begging people to give him a one-piece robe. But although there were people who offered it to him, P'u-hua refused to accept any of their offerings.

Lin-chi sent the monk in charge of temple affairs to buy a coffin. When P'u-hua returned to the temple, Lin-chi said, "I've made this one-piece robe for you." P'u-hua lifted up the coffin on his shoulders and went off with it. He paraded all over town, calling out, "Lin-chi has made this one-piece robe for me! I'm going to the east gate of the town to take leave of this world!" The townspeople trailed after him to see what would happen. P'u-hua said, "I'm not going to do it today. But tomorrow I'll go to the south gate of the town to take leave of this world."

After three days of this activity, no one in town took his proclamations seriously anymore. Then, on the fourth day, when there was no one trailing after or watching him, P'u-hua went all by himself outside the city gates, lay down in the coffin, and asked a passerby to nail down the lid.

Immediately, word of this event spread all over town, and people came to find the coffin. But when they opened the lid, they saw that any trace of his body had completely vanished. All they heard was the clear, sharp sound of his hand bell tinkling in the air before it, too, faded away.

Discussion

This kōan is cited from LL record 47 (Taishō 47:504b), which contains a half dozen passages about P'u-hua's complex relation with Lin-chi as well as his manner of dying, including record 55 (Taishō 47:505b–c) and record 69 (Taishō 47:506c). As also depicted in case 16, P'u-hua, as a kind of *pratyeka buddha* or irregular, unaffiliated monk, is at once a complement to and a foil for Lin-chi. This Zen master is assisted and challenged by P'u-hua, who on several occasions one-ups or embarrasses Lin-chi by turning over dining tables or braying like a donkey. Yet Lin-chi seems to accept the role of this nemesis, and the recorded sayings text devotes considerable attention to his eccentric counterpart.

Whereas cases 52 and 55 deal with the giving of life either inspired by devotion or love or as a punishment, this case is one of numerous examples in early Zen literature of monks demonstrating an ability to conquer ordinary mortality. This occurs when a master is able to predict or regulate the timing and posture (such as sitting in the lotus position) at the moment of dying, which transforms death from a source of pollution to a manifestation of supreme purity. Furthermore, the posthumous disappearance of P'u-hua's body is in accord with images of miraculous afterlife occurrences of Buddhist saints and Zen patriarchs, including empty coffins and pristine bodies that have not decayed.

This pattern was established in Zen records with the account of the Emperor giving instructions for Bodhidharma's grave to be opened and finding an empty coffin with only one leather sandal inside. This amazed the court, which had heard the rumor that Bodhidharma was seen walking back to India on a single sandal. There are also reports that at the time of his demise Bodhidharma exchanged skeletons with Hui-k'o, who literally grasped his "skin, flesh, bones, and marrow," to cite the kōan about transmission from the first to the second patriarch. Also, the third patriarch made the sign of a "gassho" greeting and then passed away. In another legendary account, the door of the fourth patriarch's stupa opened by itself without any cause a year after his death and the body of the master looked as though he were alive, so that his disciples did not dare close the door.

When the fifth patriarch decided that his work was done he announced he would go away and he entered his chamber. While sitting quietly, he passed away, but only after delaying the date so that it did not fall on the anniversary of the Buddha's attainment of parinirvana. In addition, the sixth patriarch predicted his death a month in advance. He left a lengthy departing poem, and made an uncanny prediction concerning the future of his school.

Other records in the Lin-chi text refer to the disappearance of P'u-hua, "body and all," but the detailed explanation of the process of his dying given in the current case clearly evokes the tradition of Taoist immortalism, which influenced Buddhist asceticism and was often combined with Zen in depictions of the achievements of attained masters. P'u-hua requests a "one-piece robe," which means he is planning to die, but he will only accept the offering from his mentor cum rival Lin-chi. Ever the trickster, P'u-hua continues to tease the community that awaits his imminent demise, but just as people begin to distrust his promise to take leave of this world he finally makes an extraordinary display of his prowess to control the timing of his death.

The image of the bell tinkling in the air until it finally fades marks a sharp contrast with the rest of the Lin-chi recorded sayings text that contains numerous passages that are rigorously iconoclastic and anti-supernatural. Lin-chi consistently uses the image of wild foxes only as a sarcastic epithet for unruly, rogue monks, and he condemns the religiosity of bodhisattva worship that looks outward instead of "killing the Buddha" and finding an exclusively inner enlightenment. Yet Lin-chi apparently also had a begrudging respect for P'u-hua, who several times bested him in this-worldly Dharma-combat and now has realized a supreme otherworldly accomplishment. The pagoda inscription of Lin-chi refers to P'u-hua as "a madman" and questions whether he was "a common mortal or a sage." But it also notes that the death of P'u-hua, after he spent time assisting Lin-chi, was in perfect accord with the prediction of Yang-shan, one of the administrators of Lin-chi's monastery.

58. Jiu-feng Does Not Concur

Pointer

Yün-chü did not rely on the power of relics, the jewels of discipline, and Jiu-feng did not admire casting off through sitting or forgetting through standing. Niu-t'ou did not need birds flocking to him with flowers in their beaks, and Huang-po did not envy sailing across a river without using a boat. Now tell me, what was their long suit?

Main Case

Jiu-feng was working as an attendant of Shih-shuang. When Shih-shuang passed away, the assembly wanted to select the monk in charge of the Dharma Hall to serve as the new abbot. Jiu-feng was not in accord with this. He said, "Wait until I question him—if he understands the meaning of our late master's teaching, I will serve him as the new master."

Then Jiu-feng asked the chief monk, "Our late teacher said, 'Cease and desist: spend ten thousand years in a single instant of thought. Pass your time as cold ashes or dry wood, or as a strip of white silk.' Now tell me, what aspect does this illuminate?" The chief monk said, "It illuminates the realm of form." Jiu-feng said, "You still don't understand the meaning of our late master's teaching."

The chief monk said, "You don't concur with me? Let's set up an incense burner." He then lit the incense burner and said, "If it is the case that I fail to understand the meaning of our late master's teaching, then I will not be able to pass away while the incense is still burning." Having said this, he sat down and immediately expired. Jiu-feng then patted him on the back approvingly and said, "When it comes to dying sitting down or standing up you have no problems. But when it comes to understanding our late master, you haven't seen the meaning of his teaching in your wildest dreams."

Discussion

This kōan is cited from TJL case 96 (Taishō 48:289b–290a), and seems to represent the flip side of the previous case's view of controlling death. Whereas case 57 valorizes P'u-hua's ability to show that he can predict and regulate the timing of his demise as well as the nature of the afterlife through the vanishing of his corpse, this case demeans and ridicules the control of death. It is seen as an inferior skill that fails to realize enlightenment and actually detracts from the chief monk's spiritual attainment. At the same time, the discourse of ridicule is possible only in a context in which the ability to regulate death was taken for granted as a necessary skill. Yet this context, which also involves elements of ancestor veneration, is reoriented in terms of a philosophical debate concerning a comparison of the state of death with deep meditation.

The case pointer makes a statement about rejecting the magical by listing several instances of masters who expressed a disregard and disdain for supernaturalism against a background of support for supernatural beliefs. Yün-chü was known as a specialist in Vinaya discipline who did not resort to the use of miraculous *sarira* or jewel-like relics that were claimed on behalf of countless Vinaya masters. The Zen monastic tradition originally grew from the Vinaya (Ch. Lü) school. Zen was a separate cloister that eventually became an independent, autonomous movement. Some scholars now argue that what was known as the Vinaya school in China actually referred not to an ideological structure but to a network of private monasteries. The new Zen school flourished in part because it was a public monastery system that was subject to greater regulation, along with financial and official support, by the central government. The government oversight also included the evaluation and registration of authentic *sarira*.

The pointer also alludes to case 4, in which Niu-t'ou of the Ox Head school was no longer visited by magical birds carrying flowers after hearing the discourse of third patriarch Tao-hsin, and to case 28, in which Huang-po criticized a monk who crossed a river by walking on water. Each of these is an example of a dramatic transition in Zen from a reliance on the supernatural imagery of relics, magical spirits, and miraculous powers to an iconoclastic, irreverent standpoint. These examples support the famous utterance of Layman P'ang that "drawing water and chopping wood are my supernatural powers and marvelous activities." In the current case, Jiu-feng rejects the kind of meditation that not only resembles a condition of death, but actually results in the controlled death of the practitioner.

The case narrative begins by referring to a problem of lineal transmission. A successor for master Shih-shuang, who was known for supervising a "dead tree congregation" in a "dead tree meditation hall," had not been selected beforehand. According to the TJL prose commentary, Shih-shuang's monks achieved a state of quietude through deep contemplation by sitting for endless hours without lying down that is often compared to being like a dead tree. Many died due to exhaustion from prolonged sitting or standing. Jiu-feng, who had been one of Shih-shuang's attendants, challenges the succession claimed by the chief monk, and this becomes, in effect, the determining factor in the transmission process. Jui-feng questions the chief monk by asking him not to take literally the master's teaching to "cease and desist . . . like cold ashes and dry wood." When the monk shows that he indeed takes the metaphor so literally that he can actually become dead, Jiu-feng's sardonic repost is to be expected.

59. A Hermit Seeks to be Saved

Main Case

A hermit living in a hut was feeling ill at ease. Every time he saw a monk he would call out, "Save me! Save me!" Many monks spoke to him, but without providing any solace. Tung-shan went to see him, and the hermit cried out, "Save me!"

Tung-shan asked, "What is it that you wish to be saved from?" The hermit said, "Aren't you the Dharma-heir of Yüeh-shan and Yün-yen?" Tung-shan humbly acknowledged that this was the case.

The hermit joined his hands in a gesture of respect and said, "I must take leave of this great family." He then passed away.

Discussion

This kōan, cited from the TSL (Taishō 47:511b), also deals ironically with the question of self-control over the timing and the event of dying. An irregular, unaffiliated, non-lineal monk living as a hermit is in a state of disturbance and anxiety and cries outwardly to be saved. Despite this ordeal he never identifies the source of his problem and refuses assistance from those who offer it. What is at the root of his condition? As in case 54, there seems to be a connection between illness and sin, and therefore between repentance and redemption.

Only after master Tung-shan arrives does the hermit begin to express his concern and thereby begin the process of offering a confession. Tung-shan's appearance recalls Chao-chou checking out the hermits in case 19, except that Tung-shan goes in order to offer help rather than a challenge. The message of this case is that the hermit's problem is based on his lack of formal affiliation with a lineal transmission. Once he makes contact with Tung-shan he apparently feels that he has received the blessing of an authentic master and is ready to die peacefully. His final comment suggests that he, perhaps on his own, has included himself in the "great family." Unlike the previous two cases dealing with the controlled deaths of P'u-hua and the chief monk encountered by Jiu-feng, this case indicates neither approval nor disapproval of the hermit's manner of dying.

In another kōan known as Tung-shan's "Disclosing Mind, Disclosing Nature," the master reveals a different level of affinity with death. This case is included in Dōgen's collection, MS case 62 (DZZ 5:158–160) and is also the basis of an entire *Shōbōgenzō* fascicle, KS "Sesshin sesshō" (DZZ 1:449–456). According to the kōan record, which revolves around several subtle word-plays, one time when master Tung-shan was traveling with master Shen-shan Seng-mi, whose name literally means "mountain god," he pointed to a road-side temple and said, "There is someone inside the temple who is disclosing mind, and disclosing nature." The way this transpires suggests a mysterious intuition that connects Tung-shan to the preacher in the chapel. The term used for "disclosing" can also be translated "explaining," "preaching," or "giving discourse," and the terms "mind" and "nature" are often used inter-changeably in Zen literature to refer to the fundamental level of reality.

Shen-shan responds, "Who is it?," which could be interpreted as a simple, innocent question or it could also be rendered as a philosophical declarative "It is who." Tung-shan then says, "When I just heard your simple question, elder brother, I attained a state of perfect death," indicating a condition of deep meditation beyond the dichotomy of life and death that is also referred to in case 60. Shen-shan asks, "Who is disclosing mind, and disclosing nature?," which, again, could be understood as a declarative, "The one dis-closing mind and disclosing nature is who." In response to the question Tung-shan says, "It is he who is alive within the realm of death."

In his extensive commentary on this relatively obscure case, Dōgen con-tinues the wordplay by dividing the act of disclosure into four categories rep-resented by his characteristic literary technique of changing the order of characters in a four-character phrase: "disclosing mind of no person," "no person disclosing mind," "disclosing mind is itself the person," and "this person itself is disclosing mind." But based largely on a sectarian agenda, Dōgen praises the handling of Shen-shan's questions by Tung-shan (one of the founders of his Sōtō lineage) and criticizes Lin-chi (founder of the rival Rinzai sect) for misrepresenting a duality between mind, as representative of evanescent individuality, and nature, as symbolic of substantive universality.

60. Tao-wu Makes a Condolence Call

Pointer

Serenely and intimately at one with the complete truth—the attainment of enlightenment right here and now. In harmony with the flux—direct realization. As swift as sparks or lightning, he cuts off all delusions and corruptions, sitting on the head of a tiger and grasping its tail or standing atop a thousand-foot cliff, or whatever is required. Is there a way to offer people a clue based on this, or not? Now consider the following.

Main Case

Tao-wu and Chien-yüan went to visit a family to make a condolence call. Chien-yüan tapped on the coffin and said, "Alive or dead?" Tao-wu said, "I won't say it's alive, and I won't say it's dead." Chien-yüan said, "Why won't you say?" Tao-wu said, "I just won't say, I just won't say."

On their way home Chien-yüan said, "Teacher, you'd better tell me right away. If you don't tell me, I'll have to hit you." Tao-wu said, "Go ahead and hit me. I still won't tell you anything." Chien-yüan then hit him.

Some time later Tao-wu passed away. Chien-yüan visited Shih-shuang and told him the whole story. Shih-shuang said, "I won't say it's alive, and I won't say it's dead." Chien-yüan said, "Why won't you say?" Shih-shuang said, "I just won't say, I just won't say." On hearing these words Chien-yüan attained sudden illumination.

One day Chien-yüan carried a hoe into the Dharma Hall, and crossed back and forth from one side of the room to the other. Shih-shuang said, "What are you doing?" Chien-yüan said, "I am looking for relics of our late master." Shih-shuang said, "Vast waves spreading everywhere, white foam reaches the sky—why are you looking for relics of our late teacher?" [Hsüeh-tou adds: Good Heavens! Good Heavens!] Chien-yüan said, "To enhance my efforts."

Fu of T'ai-yüan said, "The late teacher's relics are right here!"

Verse Commentary

> Hares and horses have horns, oxen and goats have none,
> Thin as a wisp of hair, high as a mountain peak,
> The golden relics are here right now, white foaming clouds
>   reaching the sky,
> There is no place to find them, even the monk who returned to
>   the West with a single sandal does not have them.

Discussion

This kōan, originally contained in CCL vol. 15 (Taishō 51:321b) and other transmission of the lamp records as well as a collection of master Ta-hui, is cited from PYL case 55 (Taishō 48:189a–190a). An abbreviated version that concludes with Chien-yüan's sudden illumination is included in MS case 29 (DZZ 5:142–144), and Dōgen also cites the case briefly in EK vol. 2 record 161 (DZZ 3:104) as part of a memorial service for the father of a nun. The case is divided into three parts: the condolence call, the illumination, and the search for relics. The main impact of the case revolves around the ambiguous significance of Chien-yüan's final phrase rendered here, "To enhance my efforts."

The kōan begins with two monks making a condolence call, which had become of the main activities linking the monastic world to mainstream society. Although Chinese society had long established Confucian procedures for mourning rites for ancestors, Buddhism introduced its own style of cremation, funerals, memorials, relic and stupa worship, and other mortuary rituals. At first these practices were only in effect for ordained Buddhist priests, for whom every stage of the burial was carried out in excruciating detail and with profound symbolism about the process of purification. But some of the practices were also gradually applied to laymen, especially supporters or followers of a particular temple. Lay families also received condolence calls during times of mourning by monks from local temples.

The refusal to say "alive" or "dead" recalls a case known as "Tao-wu's separation from this body," which originally appears in CCL vol. 14 and is included in MS case 252 (DZZ 5:256): "Tao-wu, visiting Yün-gan, who was very sick, said, 'When we take leave of this physical body, what becomes of us and where can we meet?' Yün-gan said, 'I will meet you at the place of non-arising and non-desistence.' Tao-wu said, 'Why don't we say that we will try to meet at a place that is other than non-arising and non-desistence?'"

In the current case, when Chien-yüan gets the message from both Tao-wu and Shih-shuang he attains enlightenment and tells Shih-shuang that he is looking for relics of Tao-wu. The question is, what does he intend to do with the relics? The critical sentence is rendered here, "To enhance my efforts," so as to dismantle mythology and show that Chien-yüan will practice and train more diligently. He is not looking for magical remains of the deceased master, but for a symbol of his own discipline and training. In other words, Zen transcends the need for supranormal powers. But the reverse interpretation and translation is also possible: "To increase my powers." According to this standpoint that is also articulated in a traditional commentary by master Liu-mi, Zen offers superior—more effective and dynamic—powers than other Buddhist schools. The final remark by Fu of T'ai-yüan, another monk at the temple, is also ambiguous. It could be taken either as an ironic way of saying that Chien-yüan's diligent practice is the true power of the relics, or as a straightforward confirmation of the discovery of the late master's relics.

What is the correct evaluation of the case's discourse on the meaning of death and supranormal powers? "I just won't say!"

ZEN FIGURES CITED

List of Zen figures with the number of the case(s) in which cited; paren-
thesis indicates the citation is in the discussion section only.

Bodhidharma, (10), (18), (19), (30), 53, (57)
Ch'ang-ch'ing, 39, 40, (44)
Chao-chou, (17), 19, 23, 26, (36), (49), (59)
Chien-yüan, 60
Chieng-mo, 3
Chih-hsien, 25
Chih-men, 41, (43)
Chih-yen, 50
Chin-niu, (39)
Ching-ching, (32)
Ch'ing-yüan, (45)
Chü-chih, (30), (37), 51
Dim Light, 27